"For people who find books about words to be
[*The Grand Panjandrum*] is a book of 'onomatomania' —an uncontrollable passion for words—and an infectiously practical book of suggestions."

—*Booklist*

"If words are your grand passion, you'll love this guide."

—Quality Paperback Book Club

"Dr. Hook virtually salivates as he takes these special words off the shelf, dusts them, and plays with them before our wondering eyes."

—Patricia Grant

"*The Grand Panjandrum* will delight you. It's a browser's paradise, a verbomaniac's mother lode."

—*Book-of-the-Month Club News*

THE GRAND PANJANDRUM

Other Books by J. N. Hook

Family Names: How Our Surnames Came to America

The Appropriate Word: Finding the Best Way to Say What You Mean

History of the English Language

The Story of American English

Spelling 1500

All Those Wonderful Names

The Grand Panjandrum

And 2,699 Other Rare, Useful, and Delightful Words and Expressions

REVISED AND EXPANDED

J. N. HOOK

Foreword by Willard R. Espy

COLLIER BOOKS
Macmillan Publishing Company / New York
Maxwell Macmillan Canada / Toronto
Maxwell Macmillan International / New York Oxford Singapore Sydney

Collier Books
Macmillan Publishing Company
866 Third Avenue
New York, NY 10022

Maxwell Macmillan Canada, Inc.
1200 Eglinton Avenue East
Suite 200
Don Mills, Ontario M3C 3N1

Macmillan Publishing Company is part of the
Maxwell Communication Group of Companies.

Library of Congress Cataloging-in-Publication Data
Hook, J. N. (Julius Nicholas), 1913–
The grand panjandrum and 2,699 other rare, useful, and delightful words and expressions / J. N. Hook.—Rev. and expanded [ed.]
p. cm.
Includes index.
ISBN 0-02-033288-2
1. Vocabulary. 2. English language—Glossaries, vocabularies. etc. 3. English language—Terms and phrases. I. Title. II. Title: The grand panjandrum and two thousand six hundred ninety nine other rare, useful words and expressions.
PE1449.H55 1991
428.1—dc20
90-24176
CIP

Macmillan books are available at special discounts for bulk purchases for sales promotions, premiums, fund-raising, or educational use. For details, contact:

Special Sales Director
Macmillan Publishing Company
866 Third Avenue
New York, NY 10022

Book design by Jennifer Dossin

10 9 8 7 6 5 4 3 2 1
Printed in the United States of America

CONTENTS

FOREWORD

The call inviting me to write this foreword came as my cassette player was reading to me the section of *Tristram Shandy* where Dr. Slop, having dealt a grievous cut to his thumb, and blaming the servant Obadiah, was formally excommunicating him in words something like these:

> May he, Obadiah, be cursed in all the faculties of his body. May he be cursed inwardly and outwardly. May he be cursed in the hair of his head. May he be cursed in his brains, and his temples, and his forehead, in his ears and his eyebrows, and his cheeks, in his jawbones, and his nostrils, in his foreteeth and grinders. May he be cursed in all the joints and articulations of his members from the top of his head to the sole of his foot. May there be no soundness in him.

Now, I am a devotee of *Tristram Shandy;* I return to it as compulsively as a suckling calf to the teat; but the words in that particular passage came at me like flung stones, making me duck, and the ringing of the telephone brought a welcome interruption. I would be delighted, I said, to turn to

J. N. Hook's *Grand Panjandrum*, where, I suspected, there would be few flung stones; the words would be more like a rainbow of butterflies pinned side by side in a glassed frame. I was right; *The Grand Panjandrum* turned out to be a grand panjandrum of a book. I am happy to describe Dr. Hook in an epithet assembled from a congeries of parts, as Dr. Frankenstein assembled his monster: Dr. Hook, I dub you a *verbidopterist.*

The butterfly words in this book are of all dimensions and colors—sapient or nonsensical; searching or superficial; cranky, feisty, seductive, or just plain fun. There's *grex* and *mumpsimus*, there's *mussitation* and *nefandous*. There's—well, I couldn't put the lexicon down.

If Dr. Slop had picked up *The Grand Panjandrum* instead of that dreadful excommunication, he would have returned much more quickly to an agreeable frame of mind.

WILLARD R. ESPY
MARCH 1991

PREFACE

It all started with *borborygmus*.

A collegienne was sitting beside the desk in my office, conferring about a report for my course in history of the English language. Noises began coming from her midsection. She shifted uneasily in her chair and turned slightly pink. One sound from her abdominal area was especially loud. She slid forward in her chair, and the pink turned to red. She was obviously becoming more and more distressed.

"Don't let a little borborygmus bother you, Eva," I said lightly. "It happens to all of us at times."

"A little what?"

"Borborygmus—intestinal growling. The Greeks had a word for it, and we borrowed it from their language a couple of hundred years ago. Unfortunately, it has never become widely known or used."

"That's too bad," she said, now more at ease although her innards were still protesting slightly. "I'm glad there's a name for this thing—makes it seem more dignified, somehow. I suppose there are other words like borborygmus."

"What do you mean?"

"Like, you know, words that tell about other common things but that most people don't know."

"Well, I've never thought much about that, specifically. But I suppose there are. Usually, of course, any word that's really needed catches on, but maybe some unlucky though meritorious words don't. I remember another example. Sometimes we want to refer to a relative from our father's side of the family, or our mother's side, and we have to say something rather verbose, like 'an aunt on my father's side' or 'one of my father's sisters.' That's all right, of course, but if we know *agnate* and *enate* we can say 'an agnate aunt' to mean one of my father's sisters and 'an enate aunt' for a sister of my mother."

"I've often thought we should have a word to distinguish a girl who is a cousin from a boy who is a cousin."

"We do—*cousiness* for the girl, but most people don't know that word. Maybe with the desire for nonsexist language they wouldn't use it anyway. But the language does make a corresponding distinction in *niece* and *nephew* and names of other relatives."

As a result of this conversation I began listing other words that I ran across—words that are not widely known or used but that could be valuable to many people. I began thinking of an article on the subject, or even a minor crusade on behalf of some unlucky, undeservedly ignored words. I began checking systematically some of the leading modern dictionaries and the older but especially scholarly *Oxford English Dictionary*, writing down any words that I thought might qualify. Quite a few of these were words that I did not remember ever hearing or reading before, and that I myself certainly had never used. Useful rare words, I found, were surprisingly numerous: for each thirteen pages in one unabridged dictionary I discovered about ten of them. The idea for an article quickly became an idea for a book.

For my own use I drew up some rough general rules for words to be included, although occasionally I decided to break one or more of them. Here are my rules:

1. Each "useful rare word" must be one that fairly large numbers of people would be likely to use, at least occasionally, if they knew it.
2. This should not be a book of "big words." Potential usefulness, not the number of syllables, is the major criterion for inclusion. When there's a common word that's as good as the rare one, there's usually no point in burdening the mind with the latter.
3. Each word included should be a real, existent word, listed in one or more unabridged dictionaries, but ordinarily not included in lists like the Thorndike-Lorge *Word Book* and often not in desk dictionaries (although exceptions here may be fairly numerous).
4. Technical words—those valuable only in highly specialized fields of knowledge—should be excluded. Technical dictionaries already exist for the use of specialists in sciences and many other fields.
5. Foreign words should for the most part be excluded, although if they meet the other criteria and have no English equivalent they may be selected. (For example, *Gleichschaltung*, which is an attempt to attain complete coordination and uniformity in business, industry, politics, culture, or what have you—a horrifying possibility that many people are working toward.)
6. Obsolete words should be included only if their deaths seem undeserved. Dialectal and Scottish words may be included if they appear useful enough.
7. Words whose meanings are clear without any explanation should not be included. (For example, *coppery*, an adjective, is fairly rare and useful but need not be explained.)
8. Rare words that, though useful, would be likely to be confused with existing common words should ordinarily not be included. (For instance, *compromis*, "an agreement between nations to submit a matter to arbitration," would probably be confused with *compromise* and should therefore be omitted.)
9. When alternative forms of useful rare words exist, the simpler or more rememberable one should be chosen. (For instance, though both *ecstasize* and *ecstasiate*

mean "to make or become ecstatic," *ecstasize* seems easier to pronounce, spell, and understand.)

I originally expected to present the entries in strictly A–Z dictionary format, but two expert consultants—my wife and our then-teenaged son—persuaded me that readability and interest would be enhanced if I used a chapter format, with only a part of the words presented in alphabetical order within each chapter. The subject matter for each chapter was decided upon somewhat arbitrarily, in light of the kinds of human endeavor, knowledge, and interests suggested by the words in my long lists. Some of the words would have fitted as well in another chapter. A comprehensive index leads readers to any words they might otherwise have difficulty in locating. It also shows pronunciations.

Unquestionably, some of the "rare" words in this book will be familiar to you. Depending on your temperament, you may either snort, "What's so rare about that?" or you may quietly pat yourself on the back for being so erudite.

How should you use this book? I hope that the material is interesting enough in itself, so that you will find it rewarding to dip into just for the fun of it, reading a chapter here and a chapter there. You certainly won't remember all the words you encounter, but some of them will probably stick with you.

Two persons may read the same chapter and then quiz each other on it.

If you are more systematic than most people, you may go straight through, actually *studying* each entry that seems potentially useful to you, and using each such word in an original sentence that clearly shows that you have made the word your own.

You may do the mastery test at the end of each chapter, and if you are not satisfied with the results, go over the chapter again and repeat the test. Or you and a friend may compete friendlily on some of the tests.

Interest in vocabulary-building is a constant in American life. Little children love to play with "new" words that interest them, and they often make up nonsense words just because they enjoy doing so. Most schoolchildren—unless the teaching is too stodgy—like to add words they can use. *Reader's Digest* spends a couple of precious pages a month on vocabulary instruction, and would no doubt receive many protests if the feature were discontinued. College professors and corporation executives yearn for students and high-level employees whose vocabularies enable them to express themselves both precisely and concisely.

Underlying most of this interest in vocabulary is the fact that words represent concepts. The word-rich man or woman is also concept-rich. Let's note a few examples of how this fact makes it valuable to possess some of the useful rare words in this collection:

- At a party you observe a couple of men who exceed not only the bounds of good taste or decorum but even those of buffoonery. Thinking that they are the life of the party, they toss a football over the heads of other guests, mimic the host, give hotfeet to unsuspecting guests, and in an excess of affection succeed in making one woman's décolletage even more décolleté. There's a word for such behavior—*baboonery*—but most people don't know it.

- A corporation sometimes pays for newspaper or magazine space or a minute on TV not to boast about a product but to make a statement on, for example, how important it is to allow increased amounts of commercial cutting of trees on public lands. The article has more wordage and less glamor than most advertising, and it usually does present some factual (though carefully selected) information. The company's name is generally in discreetly small type—say, The Wagontrain Paper Company. If one is able to attach a label to this kind of production, doing so helps to clarify the concept and the purpose. The word is *advertorial*, obviously a blend of *advertisement* and *editorial*.

- Until I wrote this book, I had never thought much about how important measurement is in our lives. I had tended to think of measurement as being merely an inches-feet kind of thing, as in building a house, or (since I am a teacher) as educational measurement. But I have found scores of examples of measuring devices that I hadn't thought about, such as *gravimeter* for measuring the force of gravity, which isn't everywhere the same, or *dendrograph*, an instrument for automatically measuring tree growth. My concept of measurement has in consequence greatly expanded.

- Almost everyone has some understanding of *pessimism* and *optimism*, but *deteriorism* and *meliorism* represent related concepts that are perhaps closer to what many of us believe. *Deteriorism* names the belief that everything human is going to the bad and that nothing can be done about it. *Meliorism* grants that this isn't the best of all possible worlds but says that things are gradually getting better and that people can help in the process. Understanding such concepts may assist any of us in the formulation of a philosophy of life.

Scores of concepts that my own mind had not previously grasped or at least not developed may be found in this book. Maybe some of the concepts will be new to you, too. I hope that after reading or playing around with some of the chapters, you will feel as indebted to Eva, my borborygmic collegienne, as I do.

A Note on *Heshe* and *Himer*

"If a person really wants to learn a word, they must use it several times in sentences." *A person* is singular, but *they* is plural. The sentence is grammatically inconsistent.

"If a person really wants to learn a word, he must use it several times in sentences." Some people object to sentences like this, on the ground that *she* deserves as much recognition as *he* does.

The lack of a common-gender pronoun in English has long been recognized, and there have been earlier suggestions on what to do about it. As an experiment, in this book I've used the following combined forms:

heshe = he or she
himer = him or her
hiser = his or her
himerself = himself or herself

Sometimes the results sound rather strange to me, and I haven't yet ventured to use these forms in a speech. Each reader can decide for himerself whether heshe prefers these forms or the status quo.

References and Acknowledgments

Some of the words added in this edition might well have been included in the first one. Kind readers have called many such to my attention. My wife's and my wide reading in contemporary materials provided most of the considerable number of recent words that I have chosen from a much larger number of possibilities. Our son Jay contributed information on music and architecture.

Four dictionaries have been especially useful, each in its own way: For historical background, *The Oxford English Dictionary* and its supplement; for neglected words in use before 1960 or the late 1970s, *Webster's Third New International Dictionary* (1961, "*Webster 3*"), and *The American Heritage Dictionary of the English Language* (1981, "*AHD*"); and, for more recently coined words and clear presentation of almost all words, *The Random House Dictionary of the English Language* (1987, the latest of the "big" dictionaries, "*RHD*").

Other relatively new words were called to my attention by encyclopedia yearbooks, by *The Morrow Book of New Words*, prepared by N. H. and S. K. Mager (1982), and by the column "Word Watch," by Anne H. Soukhanov, in *The Atlantic*. And, of course, *The New York Times* kept me up to date in many ways.

1

SOME PEOPLE YOU MAY KNOW

People-watching fascinates people more than anything else does. That's why gossip flourishes and why storytellers have always been in demand and why movies and television programs (nearly all about people) attract millions of viewers. We—most of us—are inveterate eavesdroppers and voyeurs.

And we talk about the people we hear and see. We classify them. We're **pigeonholers** by instinct—a good thing, too, for science and the arts and business and everything else important that we do consist mainly of putting like things together and putting the unlike things somewhere else. Classifying is basic to human thought.

In our classifying of people, though, we're not usually very methodical, except possibly when we're using occupation as a basic descriptor. We're more likely to classify on an emotional basis, and often, as some of the words in this chapter will show, we're rather unkind.

I'll start with what we call some of the kiddies.

A **gamin** is a rude, impoverished, and badly dressed young boy who spends much time playing in the street or getting into mischief there. His sister, a **gamine,** is perhaps eight to fourteen years old and is generally like her brother in many ways. Sometimes, however, *gamine* is used less pejoratively to mean a tomboy or a pleasantly saucy little girl who is cute despite her impertinence and the smudge on her cheek. Possibly when she is a little older she will be a **hoyden**—high-spirited, bold, boisterous, carefree, perhaps tomboyish and a little wild, but usually not immoral. Some women are **hoydenish** even in their twenties.

Either the boy or the girl may be called a **grig,** a joyous, open, lively, small, or young person: <What a grig my little girl was!> If the child is bad-mannered, said Gelett Burgess about 1900, heshe is a **goop**—a word that later came to mean a boob or a dope of any age. In our time goopishness sometimes comes about because the youngster is a **latch-key child** or **door-key child**—one who is from a broken home or a home where both parents work and who therefore must usually be on hiser own, as symbolized by carrying the door key. The term is generally used in pity, although to sociologists it may be a serious classificatory designation: <Because both parents worked until late in the evening, Beth was a latch-key child.>

We have no standard word for a half-grown person, since *youth* may extend up to age twenty or so. **Halfling,** a Scottish word, could be taken over for this purpose. **Hobbledehoy** is a good old word for an awkward adolescent boy. A **Willie-boy** is a young man who dresses and acts like a dandy or an effeminate person: <a real Willie-boy with his curled locks and ruffled shirt>. **Flirtigig** is a dialectal British expression for a giddy girl who is somewhat boy-crazy and who has no interest in the serious aspects of life. There should be a comparable masculine expression, but I know of none. **Honeydew,** best known to most of us as a kind of melon or something eaten by a character in Coleridge's "Kubla Khan," may also be the sweet stuff deposited by aphids on leaves, or tobacco flavored with molasses, or a gentle orange color, or an unusually sweet girl: <"Why, Honeydew," said the colonel, "one li'l julep won't hurt anyone.">

A **Pollyanna** is usually sweet, too—saccharine, in fact. In 1913 Eleanor Porter wrote a best-selling novel by that name about an ever-cheerful girl who looked on the bright side of everything and was constantly optimistic—"the glad girl" was her epithet. Anyone who shares this happy outlook is a Pollyanna; heshe is **Pollyannaish** and holds a belief in **Pollyannaism.**

A **rareripe** was originally simply a fruit or vegetable that ripened early. Then by extension it came to mean a physically, emotionally, or mentally precocious young person: <At age fourteen he showed that he was a rareripe not only by mastering calculus but also by taking charge in his fatherless home.>

It seems a bit odd that *co-ed*, which is a shortened form of the adjective *coeducational*, has taken over as the designation for a female college student. It is a bit demeaning in a way, as if education is really intended for males but that females are allowed to be "educated with" them. On the rare occasions when sexual differentiation is necessary in referring to students, **collegienne** may be preferable to *co-ed*.

A favorite hobby of many young—and some not so young—persons is represented by three synonymous nouns, each meaning one who greatly likes and/or collects phonograph records: **discophile, gramophile,** and **phonophile.** (Words like *cassettophile* and *C-Dophile* aren't yet in any dictionaries, as far as I know.)

There are thousands of classificatory terms relating to occupations, as publications of the U.S. Bureau of Labor Statistics reveal. Here I'll suggest a few usually ignored by the bureau.

Idleman (plural *idlemen*) is an undeservedly archaic word. An idleman is a wealthy person who does not work: <The secret ambition of many of us is to become idlemen, but some millionaires, despite all their money, have refused to do so.> Some of us, too, might not mind being **Weary Willies.** In the days when tramps roamed the country, one nickname for them was *Weary Willie*, although the term was broadened to include anyone who tried to avoid work: <He's such a Weary Willie he hates to tie his own shoelaces.>

A **grifter** loves money but deplores working for it or getting it by physical violence, so heshe uses hiser wits. Heshe forges checks, loads dice, stacks the deck, sells the Verrazano-Narrows Bridge, bilks the gullible. All hiser techniques collectively are known as **grift.** As a verb, *grift* means to engage in or obtain money by such illegal dealings. A **chairwarmer,** in contrast, steals legally. Heshe is an employee who isn't really needed or who loafs along and accomplishes little in hiser work: <If American industry could eliminate all chairwarmers, including many executives, profits would soar, and consumer prices could drop.>

It's no doubt much more pleasant to be a chairwarmer than a **toadeater.** A mountebank in medieval days sometimes had an assistant who ate (or pretended to eat) a toad. Then the mountebank would demonstrate his skill by expelling the "poison." Obviously such a toadeater had to be a very servile fellow, and the term has come to be used for anyone's follower who is highly obsequious and willing to do anything requested by hiser superior. **Toady,** a shortened form, is a synonym. **Lickspittle** is a disgustingly picturesque old word also sometimes used as a synonym.

In ancient Sparta a **helot** was a serf who had to stay with the estate on which heshe was born, could be freed only by the government, and sharecropped for hiser master. A modern *helot* may also in some countries be a serf, but may also be anyone in any country who is greatly exploited and who has few rights. Hiser condition is **helotism** or **helotry.**

Terms for criminals or near-criminals abound, and since many of them are slang, they often fall into disuse in a few years. Perhaps **heavy man,** for instance, is already out of date; it means a professional criminal whose activities lead or may lead to violence. Heshe engages in a **heavy racket**—any crime that may result in death or injury. The **moll-buzzer** may or may not be in a heavy racket; heshe specializes in stealing from women. The **porkchopper** is not usually a heavy man. He (rarely she) is a labor-union official more interested in his own well-being than in that of the members. *Porkchopper* is a derisive term for him, **pork chops** being slang for the illicit payoffs or other economic advantages he receives.

In politics the porkchopper's equivalent may be the **highbinder.** In about 1806 New York City had to combat a gang of ruffians known as the High-binders. Losing its capital letter, the name became a synonym for thug and later for an organized group of Chinese murderers. Still more recently it has come to mean a swindler, a confidence man, and especially a corrupt politician. Because of association with *spellbinder, highbinder* suggests a crooked politico who is also an effective but deceptive speaker.

Not necessarily crooked but seldom a trusted member of hiser society is the **chancer** or the **boomer.** In parts of Africa a person who comes into a country just to earn some money or make a quick profit and then get out is a chancer. In Alaska a similar person, lured by rumors of high wages or high profit potential, but without any dedication to Alaska itself, is called a boomer.

I'll turn now to a mixed bag of folks, some of whom you are almost sure to encounter at the next cocktail party you attend.

If you have an acquaintance who is a **shifter,** you will find that in an argument heshe will shift ground, perhaps abandoning what heshe said yesterday in order to make a different point that is helpful now. Thus if heshe is a lawyer, heshe may argue against the admissibility of wiretap evidence when doing so may help hiser client, but argue for it when doing that may help. The shifter is somewhat like the **timeserver,** who used to be called a *trimmer,* "one who trims his sails according to the direction of the wind." A timeserver "serves the time," that is, adjusts opinions and actions for hiser own benefit in accordance with conditions.

The person who tries to be the life of the party may be a **witling,** a person with limited understanding or verbal grace but nevertheless a desire to be funny. The witling isn't a neonate; Oliver Goldsmith knew him in the eighteenth century, when he wrote: <"Ye newspaper witlings! Ye pert scribbling fools!">

The **decorist** (accent the second syllable) at the party is a stickler for decorum, for propriety, especially in the arts, in which heshe generally dislikes the experimental and detests anything that seems shocking. In Australia a puritanical decorist is a **wowser,** a person who objects, for instance, to Sunday movies, nudity or near-nudity on beaches, and the use of *damn* on television.

The decorist may also be a **routineer** or a **misoneist.** The former prefers or insists upon following regular routines whether or not they are suitable to the occasion: <Untold numbers of soldiers have been killed because their officers were routineers.> A misoneist (whose beliefs are lumped together as **misoneism**) dislikes or distrusts anything new. Heshe longs for the good old days, believes that yesterday was better than today and that today is better than tomorrow will be unless people start "holding the line." Heshe is like the New Englander to whom on his hundredth birthday a reporter said, "I guess you've seen a lot of changes in your lifetime." He replied, "Yep. An' I've been agin ever' one of 'em."

Almost certainly there will be some **poseurs** at your party—people who pretend to have qualities that they really don't: <a poseur who intimated that his research would result in a complete reevaluation of Herman Melville's writing>. Among the poseurs are the **philosophasters,** who dabble a bit in philosophy and make believe that they know a great deal about it or are good at constructing it. (And what should we call those who dabble in psychology? *Psychologasters?*)

In one corner the **facticide** is impressing the **gobemouche.** *Facticide,* by analogy with *homicide,* means fact-killing and also means the person who does such killing; heshe alters or deletes facts or twists them viciously. *Gobemouche* comes from French *gober* "to swallow" and *mouche* "a fly." A gobemouche will "swallow anything"—is gullible, credulous: <Gobemouches are often sent to bring back left-handed monkey wrenches and skyhooks, or to hold the bag in a snipe hunt.> A **roundheel** is somewhat similar—a person easily victimized or overcome, a pushover: <He'll be easy to rob. He's just a roundheel.> <The girl's female acquaintances spitefully claimed that she was a roundheel.>

Maybe you'll find a **oncer** nursing hiser glass of ginger ale at this cocktail party. The oncer does something once and no more: <He was a real oncer—smoked a cigarette at eighteen, took a drink at nineteen, fathered one child, and worked only one day in his whole life.> An **ill-willer,** the opposite of a well-wisher, can hardly conceal hiser hope that the party will flop or that somebody will shoot the host or at least seduce the hostess. The **quidnunc** (literally "what now?") would also be made happy by a few minor seductions or other falls from grace, for heshe is a busybody who delights in reporting and speculating about other people's business, particularly trivia.

If you're lucky, there may be a few people present whom you'll like pretty well. Maybe, for instance, a **subtilist,** who will challenge your intelligence with hiser subtleties, or a **sarcast,** whose sarcasm you will enjoy. The **persifleur's** banter, frivolous talk, and mild derisiveness may also amuse you. The **causeur** who holds forth with one group is an easy talker, frequently witty, pleasant to hear. (A **causeuse** used to be a talkative woman but is now a piece of furniture—a small sofa comfortable for two persons to sit on for a long chat.) **Causerie** is a light conversation or a chatty piece of writing.

If it's a very respectable party, among the guests may be an **eminento,** a **sedens,** or even a **cenobite.** Since English lacked a single word meaning an eminent person, we went to Italian and borrowed *eminento:* <In this town Sam Stock is certainly the eminento.> A sedens, often an old-timer, is a person who remains in the vicinity where he was born—possibly, for instance, marrying the girl next door, another sedens. The word comes from Latin *sedere* "to sit," which is also the source of the familiar *sedentary.* The adoption of the stay-here way of life preferred by **sedentes** (the plural of *sedens*) is **sedentation,** although this word may also mean adoption of sedentary habits in preference to an active life. A **cenobite** is a religious person living with a group, as in a monastery or convent. The religious community itself may be known as a **cenoby.** Both words come from Greek *koinobios,* "being in community." <Dwellers in certain serious-minded communes consider themselves cenobites.>

Other People

abecedarian *adj, n* When your toddler is learning the alphabet, heshe is an abecedarian. By extension, a beginner at anything may be called by that name. As a modifier, *abecedarian* may mean pertaining to the alphabet, alphabetically arranged, or, again by extension, rudimentary—since knowledge of an alphabet is the beginning stage in much learning.

alleger *n* Oddly, this word for one who alleges is not in my *Webster 3*, although it is in *RHD*. It seems to me much better than *allegator* (which *Webster 3* does have), because the latter term could easily be confused with the name of a large reptile.

bridgebuilder *n* A peacemaker, an arbitrator. The bridgebuilder helps each opposing side to understand the positions of the other, and tries to reconcile differences in a way fair to all.

catechumen *n* It is well known that catechism is instruction in religion, specifically in the religious beliefs of a given church or denomination. Less well known is the fact that a person receiving such instruction is a catechumen.

cockalorum *n* A bantam rooster struts about as if he rules the world. A person who resembles the rooster by strutting or boasting or putting on airs is a cockalorum. The word is also used to refer to boastful talk like the braggadocio reflected in some nineteenth-century tales of the American frontier: <the cockalorum of one of Mark Twain's frontiersmen>. A variant is **high cockalorum,** which British schoolboys playing leapfrog used to shout, and perhaps still do. The expression is more generally, however, one of the rather numerous and slangy expressions disparaging someone in a position of leadership, comparable to *big shot* or *high-muckety-muck*.

cocooning *n* Some sociologists say that more and more Americans, tired of the increasing discomforts and cost of travel, take their vacations at home, in effect wrapping themselves in a cocoon away from crowds and hurly-burly.

conky *n* Slang for a person with an unusually large nose: <Jimmy Durante, a conky, was nicknamed "Schnozzola.">

cotquean *n* Today a man who shares household chores with his wife may be considered an exponent of equal rights for the sexes, an enlightened and nonsexist man. Once, though, he would have been called a cotquean (literally "cottage woman"), a word that still earlier meant a manlike, coarse woman who was reportedly as well-equipped with profanity as a fishwife. Perhaps we are kinder in our speech than people used to be, but if you are ever in an untender mood you may want to refer to either a womanly man or a manly woman as a cotquean, although in either case you may suffer physical damage.

couch people *n* No, they're not the same as *couch potatoes,* those people who sit for hours hypnotized by a TV screen. Couch people are homeless folks who drop in on friends or relatives for a week or a month or until their welcome is gone. In today's small houses or apartments they often must sleep on couches.

cultural focus *n* Whether you live in New York or New Guinea, Paris or Sevastopol, you and your fellow citizens inevitably develop a cultural focus that is unique to your community. Although no two individuals are alike in all ways, your community as a whole will emphasize some cultural ingredients or foci more or less than other communities do, creating a pattern or a mixture not quite like that anywhere else. Even great diversity among individuals and groups, as in New York City, in itself helps to create a cultural focus.

cultural lag *n* A cultural lag exists if one facet of a community lags behind some of the others. For example, there is a cultural lag if schools, libraries, and support for art and literature are less emphasized than industry and sports.

cultural pluralism *n* A live-and-let-live condition in which substantial differences in beliefs and practices are not only accepted but also valued, except when they harmfully interfere with the beliefs and practices of others.

dabster *n* A person who dabbles with a task (or anything else) but is not highly proficient at it and does not devote much time to it is a dabster: <Both Churchill and Eisenhower were dabsters in painting.>

deadhead *n* In general a deadhead receives a service of some sort without paying for it, for example, a complimentary ticket to a show or for transportation: <Part of the railroads' financial troubles arose because so many passengers were deadheads.> Heshe may also be a noncontributor to an organization or a business—a chairwarmer: <Although her father founded the company, Mrs. R. is a deadhead on the board.> A truck, plane, or freight car returning without cargo is also a deadhead.

declarant *n* An alien who has taken out hiser first naturalization papers, thus declaring that heshe intends to become a citizen of the United States.

deculturate *v* When nation A conquers and occupies nation B, it often attempts to extirpate or replace B's religion, journalistic practices, and other parts of its culture, including much of its social and political structure. Or, for a quite different example, when a sheltered, overprotected person goes to college heshe will be exposed to new experiences and encounter new concepts, come to question and perhaps alter many beliefs and practices learned in childhood, and thus be simultaneously deculturated and acculturated.

docent *n* Less often used in American universities than the corresponding *Dozent* is in Germany, *docent* is a handy designation for any college-level teacher below a professorial rank. Without it, we must either specify the particular rank (as assistant, associate, lecturer, etc.) or use several words instead of one.

embusqué *n* A person who tries to get out of military service, especially by legal or quasi-legal means, is sometimes called an *embusqué*, from a French verb for shirk.

éminence grise *n* Cardinal Richelieu, prominent French statesman of the seventeenth century, was called *Éminence Rouge*, "red eminence," because of his power and his red cloak. His trusted subordinate was Père Joseph, who wore a more ordinary gray habit and was nicknamed *Éminence Grise*, "gray eminence." Ever since that time a confidant or confidante to whom considerable power has been unofficially granted has been called an éminence grise: <Edwin Meese was the éminence grise of the Reagan administration.>

empathy *n*, **empathetic** *adj* Empathy is like sympathy but suggests an even closer relationship. Sympathetic people try to be understanding and compassionate, but empathetic people feel that they are inside someone else's mind and emotional being, feel that they *are* the other person for a while. They live with and share the other's joy, sorrow, pain, fear, love. Readers are often empathetic toward ("identify with") one or more fictional characters.

escapologist *n* An *escapist* evades unpleasant reality, as a rule, by reading about pleasant but basically unreal activity or by engaging in imaginative flights. An *escapologist*, however, turns to drink, merrymaking, and revelry for hiser escape. The term is an informal one, usually not in a psychologist's lexicon.

flagger *n* The feminist movement has made many changes in the word forms of choice. Almost everyone knows that *stewardess* has been replaced by *flight attendant*, *policeman* by *officer* or *police officer*, *fireman* by *firefighter*. Along Indiana highways recently—perhaps elsewhere, too—the old warning FLAGMAN AHEAD has been replaced on sparkling new signs by FLAGGER AHEAD. (*Webster 3* defines *flagger* as "a wild iris.")

flaneur *n*, **flaneuse** *n*, **flânerie** *n* In Old Norse *flana* meant to wander about; the French took it over, eventually, in the form *flâneur* "one who wanders about aimlessly, a vagrant, an idler." In English the flaneur usually is not a vagrant, but he is an unsettled person, an idler, a person with little concern for others; sometimes he is quite intelligent but does not persist in any serious activity. His female counterpart is a flaneuse, and their mutual occupation (or lack of it) is flânerie.

folk society *n*, **speech island** *n* A sociologist usually thinks of a folk society as a small, rather isolated group of people—say, in a remote Appalachian valley—who tend to cling to their own traditions, habits, and speech, though not necessarily rejecting the advantages and temptations of the outside world. Because their language often retains old-fashioned words and usages, the linguist may think of them as constituting a speech island. (See also *speech community* in Chapter 16.)

gentrification *n* Upper- or middle-class families (the gentry) buy up property in a rundown area and gradually renovate and move into it. The neighborhood becomes "better" as a result of this gentrification, but the displaced persons must try to find housing somewhere else.

hacker *n* A person who has little experience or skill in a sport, even though heshe may have great interest in it, is a hacker. The word is perhaps related to *hack*, shortened from *hackney*, meaning a professional writer with low literary standards and accomplishment. A computer hacker at first was only an enthusiastic computer programmer or experimenter, but later the word became mixed up with the pejorative *cracker* "computer criminal" and added the connotation "a person who tries to gain possibly illegal access to the computer files of others."

hardcase *n* A hardcase is ordinarily a hardened criminal but may also be a very impoverished, crippled, or otherwise pitiful person: <Who would have suspected that such a sweet girl would ever become a hardcase?> <my arthritic aunt, a real hardcase>.

hierophant *n* A hierophant is a spokesman, advocate, or interpreter of an idea, ism, political party, etc.: <Jefferson and other hierophants of liberty>. A *sycophant* differs from a hierophant in being servile and flattering.

japer *n*, **jape** *vi, vt* **japery** *n* To jape is to joke, especially in a jeering, taunting, or deceptive way. A japer is one who japes, and japery is unpolished, often unkind jesting, sometimes including practical jokes or trickery.

jollier *n* The verb *to jolly* may mean to banter, to joke with; to tease, coax, and flatter. A jollier is someone who jollies: <A clever jollier, he quickly cajoled her into taking

the oars.> A jollier may also be a potter or a shoemaker using a tool called a *jolly*.

klutz *n,* **deklutzification** *n* From the Yiddish *klots*, "wooden beam," *klutz* refers to a stupid, clumsy, or awkward person. <Cyril called his country cousin "an ignorant klutz" and said that his deklutzification would take years.>

laglast *n,* **laggardly** *adv* A laggard is one that lags, falls behind, loiters. *Laggardly* means like a laggard, or being laggard: <The sun crawled laggardly across the sky.> <"Be leaderly, not laggardly," his father admonished him.> A laglast is one who comes at the very end: <In classes he was a laglast, but in basketball he set scoring records.>

libertarian *n, adj* To a sociologist a libertarian argument goes like this: "Every person should be free to believe whatever heshe pleases and to do whatever heshe wishes—to the extent that the deeds do not interfere with the rights of others or harm them in any way." To a theologian, *libertarian* means this: "People are not predestined to do anything. Outside events and especially their own free will determine what they are, what they do, what they become."

morosoph *n* By etymology a sophomore is a wise fool, but that meaning is virtually forgotten in schools and colleges. *Morosoph* comes from the same Greek words, and means learned fool: <Professor Gregg is a morosoph who understands relativity but can't drive a car.>

obscurant *adj, n,* and related words. One who willfully hides information, especially to prevent others from attaining knowledge or wisdom; also, tending to obscure, pertaining to the act of obscuring. The person who practices or believes in **obscurantism** may be called an **obscurantist** as well as an **obscurant:** <Some professors, like some poets and painters, prefer obscurantism to clarity.>

old boy (old girl) network *n* A group of men or women with backgrounds and interests in common often cooperate ("I'll scratch your back if you'll scratch mine") in political or business endeavors or in support of a cause. The organization is almost always as informal as its name—no formal meetings, no minutes, no organizational announcements. <The congressman declared that old boy networks were responsible for many of the finaglings of certain savings and loan associations.> <In our town the leading old girl network consists of graduates of Wellesley, Smith, and the like.>

outsettler *n* A settler who lives outside a given region:<outsettlers over toward Hastings>.

overdog *n* Everyone knows about (and usually sympathizes with) the underdog, but the overdog is seldom mentioned. Heshe is anyone who belongs to a dominating, highly privileged group: <The northern Chinese were at that time the overdogs.>

panjandrum *n* Samuel Foote, an eighteenth-century English writer, created some nonsense about Picninnies, Joblillies, Garyulies, "and the Grand Panjandrum himself, with the little round button on top." The other characters have almost vanished from human memory, but *panjandrum* survives as the name of a pompous, pretentious official with considerable power, which heshe is likely to use unwisely.

patrioteer *n* A patrioteer is a flag-waver, a chauvinist or jingoist, a person who pretends to great patriotism but uses hiser assumed love of country for hiser own ends: <patrioteer merchants who wore their lapel flags and spoke of the need for sacrifices but increased the prices of all their goods and kept their sons out of the army>.

philomath *n* The *math* in this word comes from Greek *mathein* "to learn." A philomath, then, is someone who loves learning, a scholar. Because of the influence of *mathematics*, a philomath is especially likely to be fond of mathematics or mathematics-related subjects.

pigeon-dropper *n* Confidence men, "bunco men," reportedly call their victims *pigeons*. A pigeon-dropper is someone who swindles, or "drops pigeons," and the occupation itself is sometimes called pigeon-dropping.

plutogogue *n* A person who favors wealthy people and tries to defend or glorify them: <Congressman Lane,

while never admitting he was a plutogogue, consistently voted for measures favoring the wealthy.>

politicaster *n* Just as a poetaster is an unimportant, untalented, would-be poet, a politicaster is an unimportant, untalented, would-be politician.

polyhistor *n,* **polymath** *n* A polyhistor or a polymath is a person with vast, almost encyclopedic learning. *Polymath* is derived from Greek words meaning much learning; *polyhistor,* from Greek for much knowing.

quick study *n* A person who learns something, such as lines in a play or a musical score, with much greater than average speed.

rabbit ears *n* Besides the literal meaning, *rabbit ears* may refer to something resembling rabbit ears, such as the two-pronged antenna on top of some television sets, a type of cactus, or a self-closing faucet on which the "ears" are squeezed together to release water. Also, an athlete who is excessively sensitive to criticism may be said to have rabbit ears.

rakehell *adj, n* Middle English had a word *rakel* or *rakil,* "rash, impetuous," which apparently changed spelling to *rackle* and then to *rakehell.* Since a rash, impetuous person has little control over hiser behavior, the ideas of rascality, dissoluteness, licentiousness, and general wildness were added. Today the word is seldom used, but rakehells are still with us: <a group of rakehells terrorizing the community> <a rakehell attitude>.

scaremonger *n* Some people love to alarm others concerning dire things that they say will or may happen; these people are scaremongers.

shanachie *n* In Ireland a person fond of telling the old tales and legends of the countryfolk is a shanachie.

social development *n,* **social process** *n* Steadily, inexorably, the social characteristics of a community, a nation, or the world change. Life in the 1990s differs from that of a half century ago, and even more so from that of the 1890s. The complex and variable ways in which social changes occur are lumped together as *the social process. Social development* is a synonym.

solivagant *adj, n* The adjective means wandering alone;

the noun, one who wanders by himerself. *Sol-* is from the Latin *solus*, "alone," which is also the source of such words as *solo, solitude,* and *soliloquy; -vagant* is from Latin *vagus*, "wandering," and is related to *vagrant.*

stump-jumper *n* Slang for either a stump-speaker or a person from the backwoods, a hillbilly.

systematism *n* **systematist** *n* Some people like to create systems—for anything from doing housework to running the government. Their tendency is known as systematism, and they are systematists.

term-trotter *n* In England, as in America, for financial or other reasons many students cannot attend college straight through but must occasionally skip a term. The British call such irregularly attending students *term-trotters.*

thaumaturge *n,* and related words. A thaumaturge (also **thaumaturgist**) is one who performs miracles. Heshe is capable of **thaumaturgy;** heshe does **thaumaturgic** acts. **Thaumatology** is the study of the performance of miracles.

tippee *n* A tipper gives tips, and a tippee receives them. <Is it more blessed to be a tipper than a tippee?>

transracial *adj* Something described as transracial involves two or more races: <transracial adoptions> <Transracial discussions among South African leaders continued.>

United Statesian *n* As is generally agreed, *American* is inappropriate as a designation of a resident of the United States. *United Statesian,* though listed in dictionaries, has never caught on. (Perhaps *USan,* pronounced yo͞o′ ĕs″ ən, would be more manageable.)

warmedy *n* A warm, friendly TV comedy intended for the whole family.

Mastery Test

Match each word with the best definition in its group.

____	1. hoyden	a. lifelong resident
____	2. sedens	b. one who likes the wealthy
____	3. discophile	c. slave
____	4. helot	d. busybody
____	5. moll-buzzer	e. lone wanderer
____	6. plutogogue	f. collector of recordings
____	7. quidnunc	g. unsuccessful humorist
____	8. solivagant	h. one who robs women
____	9. witling	i. one who is easily overcome
____	10. roundheel	j. a spirited, tomboyish girl
____	11. chairwarmer	k. one who hints
____	12. decorist	l. deceitful but eloquent politician
____	13. subtilist	m. toadeater
____	14. misoneist	n. ragged boy
____	15. japer	o. precocious young person
____	16. highbinder	p. one who does not earn hiser salary
____	17. gamin	q. a person distrustful of innovations
____	18. lickspittle	r. what an oversensitive athlete has
____	19. rabbit ears	s. stickler for conventional good taste
____	20. rareripe	t. an often cruel joker
____	21. facticide	u. credulous person
____	22. gobemouche	v. distorter of information
____	23. Pollyanna	w. classifier
____	24. polyhistor	x. lover of learning
____	25. grifter	y. unreasonably optimistic person
____	26. philomath	z. swindler
____	27. pigeonholer	aa. unusually knowledgeable person

2
PEOPLE'S INTERRELATIONSHIPS

Ecology, as is well known, is a study of interrelationships. **Human ecology** is the study of the interrelationships of people with people and of people with the institutions that they themselves have created, such as government, money, trade, and social groups. In this chapter we'll look at a few of the words used to refer to some of these interrelationships.

Cooperation between people often results in accomplishments that one person alone would find impossible. It is odd, then, that we often refer to someone's performing a task *singlehanded* but that **doublehanded** is seldom used. Certainly two people often do work together: <Doublehanded, they caught the whole gang.>

People who act together may be said to **coact.** If they get along harmoniously, perhaps it is because they are **simpatico**—a Spanish word (earlier Latin) that has no exact English equivalent. *Congenial* may be closest, but *simpatico* adds some sympathy and perhaps empathy. Two persons are simpatico if they get along well together and almost instinctively recognize the moods and wishes of each other. Maybe also they are **bonhomous.** In French a *bonhomme* is a good-natured man, and *bonhomie* is geniality or good nature. The English borrowing *bonhomous* means warmly friendly and easy to get along with: <Although my uncle knew he had cancer, he was the most bonhomous person I have ever known.>

A leader-follower relationship almost always develops when two or more persons are together. An unusually honest parent, filling in a college admissions form concerning his son, answered the question "Is he a leader?" by replying, "No, but he is an excellent follower." The boy was admitted with the explanation "So far we've admitted five hundred leaders, and it's about time to get a few followers." People who can follow a leader, obediently yet intelligently, demonstrate **followership,** a quality almost as rare as good leadership.

The good leader demonstrates **manuduction.** Picture someone taking a stranger by the hand (Latin *manus*) and leading himer (Latin *ducere*) to wherever heshe should go. Such "hand-leading" is literally what manuduction is. Practically, it is any act of leading or guiding, or any book, article, set of instructions, etc., that may serve as a guide.

Psychologists recognize the need to belong as something important to human beings. Some years ago *McCall's* magazine built a profitable subscription campaign on its advocacy of family *togetherness,* thus rescuing that useful word from undeserved obscurity. **Belongingness** merits no less: "the quality or state of being essential, integral, or important," says *Webster 3.* <The saddest thing about the man without a country, or any other outcast, is that he has lost his belongingness.> Whether what one belongs to is a family, a street gang, a political party, or a group of lovers of dictionaries, the belongingness provides a sense of companionship if not solidarity.

Belongingness sometimes results from **comity:** friendly, considerate behavior between persons, groups, or nations. The word comes from the Latin *comis,* "courteous," and is related to a Sanskrit word meaning "he smiles." (Among American Protestant churches, *comity* refers to the custom of not trying to lure members away from one another.)

Any group that stays together for a while develops its own characteristics. *Personality* refers to the behavior or idiosyncrasies of an individual, and **syntality**—surprisingly little used—refers to the behavior or idiosyncrasies of a group: <the kindly, cheerful syntality of the village's inhabitants>.

Unfortunately, people don't always live harmoniously or constantly illustrate comity, bonhomie, or other pleasant relationships. As an illustration, city dwellers and rural folk have seldom thoroughly understood, respected, and liked one another, as the language reveals in words like *hick, rube,* and *city slicker.* (*Heathen* was originally a city person's term for one who lives on the heath. Christianity usually reached rural areas later than it did urban ones, so *heathen* took on its current meaning. Heathens are people in the sticks who haven't even heard the Word.) **Cityness** and **citified** are terms used by some country people to disparage qualities they dislike in their city cousins: arrogance, boastfulness, superciliousness, and lack of awareness of the elemental things of life.

A **ruralist** is someone who speaks out in favor of rural as opposed to urban life. To the linguist a **ruralism** is an expression associated with the country: <*Cuppin* for "cowpen" is a ruralism still heard in some areas.> But ruralism is also a belief in the superiority of the country over the city: <staunchly upheld ruralism>. The meanings of **urbanist** and **urbanism** are not related to or opposed to those of *ruralist* and *ruralism.* An urbanist plans cities. Urbanism is (1) city planning, (2) urbanization, or (3) a way of life characteristic of many city-dwellers. <Urbanism appealed to him. "There's so much to do here," he said.> **Rurban,** a blend of *rural* and *urban,* is an adjective meaning living outside a city but not on a farm, or pertaining to a place mainly residential but with some farming: <Perhaps rurban people live in the best of all worlds.> **Rurigenous** means born in the country, or from the country: <Most American presidents have been rurigenous or at least rurban.>

Many of mankind's arguments, even wars, have arisen because people tend to be **ethnocentric. Ethnocentrism** is like provincialism—a belief that one's own environment and customs and beliefs and appearance are best. It results in looking at other racial or cultural groups with disfavor, disdain, or hostility, and in assuming that because their looks and mores are different, the other people are inferior. The ethnocentric person regards hiser own race or cultural group as a proper norm, which other races or cultural groups have failed to equal.

But when people are able to overcome their divisive forces, they often learn to enjoy being with one another. In Australia, for instance, **mateship,** "fellowship, regard for everyone else as an equal," is a prized virtue. In America we perhaps have less of it than a Christian country should, since mateship is clearly related to the biblical injunction "Love thy neighbor." Australia is also the home of the **corroboree,** based on a native New South Wales word for a noisy, high-spirited, uproarious party. (A person taking part in such an activity is *corroboreeing.*) The event is certainly not unknown in the United States, so we might as well adopt the name for it. A British variety of celebration is commemorated in the verb **maffick.** In 1900 the town of Mafeking, in South Africa, was under siege by the Boers. When British forces drove away the besiegers, rejoicing in England was unparalleled. From *Mafeking* came *maffick:* to celebrate with great boisterousness.

Sometimes when a Haitian needs assistance, a group of friends or neighbors will assemble and, usually to the accompaniment of singing and rhythmic music, help himer to finish hiser task. Such a group is called a **combite** (second syllable like "beet") and is not unlike the old-fashioned USan barn raisings, cellar-digging bees, and other helpful endeavors that industrialization and urbanization have now almost eliminated.

Other Words About Human Ecology

baboonery *n* Although somewhat like *buffoonery, baboonery* suggests attitudes and especially conduct that are not only funny and clownish but also grotesque, degrading, and perhaps cruel. Practical jokes that cause genuine distress may be examples, as may the activities in old-time hazing of college freshmen.

barrio *n* In Latin-American countries and the Philippines a ward or district is called a *barrio.* In the United States the word is becoming increasingly known as a synonym for *Spanish-speaking neighborhood.*

camorra *n,* and related words. This word, from Italian, names a group of people who work together for a cause that others regard as dishonest or dishonorable: <a camorra of plotters trying to corner the supply of sulfur>. A member of the camorra may be called a **camorrista** or a **camorrist,** pluralized as **camorristi** or **camorrists.**

canard *n* Cooks, at least French cooks, know that *canard* means flesh of a duck. But what is the meaning of the word in a phrase like "a vile canard"? Well, the French have an expression, *vendre des canards à moitié,* which means to half-sell ducks. I don't know how one half-sells a duck, but it must be a dishonest act, because the French expression has come to mean to deceive, to cheat. The English took over the duck part, *canard,* and used it to mean a deceptive story, a false report, a rumor without foundation. So today's politician may thunder that his opponents who accuse him of wrongdoing are guilty of "vile canards," even though ducks were never mentioned.

cark *vi, vt* Latin *carrus,* the source of our *car,* means wheeled vehicle, and Late Latin *carricare* means to load on a wheeled vehicle. Middle English adopted the verb as *carken* "to load, to burden." Soon it took on a figurative sense of to load or burden (someone) with trouble or anxiety, or, intransitively, to be troubled or fretful or to work while burdened with trouble: <His wife's ill health carked him still more.> <always carking but still trying to be cheerful>.

catbird seat *n* A former New York baseball announcer popularized the southern expression *sitting in the catbird seat,* "in a highly advantageous position": <Ahead 10 to 3, the Yankees are really sitting in the catbird seat.> <Rogers is now in the catbird seat in the corporation, for he owns nearly 60 percent of the stock.>

ceremonialist *n*, **ceremonialism** *n* Someone who likes much emphasis on ceremonial forms or rites, especially though not necessarily in religion, is a ceremonialist; heshe usually prefers a ritualistic church such as the Roman Catholic or the Episcopalian. The following of or preference for such ceremonies is ceremonialism.

chest beating *n*, **chest thumping** *n*, **breast beating** *n* The three aren't quite the same. Chest beating is an excessively dramatic confession of errors. Chest thumping is boastful and arrogant conduct and self-glorification. Breast beating is most often a noisy expression of grief.

chummage *n* Persons strangers to each others initially, such as soldiers or college students, are often quartered in the same room. The practice of such quartering is called *chummage*, perhaps because it often results in chumminess. <Chummage of male and female students is still forbidden by this college.>

compossible *adj* *Compatible* and *compossible* are similar in that both mean capable of existing together. But *compatible* suggests that the coexistence is harmonious or even pleasant, while *compossible* means only that the coexistence is not impossible: <The tenets of the two religious sects were compossible but hardly compatible.>

conclamant *adj*, **conjubilant** *adj* Conclamant voices are those that shout together, often in protest: <conclamant warnings of doom>. Conjubilant voices also shout together, but always in joy: <the conjubilant cheers of the basketball fans>.

correctitude *n* Correctitude is not just any sort of correctness; rather, it is correctness of behavior, especially adherence to rules of etiquette: <Emily Post was then the nation's foremost explicator and advocate of correctitude.>

criminogenic *adj*, **criminogenesis** *n* Whatever may produce or lead to crime or criminality may be described as criminogenic: <criminogenic ghettos>. *Criminogenesis* means the origin of crime: <Criminogenesis is often attributed to lack of parental discipline.>

curtain lecture *n* Alas, even lexicographers are sometimes sexist pigs, as when they define *curtain lecture* as a censorious lecture by a wife to her husband, often in bed. Don't husbands ever give curtain lectures?

dehort *vt* If you *exhort* someone, you encourage himer to do something; you egg himer on or plead with himer to do hiser best. The antonym of *exhort* is *dehort*, "to discourage a person from proceeding, to advise against": <I wanted a jury trial, but my lawyer dehorted me.>

desuetude *n* Desuetude is a state of inactivity that suggests that some long-established custom is being abandoned: <The courtesy once characteristic of retail clerks seems to have fallen into desuetude.>

discombobulate *vt* If you ever need a somewhat humorous verb for "to upset, to disconcert," try *discombobulate*, which is one of those pleasant monstrosities that our nineteenth-century ancestors liked to construct on the base of some other word—this time perhaps *discompose* or *discomfit*.

Engel's law *n* Ernst Engel was a late nineteenth-century German economist who described what is now a familiar phenomenon: In comparison with the poor, wealthy people spend a smaller proportion of their income for food, about the same proportion for housing and clothing, and a higher proportion for recreation, education, and medical care. The generalization is now called *Engel's law*.

esclandre *n* A public quarrel, an open insult, shocking behavior—anything of the sort that may result in scandal or gossip.

factional *adj*, **factious** *adj* These two words are not quite synonyms, though both have to do with factions, such as splinter groups within a government. *Factional* means "pertaining to factions, characterized by factionalism," but *factious* refers more often to "a tendency to create factions, divisive." <Factional disputes are frequent.> <His factious inclinations led to a three-way split among New York Democrats.>

foofaraw or **foofarah** *n* A foofaraw is much ado about nothing, a disturbance caused by a trifle. The word is also a slangy term for overly ornate clothing.

Greek gift *n* The "gift" by the Greeks to the Trojans of a huge wooden horse was an act of treachery, since the horse was filled with Greek soldiers who succeeded in capturing Troy. So for centuries *Greek gift* has symbolized any gift or favor presented deceptively for nefarious purposes: <Many a young man has brought Greek gifts to a girl, and many a girl has presented her body as a Greek gift.>

handsel *n* It is difficult to understand why this useful word fell out of favor. It refers to a gift made as a token of good luck—e.g., a graduation present, wedding present, New Year present, or opening-of-business present. It may also be earnest money paid to confirm a purchase.

liaise *vi* The verb based on *liaison* is little known, but can be useful in either its meaning "to make liaison with" or its meaning "to serve as a liaison": <Dr. Cray was selected to liaise at once with the Chilean ambassador.> <He liaised successfully with the kidnappers.>

mala fide *adj, adv* The expression *bona fide* "in good faith, genuine" is well known, but its opposite is rarely heard. It refers to acting in bad faith, with the intention of deceiving or defrauding: <a mala fide interpretation of the law> <swore mala fide> <the mala fide buyer>.

mass society *n* Mass society is the impersonalized, largely urban society in which identities appear submerged in the crowd. Mobility is high, but the individual finds, wherever heshe goes, essentially the same products, the same jobs, the same pastimes, the same beliefs.

maturism *n* If a society develops as far as it is capable, its forward movement ceases and the most it can hope for is avoidance of retrogression. This unsatisfactory state is called *maturism:* <The goal is maturity without maturism.> Individuals, too, may reach maturism, although the wise avoid it by at least minor alterations of their course.

meeting seed *n* "Gotta go back a minute, Ma. Fergot my meetin' seed." That's what an old-time churchgoer might have said, referring to the small fruits or aromatic seeds that some parishioners used to chew to keep awake during long sermons. <Meeting seeds should be available to today's college students.>

objurgate *vt,* and related words. To objurgate is to condemn or decry, to castigate harshly and often profanely: <Consumers increasingly objurgated the greed and deception of big business.> The noun form is **objurgation;** the adjectives are **objurgative** and **objurgatory.** One who objurgates is an **objurgator.**

opprobriate *vt* To opprobriate is to regard with opprobrium or speak or write with opprobrium—with distaste, contempt, sometimes hatred, or even scurrility: <Nineteenth-century politicians often opprobriated their opponents viciously.>

oppugn *vt* To oppugn an opponent is usually to express doubts of his honesty, truthfulness, or other good qualities; less often it means to fight against (which is the etymological meaning): <Each candidate oppugned the other's veracity.>

palter *vi* A character in Sir Walter Scott's *Quentin Durward* says, "If you palter or double in your answers, I will have thee hung alive in an iron chain." Paltering is not usually so harshly punished, though it consists of speaking or acting insincerely, using trickery or deceit, and playing false. Less objectionably, *palter* may also mean to bargain, to haggle: <I'll pay what you ask, because I have no time to palter.>

prévenance *n* From a French verb meaning to anticipate, *prévenance* means anticipating the needs of others, or an example of such anticipation: <British servants were long famed for their prévenance; they always seemed to know what the master or mistress or guest might require and when.>

psychosocial *adj* Pertaining to both psychological and sociological considerations: <psychosocial rather than economic problems in their partnership>.

punctilio *n*, **punctilious** *adj* In Italian *puntiglio* is a small point, a point of honor; Spanish *puntillo* is similar. English *punctilio* means a small detail in a ceremony, a bit of behavior that one carefully observes: <The groom's family was unaware of some of the punctilios that the bride's family considered essential.> *Punctilious,* "attentive to details and conventions," is based on *punctilio.*

reference group *n* Usually a person knows or knows of a group that heshe admires and wants to emulate; heshe shares their interests, attitudes, and societal values. They are hiser reference group: <Unfortunately the reference group of the young slum-dweller is often one that turns himer toward crime.>

rencontre or **rencounter** *n* French for an accidental or hostile meeting; English for a duel or other combat between two individuals or groups; by extension, a nonviolent meeting of opponents, as in an argument; also, a casual meeting: <a bloody rencontre> <a spirited rencontre concerning American policy in the Mediterranean> <a chance rencontre with an old friend>.

sequacity *n* A tendency to follow or to be servile: <Sequacity used to be what officers most wanted to instill.>

sub rosa *adv,* **sub-rosa** *adj* Literally "under the rose." According to mythology, Cupid once gave a rose to Harpocrates, the god of silence, to keep him from telling anyone about the love life of Cupid's mother, Venus. Following the spirit of the legend, in some state councils a rose was hung over the table to indicate that everyone present was sworn to secrecy. Anything now done sub rosa is done secretly, in the hope that no publicity will emerge: <They met sub rosa.> <a sub-rosa decision>.

Mastery Test

Match each word with the best definition in its group of ten.

____	1. canard	a. secret, associated with a flower
____	2. catbird seat	b. a guide, associated with the hand
____	3. sub rosa	c. clownish conduct, associated with the wilds
____	4. cultural pluralism	d. a favorable position, associated with a wild bird

___ 5. manuduction	e. condemnation or exhortation, associated with marriage
___ 6. rurigenous	f. a wild party, associated with down under
___ 7. corroboree	g. sleep inhibitor, associated with church
___ 8. baboonery	h. a false rumor, associated with a duck
___ 9. curtain lecture	i. associated with the country
___ 10. meeting seed	j. acceptance of others' beliefs
___ 11. foofaraw	k. in bad faith
___ 12. handsel	l. the "personality" of a group
___ 13. mala fide	m. end of forward movement
___ 14. maturism	n. exaltation of one's own group
___ 15. simpatico	o. friendly, considerate behavior
___ 16. comity	p. a group of helpful neighbors
___ 17. syntality	q. good-luck gift
___ 18. ethnocentrism	r. group working for a dishonorable cause
___ 19. combite	s. much ado about nothing
___ 20. camorra	t. congenial and understanding
___ 21. cark	u. annoy, upset
___ 22. compossible	v. burden with trouble or anxiety
___ 23. chest thumping	w. divisive
___ 24. conjubilant	x. rejoicing together
___ 25. dehort	y. condemn

___ 26. discombobulate	z. capable of existing together
___ 27. factious	aa. express doubts of (someone's) honesty or motives
___ 28. objurgate	bb. advise against
___ 29. oppugn	cc. foreseeing of the needs of others
___ 30. prévenance	dd. self-glorification

3
OF HUSBANDS, WIVES, AND A FEW OTHER RELATIVES

Words to describe marrying and the institution of marriage are almost as numerous as the customs themselves. Not everybody, though, likes the thought of spending a lifetime—or even a night—locked to another. A **misogynist,** for example, is one who hates women; **misogyny** is that sort of hatred; the adjective is **misogynic** "hating or distrusting women." **Misandry** is hatred of men; a person who hates men is a **misandrist,** and heshe may be described as **misandric.** *RHD* lists *misandrist* but not *misandric.* Surely haters of men are numerous enough to warrant use of all three words. **Misogamy** is hatred of marriage—the members of the opposite sex may be OK, but marriage to one of them is undesirable. A **misogamist** is one who hates marriage, and the adjective **misogamic** means marriage-hating.

But most people, it seems, aren't misogamists and do get married. If as a result of law or custom one marries within a specific group, heshe is practicing **endogamy:** <Endogamy has been usual in the caste system of India.> If heshe marries outside hiser own group, the practice is **exogamy:** <Exogamy is fairly frequent in the United States; the merchant prince sometimes weds the poor dancing girl.> In that case the party with lower status may be said to **outmarry** himerself. (Intransitively *outmarry* may mean to marry outside one's group: <Plain folks talk about *outmarrying*, but sociologists call it *exogamy.*>)

In some societies, tribal rules specify certain marital choices; mating in accordance with those rules is **preferential mating.** For instance, **levirate** is a form of preferential mating in which the brother of a deceased man is expected to marry the widow, and **sororate** is the custom of marrying a wife's sister after the wife dies or proves barren.

If two people, living far apart and not meeting, correspond, exchange photographs, and decide to marry, such a marriage is a **picture marriage.** It sometimes occurred in America when a Western pioneer man made arrangements with a woman in the East or in the "old country." If contact was made through a matrimonial agency catalog, the woman could be called a **catalog bride.**

A **trial marriage** is a legal marriage, but the husband and wife agree that it shall last for only a limited trial period unless at the end of that time both agree to continue it. **Companionate marriage** may be only a fancy term for living together or it may be a form of marriage in which neither party is financially responsible to the other and that may be terminated at any time by either partner.

In a December 1974 *Newsweek*, Jane Otten raised the question of what one calls the man living with but not married to one's daughter, or the woman living with one's son. The questions have still not been answered definitively. Otten dismissed *friend, roommate, companion, swain, lover, paramour, consort*, and a few others, and facetiously suggested *lover-in-law, out-law*, and *checkmate*. Possibilities that others have tried include *symbiant, shackpartner, shacker-upper*, and the acronym *posslq*, pronounced "posselcue" and meaning "person of opposite sex sharing living quarters." It is said to be used sometimes—at least internally—by the Bureau of the Census and the Internal Revenue Service. *Co-*

habitant has probably been tried by someone, but I don't remember seeing it. An unexplored possibility: Adapt the Spanish *compañero* for a male companion, and *compañera* for a female. The tilde (˜) above the *n* should be dropped to distinguish these words from the authentic Spanish.

Some people apparently like marriage so much that they can't get enough of it. Polygamy, especially the early Mormon custom of taking several wives, was also known as **plural marriage** or even **celestial marriage.** A wife in such a marriage, particularly any except the first, was a **plural wife.**

Polyandry is (for a woman) the perhaps delightful possession of two or more husbands at the same time. In **fraternal polyandry** her husbands are brothers. In **monandry** she has only one husband at a time. A woman practicing polyandry is **polyandrous** or **polyandric** and is a **polyandrist.** When a man has two or more wives, he is engaging in **polygyny;** if they are sisters, he is enjoying **sororal polygyny.** A man with plural wives is **polygynous** and is a **polygynist.** A **quadrigamist** is usually one who has four wives or husbands at once, but may also be one whose four mates are serial rather than concurrent. *Webster 3* also lists *bigamist* and *trigamist,* but seems not to have found any term for having more mates than four. Incidentally, *polygamy* is a more general term than any of the above, referring unspecifically to possession of two or more mates at a time. Random mating, as practiced by insects and some higher animals, is called **panmixia.**

An **uxorious** man is excessively fond of his wife, spoiling her shamefully and often bowing to her whims. I know of no comparable word to describe a woman. But neither, it seems, is there a feminine counterpart of **uxoricide,** "the killing of one's wife."

A **gravida** is a pregnant woman, a **nulligravida** one who has never been pregnant, a **primigravida** one who is pregnant for the first time, and a **multigravida** one who has been pregnant more than once. Adjectival forms include **primigravid** and **multigravid.** Sometimes numbers accompany *gravida* to indicate the precise number of pregnancies: <a 3-gravida> <a gravida three> <a trigravida>. The Latin original means heavy and is also the source of our adjective *grave,* our noun *gravity,* and our verb *grieve.*

Comparable is **-para,** a term for a woman who has had a specified number of children: <a twenty-nine-year-old para 3> <a tripara>. A **multipara** has given birth to more than one child, a **nullipara** to none. Adjectives include **primiparous** or **uniparous** and **multiparous.**

It is no news that marriages sometimes break up. **Unmarry** is a handy, inclusive word that covers all possible means of terminating wedlock: divorce, annulment, desertion, or anything else (except possibly death), whether legal or not. One type of unmarrying is the **migratory divorce.** In Nevada, say, Mary Jones divorces Harry Jones, who lives in Michigan. This is a migratory divorce, as is any divorce granted outside the state of residence of the defendant. In some dialects Mary Jones, now a divorcée, is called a **grass widow,** since her husband is still on the grass and not under it. In other dialects she may be a **widow bewitched,** a name that suggests the high regard in which husbands are still held in a few places.

A **nuclear family** is one's immediate family; specifically father, mother, and their children constitute such a family. If you add grandfathers, grandmothers, and other moderately close relatives (but often excluding in-laws), you have an **extended family.** If you go beyond that to include all cousins, no matter how distant, and uncles and aunts and each person married to any member of the family, you have a *clan.* And if relationship is not considered, so that persons unrelated to clan members are included, you have a *tribe.*

Sib may be short for *sibling* "brother or sister," but more broadly may mean any blood relative, such as aunt, uncle, or cousin: <All those present were sibs; in-laws were barred.> As an adjective, *sib* may mean related by blood: <George is sib to Helen, but I don't know just how close.>

We make distinctions of gender in *father* and *mother, grandfather* and *grandmother, uncle* and *aunt,* and *nephew* and *niece,* but nobody knows whether our *cousin* is male or female unless we specify "the cousin who is a girl" or ". . . a boy." Why don't we use, for the girl, **cousiness,** a word that goes back to at least the fourteenth century? <My cousin came, but my cousiness stayed away.>

Half brother and *half sister* are familiar words, but these are less so:

half aunt the half sister of one's mother or father
half nephew the son of one's half brother or half sister
half niece the daughter of one's half brother or half sister
half sib one's half brother or half sister
half uncle the half brother of one's mother or father

Oddly, **avuncular,** "unclelike; pertaining to an uncle," seems better known than the much simpler and more obvious **auntly,** "auntlike; pertaining to an aunt": <the avuncular appearance of the network newscaster>. <Although only five years older than I, she seemed more auntly than sisterly.> The noun forms **auntship** and **aunthood, uncleship** and **unclehood** also have occasional uses: <Unclehood did not appeal to him.>

Two useful adjectives are **agnate** and **enate.** A person related to you on your father's side is *agnate* (from Latin for "born in addition to"). Relationship on your mother's side is *enate* (from Latin for "born out of"). Thus your father's sister is your agnate aunt, and your mother's sister your enate aunt.

The term *distaff side* (of a family) is a familiar one, using *distaff* "a staff with a cleft end for holding wool or flax" to stand for *mother's.* **Sword side,** the little-known antonym, also uses sexual imagery and stands for the father's side (of a family).

All in the Family

avatar *n* Sanskrit had a word *avatāra,* "descent." In English an avatar is a person who seems to be a descendant, indeed a replica or a reincarnation, of someone (usually famous) from the past: <In his ability to tell an exciting long story in verse, he is the avatar of Homer.> We also use the term to refer to a person as the embodiment of an abstraction: <the very avatar of statesmanship>.

boomerang baby *n* Not a baby but a grown or almost grown daughter or son, often a college graduate, who returns to live—maybe for months or years—with hiser family.

by-child *n* A kinder word than *bastard* for an illegitimate child.

cenogamy *n* A marriage or living-together arrangement in which two or more couples share mates.

computer dating *n* Dating that results from computer output, after information has been fed in about the ages, physical descriptions, hobbies, etc., of many men and women. The computer locates pairs who will supposedly be compatible for a date or a longer relationship. <Joe and Sally met through a computer dating bureau.>

digamy or **deuterogamy** *n* These words are synonyms, each referring to marriage of a person for the second time. They differ from bigamy in that the marriage they refer to is serial, not simultaneous.

dink *n* An informal acronym for "double income, no kids." A childless, two-income family. <Dinks are becoming more numerous, perhaps because difficulties of rearing children seem to be increasing.>

displaced homemaker *n* Roberta was married to Clyde for a number of years, and on tax forms reported her occupation as homemaker or housewife. But Clyde died, or the two were separated or divorced. Roberta is now a displaced homemaker and faces unfamiliar social, financial, and other problems.

filiopietistic *adj* Veneration of one's ancestors and of their values and accomplishments is in most societies considered desirable and praiseworthy, but when it is carried to foolish extremes, it is described pejoratively as *filiopietistic:* <Filiopietistic adherence to human sacrifice is described in Shirley Jackson's famous short story "The Lottery.">

foremother *n* Any female ancestor. The word is used most often for pioneer women who endured the hardships of early rural life, but historians use it also to honor better-known women such as Revolutionary warrior Molly Pitcher, independent-minded Abigail Adams, and the much more recent Marie Curie, codiscoverer of radium.

hypergamy *n,* **hypogamy** *n* In a society without a strong caste or class system, hypergamy and hypogamy have less significance than in the India or England of the past. Hypergamy is marrying someone on one's own social level or above it; the son of a noble, for instance, marries the daughter of a noble or perhaps a princess. Hypogamy is marrying someone beneath one's rank. Even in a democracy the concepts exist, although wealth or educational level or even military rank is generally substituted for social rank; for example, the expression "She married beneath her" suggests a belief that hypogamy exists.

matricentric *adj,* and related words A family centered upon the mother is described as *matricentric* or **matrifocal;** upon the father, **patricentric** or **patrifocal.** When a person's ancestry is traced through the mother's side of the family, we speak of hiser **matrilineage;** through the father's **patrilineage.** Inherited traits derived mainly from the mother and her forebears are lumped together as **matrocliny;** from the father or his side of the family, **patrocliny.** <Max looks just like his dad. Patrocliny seems dominant also in his athletic build.> A couple who reside with or near the wife's family is **matrilocal;** the husband's, **patrilocal;** and if the couple lives somewhere else—say, another state—**neolocal.**

mismarriage *n* A marriage that should not occur, whether because of incompatibility or some other important reason.

mismate *vi, vt* To mate unsuitably: <J.G. Holland, 1858: "A mismated match is much worse than unmated life.">

mutual child *n* Judy has a child by a former marriage, and her present husband, Kevin, has one by a previous marriage as well. Judy and Kevin are also the parents of Carol, their mutual child.

neonate *n,* and related words. A neonate is a newborn child, or a child up to the age of one month. The adjectival form is **neonatal.** Related words are **antenatal** "before birth," **intranatal** "during birth," and the familiar **post-natal** "after birth."

palimony *n* Similar to alimony, but paid to a former mistress, lover, or other unmarried partner—usually but not necessarily of the opposite sex.

paranymph *n* In ancient Greece a bridegroom went in a chariot to bring the bride home, and (presumably to keep him company) he took along another man, a *paranymphos*, "beside the bride." Alternatively the bride might come to the groom and bring her paranymphos, a female friend. Today *paranymph* is used, though infrequently, to mean either best man or bridesmaid. Sometimes the word is also used for someone who speaks on behalf of another, as John Alden on behalf of Miles Standish asked for the hand of the lovely Priscilla Mullins. (It turned out that she liked the paranymph better than the suitor.)

philander *vi* Greek *philandros* meant "loving men" or "loving one's husband." But many pastoral poets must have thought that it meant "lover," and used it as a man's name in thousands of poems. Now it has become a verb for "flirt" or "make love outside one's marriage." It is generally used of a man, not a woman, although incidents of female philandering have been reported.

philoprogenitive *adj* Basically one is philoprogenitive if heshe likes to produce offspring or tends to do so: <the almost universal philoprogenitive drive>. It may also mean loving one's offspring and one's descendants: <Most wealthy parents are sufficiently philoprogenitive that they try to leave substantial estates for their children and grandchildren.>

proxy marriage *n* A marriage ceremony in which an authorized representative of an unavoidably absent bride or groom stands in for her or him. For instance, in wartime such a marriage was occasionally arranged for or by a pregnant woman, with the written consent of the father-to-be, who was in military service.

punalua *n* Punalua was a form of group marriage once practiced in Hawaii in which two or more brothers or other related males married two or more sisters or other related females.

putative marriage *n* A putative marriage is one that has been properly formalized but is nevertheless invalid in the state where it was performed, because of some legal impediment such as too-close blood relationship. However, the putative marriage may possibly be considered legal if it was entered into in good faith.

sannup *n* *Buck* was a term often used to designate a male American Indian, whether married or unmarried. *Sannup* specifies a married American Indian man.

sonship *n* The relationship of son to father: <Since his father was in jail, sonship held few pleasures for Henry.>

sororicide *n,* and related words. Sororicide is the killing of one's sister, or one who kills hiser sister. Similarly:

fratricide (brother)
matricide (mother)
patricide (father)
maritocide (spouse)
parricide (father, mother, other close relative, or a national leader regarded as a father)
filicide (son or daughter)

Also:

avicide (bird)
felicide (cat)
vermicide (worms, especially parasites)

spite marriage *n* Bob loved Eloise. Rebuffed by her, he quickly married Karen, "to show Eloise that she's not the only fish in the sea," as he told a friend. Such a marriage, motivated primarily by a desire to hurt or get even with someone else, is a spite marriage.

wive *vi, vt* One of those interesting words that can have opposite meanings. To wive can be either to take (a woman) for a wife or to become the wife of (a man).

Mastery Test

Mark each statement *true* (T) or *false* (F).

____ 1. A *misogamist* is likely to marry several times.
____ 2. In *exogamy* one marries outside hiser social class.
____ 3. A *polyandrous* woman has more than one husband.
____ 4. A person who is *avuncular* is seldom likable.
____ 5. *Uxorious* men are hard for their wives to get along with.
____ 6. A *primigravida* has never been pregnant until now.
____ 7. A *migratory divorce* is granted in a state other than that where the defendant legally resides.
____ 8. Grandpa isn't part of your *nuclear family.*
____ 9. Your aunt can be your *sib.*
____ 10. You can't have a *half niece* unless you have a half sister or half brother.
____ 11. An *enate* relative is one on your father's side.
____ 12. *Hypergamy* is marrying below one's social level.
____ 13. A *matrilocal* family live with or near the wife's family.
____ 14. A *paranymph* is like a dryad or a naiad.
____ 15. *Philoprogenitive* people don't like children.
____ 16. A *neonate* is an unusually bright child.
____ 17. A recently performed *putative marriage* is likely to be annulled.
____ 18. A *maritocide* is a married woman who deserves to be killed.
____ 19. A *spite marriage* is motivated by spite toward a third person.
____ 20. *Digamy* refers to remarriage after the death or divorce of the first spouse.
____ 21. A *picture marriage* is an especially beautiful wedding.
____ 22. *Celestial marriages* are made in heaven.

___ 23. A *sororal polygynist* has two or more wives who are sisters.

___ 24. A *nullipara* has given birth to no children.

___ 25. *Widow bewitched* is a dialectal term for *grass widow.*

___ 26. *Filiopietistic* is a word used to praise someone for respecting hiser ancestors.

___ 27. The mother is primarily responsible for holding together a *matricentric* family.

___ 28. *Punalua* is a Hawaiian word for *aunt.*

___ 29. A *sannup* ordinarily lived with a squaw.

___ 30. *Misandry* is hatred of women.

4

PIECE OF MIND (PSYCHOLOGY)

It is a common misconception that psychologists are mainly interested in mental unbalance, in oddballs such as sex perverts, in bizarre actions. In reality, psychologists study all sorts of mental processes and behavior. They are interested in the workings of the nervous system, in (to borrow a once well-known title) "why we behave like human beings," in the emotions and ways of thinking that most or all people share. So, although they do not ignore the highly eccentric, they are no less concerned with the "normal" (but won't try to define that undefinable word).

For instance, **ambitendencies** are common. When many of us fill out our income tax forms, we are pulled in two directions: to be completely honest (and safe) or to cheat a little and save ourselves some money (but perhaps get caught). Any such opposing tendencies—and not just with regard to money—are ambitendencies.

For another example, psychologists are interested in the thinking process. To **ideate** is to have ideas or thoughts, to conceive, imagine, or recall, or to invent through thinking rather than through manipulation of physical objects. **Idea-**

tion, then, is the capacity or ability to ideate, the power to receive and interrelate ideas. **Ideational** and **ideative** are synonymous adjectives that mean pertaining to thinking—especially abstract thinking. And **ideaphoria** is a tendency to have ideas, especially the capacity to think creatively. Many psychologists attempt to discover what the processes of ideation are, and why some persons have greater ideaphoria than others.

The study of child growth and development is another concern of psychology. For example, instead of shaking their heads over the incomprehensibility of teenage behavior, psychologists study it and seek to understand and explain it. It may be significant that although the layman often uses the nouns *adolescent* and *adolescence*, the psychologist often uses the verb **adolesce,** a fact that suggests that heshe is viewing a process, a continuing series of events, rather than a more or less homogeneous thing. Adolescing is a very active, constantly changing process of bodily, mental, and emotional development and varies greatly from individual to individual: <Adolescing combines pain with exuberance, apathy with enthusiasm.>

Psychologists also study memory. **Mnemonic** devices are those intended to remind one of something else; for example, the string tied around one's finger so that one won't forget to mail a letter, or learning "The princi*pal* is your *pal*" as a spelling aid. *Mnemonic* comes from Greek *mnemon* "mindful." **Mneme,** which means the continuing effect of the past experience of the individual or the race, is from a related Greek word *mnēmē*, "memory." Psychiatrists, well aware of mnemes, try to probe an individual's early years to find explanations of present conduct or feelings. (Anthropologists interested in mnemes may try to explain present human characteristics on the basis of what our distant ancestors were like.)

Greek *mnasthai*, "to remember," appears in other words. One is **panmnesia,** literally "all memories." All mental impressions, some psychologists believe, remain in the memory as long as a person lives. This retention is panmnesia: <Psychiatrists who delve into childhood memories appear to

believe in panmnesia.> Sometimes a person "creates" images, stories, etc., that heshe doesn't actually invent but rather remembers subconsciously from some earlier experience. Heshe is not consciously aware of the lack of originality. **Cryptomnesia** is the name given this phenomenon: <The accused plagiarist claimed that cryptomnesia was to blame—that he could not remember ever having read the borrowed passage.> **Paramnesia** is the name given to two quite distinct mental phenomena, both of which most people occasionally experience. One is an inability to recall the meaning of some familiar words, as in "I've forgotten whether the benediction comes first or last." The second is a feeling that one has previously visited a place or has had an experience that is actually happening for the first time.

Psychologists have helped to clarify just how concerned each of us is with hiser own ego. Unless we are extreme psychotics, and sometimes even then, we all have a conscious or unconscious need to protect the way we feel and think about ourselves. So we react in a bristly fashion when someone demeans us or says or does anything that could make us think less of ourselves. Such defensive reaction is called **ego-defense. Ego-expansion,** also important, is self-fulfillment, the widening of self-awareness, the deepening of one's opinion of oneself: <Securing the department headship served him mainly for ego-expansion, since the increase in salary was small.>

The respective roles of the sexes, their similarities and their differences, necessarily are the concerns of some psychologists. For instance, they try to define **manness** and **womanness,** which are not quite the same as *manliness* and *womanliness. Manness* and *womanness* refer to the distinctive features, the "essence" of being a man or a woman, whereas *manliness* and *womanliness* (from *manly* and *womanly*) suggest more the appearance and the superficial actions. A young boy and girl may possess "manliness" and "womanliness" but not ordinarily the deeper "manness" and "womanness": <In *Giants in the Earth* the manness of Per Hansa and the womanness of his wife, Beret, are in constant but not open conflict.>

Other Psychological Words

abience *n,* **adience** *n,* and related words. If you have a tendency to withdraw from members of the opposite sex or from snakes or from anything else, your tendency is called *abience.* (Latin *ab* means away from, and the rest of the word comes from *ire* "to go.") *Adience,* its antonym, is a tendency to move toward a given stimulus. (Latin *ad* means to or toward.) The adjectival forms are **abient** and **adient.**

abreact *vt,* and related words. Psychoanalysts often encourage their patients to recall and talk about long-repressed experiences and feelings—a supposedly healthful, cathartic act. The patients who do so are said to *abreact* (literally "react from") the emotions. The confessional or any other encouragement to the release of suppressed memories is also said to be **abreactive** or to cause **abreaction.**

adultoid *adj, n* An immature person or animal resembling an adult: <the wizened, adultoid features of ten-year-olds who worked in nineteenth-century factories>.

ambivert *n,* **ambiversion** *n* An extrovert figuratively turns outside himerself, showing greater interest in other people. An introvert turns inside himerself, paying little attention to others. Most of us, however, are ambiverts: We pay considerable attention both to ourselves and to others. Oddly, though, both *extrovert* and *introvert* are well-known words, but comparatively few people know *ambivert* or *ambiversion,* which is an approximate balance between extroversion and introversion.

anomie or **anomy** *n* One meaning of this word is anarchy, lawlessness, but since *anomie* or *anomy* has no advantages over its synonyms, I'd not use it for this purpose. However, a second definition is useful: a personal state symptomized by isolation, anxiousness, and general disorientation to society: <After his bankruptcy his anomie increased. He even shot at boys swiping apples from his orchard.>

autism *n.* **autistic** *adj* Almost everyone engages in occasional fantasy, imagining himerself in (usually) pleasant but unlikely or impossible circumstances. When carried to an extreme, however, such fantasy can result in partial or complete withdrawal from actuality; it is then called autism, from Greek *aut(o)*-"self." *Autistic* is the corresponding adjective.

avoidant *n* A person who takes special measures to avoid unpleasantness. Heshe will cross to the other side of the street to avoid meeting an old posslq.

brain spa *n* "You park your car [in the parking lot of my Marin County, California, brain spa], you run in, you get your anxiety released," Randy Adamadama told *The New York Times.* Inside such a "spa" you listen to New Age music or soft bird calls or the sounds of gentle ocean waves, while your begoggled eyes observe color patterns in constant motion, as from a color organ. The Synchro-Synthesizer, as the whole shebang is called, was invented by Denis E. Gorges, some of whose loyal followers pronounce his name "gorgeous." His invention is intended to reduce excessive stress.

cataplexy *n,* **cataplectic** *adj* After a great fright, shock, or fit of anger, have you ever simply been unable to move for a short time? If so, you were afflicted with cataplexy, from a Greek word meaning to strike down, terrify. The adjectival form is *cataplectic.*

clairaudience *n,* **clairsentience** *n,* and related words. Clairvoyance, as many people know, is the power of "seeing" distant or hidden things, sometimes including future events. *Clairaudience* refers to "hearing" things not present, and *clairsentience* to "feeling" them, as, for example, a twin has been said to feel pain when hiser faraway sibling is injured. Corresponding adjectives are **clairaudient** and **clairsentient.**

coconscious or **coconsciousness** *n* Apparently the human mind works on at least three levels: *consciousness,* a level of awareness; *subconsciousness,* a level that we are not but can be made aware of; and *coconsciousness,* mental processes that exist alongside the others but differ markedly from them, as in schizophrenia. Assuming that the personality of Dr. Jekyll was the "normal" or "real" one, his coconscious took over when he became Mr. Hyde.

cognitive consonance, ______ **dissonance** *n* Most of us have many internal contradictions. The emotional part of our being sometimes goes one way, the rational another. Or our rational conscience tells us we shouldn't do something but our emotions make us do it anyway. We are victims of cognitive dissonance, a cacophony not of sound but of emotions, thoughts, and actions. Maybe a few people (although I've never met any) possess pure cognitive consonance, with everything in harmony.

collective unconscious *n* Each of us is the product not only of our own experience but also of the experiences, thoughts, and feelings of all our ancestors, although we are largely unaware of these, important as they are in our motives and daily actions. The aggregate of this inheritance is called the *collective unconscious*, or perhaps more ambiguously the *racial unconscious*.

conation *n*, **conative** *adj* In psychology, *conation* refers to the mental processes or behaviors that lead toward some action or change. Psychologists list as its ingredients impulse, desire, volition, and striving. It is a conscious urge to perform, and thus is different from *cognition*, which means knowing, and from *affection*, which means feeling. <The perpetual student is ruled by cognitive desires, but the administrator and perhaps even the artist are governed by conation. Their conative drives are likely to be especially strong.>

countercathexis *n (pl. -es)* *Cathexis* is a psychological term for the concentration of emotional energy (especially sexual drive) on some one person or thing. Countercathexis, then, is opposition to such concentration—an attempt to block from consciousness objectionable notions and impulses: <His complete absorption in his work was no doubt the result of countercathexis.>

counterconditioning *n* Let's say that you are trying to stop smoking and that you chew gum instead. Your substitution of a supposedly good habit for a bad one is an example of counterconditioning.

criminosis *n* Psychologists and psychiatrists often are asked to treat psychoneurotic persons who as a result of their mental problems commit or tend to commit criminal, vandalistic, or other antisocial acts. Such behavior or tendency is called criminosis: <His criminosis first became apparent when he stole or destroyed classmates' papers, books, and school supplies.>

crisis center, _____ shelter *n* A *crisis center* is a facility a person may call or visit for informed advice or other help during a personal crisis, such as a strong urge to commit suicide. A *crisis shelter* will receive battered spouses, children who feel endangered, or others who need refuge for a short period.

dementia *n*, **amentia** *n* Dementia is mental deterioration, often combined with apathy. Amentia, however, is mental deficiency, undeveloped mental capacity.

destress *n* To reduce stress. <The music of Mozart usually destresses Elizabeth.>

double bind *n* Sometimes a person receives contradictory signals or messages from a single source, and loses regardless of which of the signals heshe acts upon. For example, Mom says, "You're getting fat" but packs cookies and cake in the child's lunch. The child is in a double bind—heshe will continue Mom's disapproval if heshe keeps adding weight, but if heshe doesn't eat hiser lunch Mom will say angrily, "So you don't like the lunches I pack!" Some psychologists say that mental disturbances may be caused by numerous double-bind situations.

dybbuk or **dibbuk** *n* In Jewish folklore a dybbuk is a wicked spirit that enters a person's body and drives himer to evil deeds unless exorcised: <Leo Rosten: "If the dybbuk is stubborn and refuses to behave . . . the *Baal Shem* orders a ram's horn *(shofar)* blown at once. That ought to do it.">

dynamic psychology *n* One who accepts or practices dynamic psychology believes that to understand the reasons for a specific human act one must know in detail the much earlier experiences of the person, not just the immediate circumstances of the act.

halo effect *n* If we form our opinion of a person on the basis of one especially prominent characteristic, we are likely to transfer that opinion—rightly or wrongly—to other of hiser characteristics. This transfer is called the *halo effect:* <The halo effect of the senator's advocacy of the consumer caused many to consider him the ideal candidate for the presidency.>

hand-minded *adj* People who prefer and are more adept at manual activities rather than mental are said to be hand-minded: <Many schools make special provisions for their hand-minded students.>

Hawthorne effect *n* According to experiments (first conducted in the Hawthorne plant of Western Electric in Illinois), people who are told that they are highly capable and are doing well will then do even better work than before, and the work of people told the opposite gets worse. The adage "Honey catches more flies than vinegar" appears confirmed. Some other experiments, however, suggest that changes resulting from praise or dispraise may not be lasting.

hypercathexis *n* One often hears expressions like "I had my heart set on that (dress, car, political office, etc.). I felt I couldn't live without it." Excessive desire for anything is hypercathexis—particularly if libidinal energy is involved. The love of a man for a woman or a woman for a man is often hypercathexis, because in reality there is never "only one" who can satisfy one's physical, emotional, and mental needs.

hypnoanalysis *n*, **hypnotherapy** *n* One tool of the psychoanalyst is hypnotism, which heshe may use to help, for instance, in bringing to the surface long-repressed memories. The procedure is known as *hypnoanalysis.* When hypnotism is used in treatment, whether by a psychiatrist or by another physician, it is known as *hypnotherapy.*

hypomania *n* Some manias are less strong, less persistent, and less significant and worrisome than others. These underdeveloped manias are hypomanias: <Although his affection for dogs was at least a hypomania, it did not rule his life.>

lostness *n* Obviously, "the condition of being lost," but less often in a geographical than in a psychological sense:

<The 1970s was a decade of lostness for the American people, with wavering or obliteration of compass points they had once thought permanently fixed.>

marotte *n* If you have a pet idea, something you believe in but that other people may ridicule, perhaps you can dignify it by calling it a *marotte.* The word is a French diminutive of *Marie (Mary),* and may also mean a holy image—which your pet idea probably is to you.

megalomania *n,* **megalomaniac** *n* Megalo- comes from a Greek word for great, large. A megalomaniac has a mania for doing grandiose things (which to himer seem "great"). Small children often dream (properly so) of greatness, fame, and even omnipotence, but when those dreams are retained into adulthood, they often are classifiable as megalomania—the disease of Hitler and of many assassins.

menticide *n* Similar to brainwashing, menticide is a prolonged and systematic attempt to replace one's ideas and attitudes with distinctly different ones: <Solzhenitsyn, in *The Gulag Archipelago,* graphically describes the mental and physical tortures used to effect menticide.>

parapsychology *n* Parapsychology involves investigation of mental telepathy, clairvoyance, psychokinesis—any such phenomena not explicable by natural laws.

pathological liar *n* For most persons who lie, prevarication is a defensive measure. For the pathological liar, however, it is a way of life. It is a symptom of a mental illness that forces himer to concoct often fanciful, absurd, and totally unnecessary lies.

psychagogy *n* In Greek, *psychagōgia* means leading souls from the lower world. More prosaically, English *psychagogy* means a way to influence behavior by recommending desirable goals: <An idealistic guidance counselor, he was basically interested in psychagogy.>

psychasthenia *n* A form of psychoneurosis in which one has doubts, fears, andor obsessions that heshe cannot combat even though heshe recognizes their irrationality.

psychodrama *n,* **sociodrama** *n* Some psychologists and social psychologists use groups to act out, for therapeutic reasons, usually unrehearsed playlets focusing on problems of individuals within the group. When the drama is intended to provide catharsis or other relief for individual participants, it is psychodrama, but when it is supposed to help resolve problems of human interrelationships, it is sociodrama.

psychogenic *adj*, **psychosomatic** *adj* *Psychogenic* means originating in the mind or in emotional conflict: <Her fights with her father were probably psychogenic.> *Psychosomatic* (*somatic* is from Greek *sōma*, "body") means pertaining to interaction of mind and body; a psychosomatic illness, then, is a physical illness arising from mental causes: <A psychosomatic pain hurts no less and is no more controllable than one arising from a blow or other physical cause.>

psycholepsy *n* Greek *lēpsis* means seizing, taking hold of. A victim of psycholepsy is seized by an attack of the blues, a feeling that all is lost, and a lack of desire to think or do anything constructive. Psycholepsy is a form of neurosis to which most people are subject, though in varying degree and duration; it often occurs after a contrasting period of jubilation.

psychosensory *adj* *Psychosensory* may mean either pertaining to sense perception: <the elaborate psychosensory nerve network> or hallucinatory—pertaining to sensory awareness not transmitted by the senses: <His being trapped in the burning house was, of course, only psychosensory, an illusion.>

reactology *n*, **reflexology** *n* Reactology is the scientific study of psychological reactions—not just reflex actions. Reflexology (originally Russian *refleksologiya*) is a study of behavior in terms of simple and complex reflexes only.

redintegration *n* Suppose that Schenectady was the scene of a traumatic experience of yours. Whenever you hear "Schenectady" now, the incident is recalled to you, and you may for a while return to your mental state of that earlier time. Such a response or revival of a former mental state when triggered by a given stimulus (Schenectady in our illustration) is *redintegration*, from Latin for to make complete again.

social psychology *n*, and related terms. Anthropologists particularly interested in the culture of societies whose members cannot read and write are specialists in **social anthropology. Social philosophy** deals with the ethical values of a society. **Social psychiatry** is application of the principles of psychiatry to social rather than individual problems. And *social psychology* is concerned with the ways in which an individual influences and is influenced by the social group or groups with which heshe has contact.

somnial *adj* Pertaining to sleep or dreams: <somnial horrors>.

somniloquy *n*, **somniloquist** *n* A somniloquist talks in hiser sleep, and somniloquy is the act or practice of talking in one's sleep. <Few people combine somnambulism with somniloquy.>

symbiosis *n* In biology, the word refers to the mutually helpful living together of two dissimilar organisms, such as an oxpecker and a rhinoceros: The bird on the back of the rhino subsists on the insects in cracks in its skin, and thus gets food, while the pachyderm gets pleasant relief. In psychiatry, *symbiosis* means the association of two persons (sometimes more) in which each depends on the other or others in some important ways. A classic example: a blind wife and a deaf husband.

syntactical aphasia *n* Loss of the ability to put sentences together—a very specific form of mental illness.

unsane *adj* Not sane. *Insane* isn't quite the same, since it refers to more or less specific mental disorders, whereas *unsane* carries only the idea of not quite normal, unwise, unconventional, or unreasoning.

Mastery Test

Match the word at the left with the most appropriate phrase in its group of ten.

___	1. abreactive	a. facing an impossssible decision

____ 2. clairsentient	b. People who think a lot have it.
____ 3. menticide	c. something that all your ancestors left you
____ 4. psycholepsy	d. a wild spirit inside
____ 5. ideation	e. loss of ability to talk coherently
____ 6. syntactical aphasia	f. describing a function of the confessional
____ 7. collective unconscious	g. a severe attack of the blues
____ 8. redintegration	h. a stimulated renewal of an earlier mental state
____ 9. dybbuk	i. able to feel something far away
____ 10. double bind	j. a form of brainwashing
____ 11. somniloquy	k. "I'm being pulled in two directions."
____ 12. ambitendency	l. perhaps describing Walter Mitty
____ 13. paramnesia	m. "My troubles started because my father hated me."
____ 14. ambivert	n. impulse, desire, striving
____ 15. autistic	o. "After the truck just missed me, I couldn't move."
____ 16. cataplexy	p. may result in unconscious copying

___ 17.	psychogenic	q.	This is most likely to occur at night.
___ 18.	cryptomnesia	r.	It could result from a phobia.
___ 19.	conation	s.	"I can't remember what a meringue is."
___ 20.	abience	t.	one interested in both himerself and others

5
VIVE LES DIFFÉRENCES

The 1960s through the 1980s saw so much openness and so many publications about sex that it hardly seems possible that any useful terms are now "rare." Perhaps naively, though, I'll suggest a few words that I seldom or never see in widely read publications.

A British dictionary of slang says that **canoodle** is of American origin, and quotes this from a British publication of 1859: "A sly kiss, and a squeeze, and a pressure of the foot or so, and a variety of harmless endearing blandishments, known to our American cousins (who are great adepts at sweet-hearting) under the generic name of CONOODLING." *Canoodle* is a valuable synonym for *caress* when a not-very-serious effect is intended. In addition, it may refer to persuasion by fondling: <He canoodled her out of five thousand dollars.>

Latin *osculari*, "to kiss," is ancestral to several English words. **Oscular** means pertaining to kissing (or sometimes pertaining to the mouth): <oscular pleasure>. **Osculation** is the act of kissing: <He put up a sign reading Free Lessons in Osculation.>

An **amorist** is anyone who is in love with love, especially sexual love. Heshe is also anyone who specializes in writing about love, painting erotic pictures, or composing especially sensual music. **Amoristic** means pertaining to **amorism.** A **carnalist** is a person who overdoes amorism, being abnormally addicted to sex and other sensual experience.

Alliciency is an obsolete word that maybe deserves renewal. Its closest synonyms are *attractiveness, allure,* and *enticement,* but it goes beyond them in suggesting an especially pleasant kind of entrapment. Its distant Latin ancestor *allicere* meant to allure; it was a kissin' cousin of *delicere,* an ancestor of our *delight.* We might refer, for instance, to the alliciency of Calypso, the nymph who detained Odysseus for seven years, or the alliciency of Lolita. **Epigamic** is semantically a relative. Birds, animals, or insects that don special apparel or perform unusual antics during courtship are described as epigamic "enticing toward mating": <the epigamic flashing of fireflies>. The word is only occasionally used for human beings, though human epigamic activities and appearance are certainly often visible: <her epigamic décolletage>.

Other Sexy Words

alloerotism or **alloeroticism** *n,* and related words. Most people address their sexual feelings and activities mainly to another person rather than to themselves—the mythological Narcissus being an exception. This "normal" tendency is called *alloerotism* or *alloeroticism, allo-* being Greek for other or different. It is to be contrasted with **autoerotism** or **autoeroticism,** which refers to self-serving sexual feelings and acts. Still another word, **amphierotism,** refers to bisexuality, a capacity for erotic reaction to members of both sexes. **Alloerotic, autoerotic,** and **amphierotic** are the adjectival forms.

ambosexual or **ambisexual** *adj* Although we happily applaud *la différence* between male and female, we often forget that the similarities between the two sexes are greater than the dissimilarities. Sexual traits or characteristics common to both sexes are described as *ambosexual*. Examples: pubic hair, the comparability of the clitoris and the penis, the presence of sexual desire.

beefcake *n* Some magazines intended principally for women feature photographs of nude or nearly nude handsome, muscular men. Such art demanded a name, and it was found in *beefcake*, by analogy with *cheesecake* (the inedible kind). *Webster 3*, in an obvious denial of equal rights, labels *beefcake* "slang" but makes no such pejorative comment on *cheesecake*. *RHD* calls both "informal."

cuckquean *n* *Cuckold* "a man whose wife has been unfaithful to him" is a familiar word in literature although less commonly used now than in the past, but *cuckquean* "a woman whose husband has been unfaithful to her" has been allowed to become obsolete. Since such women undoubtedly still exist, perhaps the word is needed even today. The alternative is an ungainly phrase such as the definition above.

Cytherean *adj, n,* and related words. A relatively unknown name for the goddess Venus is *Cytherea*. A follower of Venus—a person in love with love, or an inordinately sexy person, especially female—is a Cytherean. As an adjective the word may mean either pertaining to the goddess Venus or pertaining to the planet Venus. **Venusian** and **Venerean** are used for the same purposes, but *venerean* (also spelled *venerian*) tends to become confused with *venereal*.

demi-vierge *n* Literally "half a virgin," a demi-vierge is a girl or woman whose speech and actions suggest lack of chastity and who engages in petting but still retains her virginity.

desexualize *vt* Although to desexualize may mean to castrate or spay, it more often refers to removal of whatever has a sexual quality or is suggestive of sex: <"Perhaps we should consider desexualizing our advertising," said one director.> It may also mean to reduce sexual drive by diverting it to, for example, music or hard work. Finally, in certain "perversions" sexuality may be altered by redirection from the genitals to other bodily areas; this, too, is considered desexualizing by many psychologists.

ego-libido *n,* **object-libido** *n* Erotic desire directed toward the self is ego-libido; that directed toward someone else is object-libido.

epicene *adj, n* Rather indeterminate sexually; having both male and female characteristics: <Elves are sometimes portrayed as epicene.> Men who do not exude masculinity are also occasionally described with this word: <"He's just a poet, a hairless epicene," she said contemptuously.>

euthenics *n sg. or pl.* A believer in *eugenics* thinks that human beings (or other living animals and plants) can best be improved through controlling reproduction—who mates with whom. A believer in *euthenics,* in contrast, thinks that improvement must come basically from betterment of environment.

forepleasure *n* Perhaps somewhat richer than *foreplay,* which usually refers to physical contacts, especially kissing and fondling. Forepleasure by no means excludes those, but it also includes such things as listening to music, reading poems or stories that stimulate affectionate responses, recalling earlier experiences, and even just quietly enjoying togetherness.

frottage *n,* **frotteur** *n* From a French verb for "rub," *frottage* refers to sexual stimulation by rubbing against someone—for example, in a crowded subway. The person who performs the act is a frotteur.

group grope *n* A slang term for an orgy or any party involving close physical contact of several or many persons.

gynecocentric *adj,* **androcentric** *adj* A group or a whole society that is dominated by women or in which a feminine point of view is dominant is called *gynecocentric; androcentric,* in contrast, means male-centered: <Because of Grandmother Marshall's unbending strength, our family is definitely gynecocentric.> <The Amazons represent the best-known gynecocentric society.>

heterosexism *n,* **heterosexist** *n* A heterosexist is a heterosexual person with strong prejudice against homosexuals. The prejudice itself is called *heterosexism.*

impuberty *n* The state of not yet having reached puberty: <While still in impuberty, she was attacked by a neighborhood gang.>

incubus *n,* **succubus** *n* From the same source as *incubate,* an incubus is literally something that lies upon, but refers especially to a being that may come in a dream and lie heavily upon someone, perhaps forcing intercourse. *Incubus* is sometimes used also as a synonym for *nightmare,* or to represent any unpleasant weight: <the incubus of economic depression>. *Succubus,* a less-used word, is the female equivalent of *incubus.*

mating group *n,* **mating isolate** *n* These two terms are synonymous for a group in which members (human or not) mate with other members of the same group but do not go outside it: <Because of its geographic remoteness the community became a mating isolate, with much inbreeding.>

philogynous *adj,* **philogyny** *n* A philogynous person is fond of women. Philogyny is fondness for women.

priapic *adj,* **priapism** *n* Priapus was the Greek god of male procreative power, the son of Dionysus and Aphrodite. *Priapic,* derived from his name, refers to the penis or an artistic depiction suggesting a penis. <The exhibit included a display of priapic sculptures.> Priapism is a painful illness in which the penis is continuously distended.

psychosexual *adj* Sexual activity (or even inactivity) has long been known to be closely related to one's mental and emotional states; analysis of it is basic to Freudian and some other psychologies. *Psychosexual* is the adjective referring to the links between sex and the mind and emotions.

Rabelaisian *adj* François Rabelais was a sixteenth-century French author whose works abounded in vigor, robust humor, caricature, and frankness that often reached vulgarity or beyond. *Rabelaisian* means like Rabelais or his works: <Rabelaisian humor> <Rabelaisian *joie de vivre*>.

sapphism *n* and related words. Sappho, a female poet who lived on the island of Lesbos about 600 B.C., is reputed to have been homosexual. *Sapphism,* named for her, means the desire of a woman for the erotic embraces of another woman or other women. Someone with such a desire is a **sapphist,** and **sapphic** means pertaining to lesbian or other erotic indulgences.

satyriasis *n,* and related words. Satyriasis is an abnormally high, even overpowering, sexual desire and drive in men. One with such a psychological disorder is a **satyromaniac.** The comparable terms for women are *nymphomania* and *nymphomaniac.*

sexology *n* The study of sexual behavior, especially in human beings.

suigenderism *n,* **altrigenderism** *n* At some time in childhood or youth, almost everyone is most attracted by others of the same sex—a time or a condition known as *suigenderism,* literally "of one's own gender." But there is generally also *altrigenderism,* a time or a condition in which one becomes attracted to the opposite sex. (*Altri-* is from the Latin *alter,* "other.")

sociosexual *adj* Pertaining to the social or interpersonal aspects of sexual relations: <Sociosexual adjustments can be difficult at any age, not just in youth.>

superfemale *n,* **supermale** *n* These words do not use *super-* in the sense of "superior." A superfemale is a sterile female who has three X-chromosomes and two sets of autosomes, and a supermale is a sterile male with one X-chromosome and three or more sets of autosomes.

transsexual *n, adj,* **transvestite** *n* A person who would like to have the physical attributes and life-style of a member of the opposite sex and has received hormone treatment and undergone surgery to lead to such a result is called a *transsexual.* A *transvestite,* believed to be most often male, likes to wear clothing and adopt mannerisms of the opposite gender.

Mastery Test

Supply the missing letters.

1. h____________m strong dislike of homosexuality
2. d__________e literally, a half virgin
3. e______e having both male and female characteristics
4. i________y state preceding puberty
5. R__________n robust, frank, uninhibited
6. p________y fondness for women
7. a______________m attraction to the other sex
8. a______t one who is in love with love
9. c_______e caress
10. a_________y pleasant entrapment
11. a__________m erotic interest in others
12. b_______e spicy picture(s) of a man
13. a_________l pertaining to sexual traits common to both men and women
14. C________n an unusually sexy person, especially female
15. d__________e to reduce sexual drive or quality
16. a___________c male-centered
17. s_______s incubus of female gender
18. s_______t a lesbian

6
WORDS OF THE FIVE SENSES

Most people react more frequently and more strongly to what they see and hear than to what they taste, smell, or feel. Perhaps that is why words relating to sight and sound are much more numerous than those for the other senses. But there are some useful words for those senses, too.

Unlike a primarily **optic** animal, such as man, that tends to orient itself through use of its eyes, a primarily **osmatic** animal, such as a dog or a bear, relies mainly on its sense of smell. **Osmics** is the science dealing with the sense of smell. **Olfaction** is the sense of smell or the act of smelling; it comes from Latin *olfacere* "to smell," but *osmics* and *osmatic* come from Greek *osm-* "odor." **Olfactory** means "pertaining to the sense of smell": <the olfactory pleasures of the countryside">.

A **nidor** is a particular kind of odor, the strong smell of meat or fat that is cooking or especially burning: <the nidor of scorched bacon>. **Redolent** is a word seen in print fairly often, but I've found that most college students don't know what it means. It refers to pleasant odors and is similar to *fragrant, aromatic:* <the man-made cave on our farm, used for storage and redolent of pickles and apples and turnips as well as the rich black earth>. It may also mean, however, reminiscent, evocative: <mountaineers' language redolent of the sixteenth century>. Especially in this sense, *of* or *with* is likely to follow the adjective.

Gustation is the act of tasting or, less often, the sense of taste. The corresponding adjective is **gustatory** or the slightly older **gustative.**

A **sialagogue** is anything that promotes the flow of saliva, "makes the mouth water." A medical term, it also may be found in more common expressions: <Magazine pictures of foods are often sialagogues.> The foods portrayed in advertisements generally look **sapid** or **saporous,** from Latin *sapere* "to taste, to have good taste." Sometimes a sapid or saporous taste may be strong but nevertheless agreeable: <the sapid taste of black walnuts> <saporous mutton>.

Both **acerb** and **acrid** come from Latin *acer* "sharp," as do the noun forms **acerbity** and **acridity,** but the kinds of sharpness are not the same. Something is acerb if it is sour to the taste, like lemon juice, or by extension sour in mood or tone: <Juvenal's acerb satire inevitably created enemies for him.> That which is acrid, though, is bitter to the taste or smell, or by extension extremely caustic or rancorous in manner or tone: <the acrid smell of burning rubber> <the acrid accusations of FDR's political enemies>. **Acrimony** and **acrimonious** are approximately synonymous with the figurative senses of *acridity* and *acrid.* **Exacerbate** "to embitter; to increase the severity of," along with its nounal and adverbial variants, also comes from *acer.* **Acidulous** means acid in taste or behavior and thus is similar in meaning to *acerb:* <an acidulous remark>.

By contrast **vapid** (noun **vapidity**) means flat-tasting: <vapid wine> but more often extends the meaning to lacking in animation or spirit: <a vapid conversation> <a vapid laugh> <vapid dinner party>. Thus *vapid* is much like *insipid,* but the latter usually has greater implication of an unamusing silliness.

A **tactile** is a person in whom the sense of touch is particularly strong, not only in experiencing but also in learning and remembering. An **audile** emphasizes hearing, a **visualizer** emphasizes vision, and a **motile** stresses motion. Thus if each of these grasps with tongs a bar of red-hot iron and plunges it into cold water, the tactile will especially note the feel of the heat and its abrupt cessation, the audile the hiss, the visualizer the glowing iron and the sudden steam, and the motile the rapid movement of hiser body. Adjectives comparable to the last three nouns are **ear-minded, eye-minded,** and **motor-minded.**

Let's look now at a few words pertaining especially to sound. *Open-eyed* is a familiar term, and **open-eared** should be no less so, since sounds, many of them worth hearing, surround us. Among the sounds are many **dulcet** ones, from Latin *dulcis,* "sweet," which is also the ancestor of the Italian *dolce* as in *la dolce vita:* <the dulcet clarinet>. By extension *dulcet* may be used for scenery: <dulcet as an apple orchard in full bloom>. To **dulcify** (also **edulcorate**) is to make sweet, pleasant, agreeable: <Baking soda helps to dulcify odorous plumbing.> <Gin always dulcified her quickly.> A **dulcimer,** a wire-stringed instrument played with little hammers, is so named because of its sweet tones, as is the less familiar **dulcimore,** a violin-shaped instrument with three drone strings and one for melody.

Many sound-words are onomatopoeic, including: **tankle,** which is like a tinkle but a little louder and a little lower in pitch; **ting,** a short, high-pitched sound, like a single stroke on a small bell: <the ting of a pebble hitting the bucket>; and **flump,** a heavy sound such as might be made by a falling human body, also the motion producing such a sound: <subsided into his chair with a flump>, or as a verb, to move or fall heavily or to drop something making the sound of a flump: <He flumped the big box onto the rug.>

A **susurrus** (accent the second syllable) is a sound like that of a whisper or a rustle: <the susurrus of wind among fallen leaves>. The adjective is **susurrous:** <a quiet, barely susurrous crowd>. To **ululate** is to howl or wail mournfully, often in a prolonged, rhythmic manner. **Ululant** is an adjective describing this manner, and an **ululation** is a long, rhythmic howl: <The hired mourners ululated until they had earned their money.> <the ululant wind sweeping around the old

house> <the ululation of the wolfpack>. Some people, wanting to concentrate or to sleep, try to cover unwanted, intrusive sounds by playing recordings of **white noise** or **white sound**—for example, rain on the roof; waves lapping a shoreline; or soft, easily ignored music.

Bombilation, also spelled **bombination,** comes from Latin *bombus,* "a deep, hollow sound," and refers to the deep droning or buzzing sound made, for instance, by swarming bees or a distant airliner. A loud vocal sound, especially one low in pitch, may be described as **stentorian.** In the Trojan War, Stentor was a Greek with a powerful voice; anyone with such a voice may today be called a **stentor.** <Before the advent of p.a. systems, a stentorian voice could be a political asset.>

Otic is a doctor's or crossword puzzler's word for "pertaining to the ear or hearing; auricular." **Otitis** is inflammation of the ear. **Tinnitus** means ringing or other sound originating in the ear itself.

The making of sound is **sonification:** <Most sonification results from percussion, friction, or air movement.> Sound level is usually measured in **decibels,** which logarithmic calculations are needed to determine. Noise has been defined as unproductive sound. Sometimes the noise level about us may be so high that permanent aural damage may result—for example, from continued use of a chain saw or considerable exposure to the sounds of a musical group with amplifiers. To prevent damage one may need **ear defenders,** which are earplugs or other protective devices.

Some people, called **synesthetes,** associate sounds with colors (or often smells with tastes, and less often other combinations of the five senses). This kind of association is known as **synesthesia** and is described as **synesthetic:** <His synesthetic sense told him that the clang of metal against metal is colored blue.>

Words referring to visual observations are so numerous that only a small handful of examples will be selected. If something rather bright twinkles or scintillates, it is **scintillant,** but if it is relatively faint, it is merely **scintillescent:** <scintillescent distant stars>. Anything that **effulges** shines forth brilliantly—not just glimmeringly or even with ordinary brightness, but with an attractive, resplendent light. Such a strong light is called **effulgence** and may be described by the adjective **effulgent.**

Something is **rubescent** when it is becoming red. The noun **rubescence** means the act of turning red: <He held the wire in the fireplace until it was rubescent.> <Her cheeks glowed with a sudden rubescence.> Sometimes rubescence or the appearance of any bright, loud colors results in **gaudery.** Clothes or furnishings that are excessively ornate are gaudery. Also, a loud, untasteful display may be called gaudery: <the gaudery of a Roman triumphal parade>. To **gaudify** is to make gaudy: <Knowing the queen's taste, Sir Reginald and his servants carefully gaudified the room where Her Majesty would sleep.>

Gaudery is sometimes **ugsome**—an archaic word worth reviving. It means horrid, loathsome, filling with dread, uglier than ugly: <a scowling, ugsome man, with scar from cheek to jaw>. **Tenebrous** is another word to describe something unpleasant, because of its dark, sinister connotations. It means murky, obscure, dim, and mysterious, and carries with it a fear of the unknown: <tenebrous as the depths of a bat-infested cave>. By extension it may mean hard to understand, obscure: <a tenebrous argument>. *Tenebrose* is a variant spelling. A fancy name for darkness is *tenebrosity.* **Tenebrism** is the style of painting of Caravaggio and his school, who made extensive use of shadows but usually relieved them with a single pinpointing ray of light.

Some sights we see only in what poets call "the mind's eye." These are **eidetic** images, vivid, nearly photographic images that some people are able to produce from memory or imagination: <She retained until she was eighty eidetic images of the small town where she grew up.>

Other Sensory Words

arake *adj, adv* *Arake* is a short way of saying "at a rakish angle"—the kind of attention-getting angle at which rakes used to wear their hats. More generally, *arake* may be used to indicate any slight deviation from the perpendicular: <Several of the hastily installed slalom stakes were knocked arake in his descent.>

arcadian (often cap.) *adj, n* Arcadia was a rural area in ancient Greece in which the inhabitants were thought to lead an idyllic, untroubled existence. Today an arcadian is any person who supposedly leads a similar life. As an adjective, *arcadian* suggests the antithesis of urban hurry and worry: <Settlers in Alaska's Matanuska valley expected to live an arcadian existence, but the harsh climate dispelled their dream.>

doless *adj* <"I feel doless today," she complained.> <He's a good man—just doless.> In the first example, *doless* means lacking in energy; in the second, lacking in ambition.

dyspathy *n* *Dyspathy* is approximately the antonym of *sympathy*, because a person who shows dyspathy fails to share in someone else's feelings, as a sympathetic person does. It is not the same, however, as *antipathy*, which is hostility, a "feeling against."

dysphoria *n* *Euphoria* is a feeling of happiness, wellbeing, and *dysphoria* is its opposite, a feeling of sadness, illness, malaise: <At last she was recovering from her long dysphoria.>

ecstasize *vi, vt* To go into ecstasy or to cause (someone) to go into ecstasy: <She ecstasized repeatedly over her triumph.> <Some popular singers ecstasize their teenage admirers.>

equanimous *adj* *Equanimity* "calmness, emotional balance even under stress" is well known, but for some reason the corresponding adjective is not. It means calm, even-tempered, poised even during trying circumstances: <Although now widowed and impoverished, she is surprisingly equanimous.>

fleer *vi, vt,* **fleerer** *n* To fleer is to smile or laugh (or laugh at) contemptuously, to mock with coarse facial expressions: <Fleering, characteristic of many of the poorer students in the high school, was often just a cover for insecurity.> One who fleers is a fleerer.

grue *n* The adjective *gruesome* is familiar, but the noun *grue* is rare. It means a horrifying effect or quality, or sometimes an attack of shivering, often caused by fear: <the grue of his clawlike fingers> <A grue seized her so violently that she could not hold the flashlight.>

gruntle *vt* To *disgruntle,* of course, means to put in bad humor. The antonym, *gruntle,* is seldom used. It means to put in good humor, to soothe: <Little Margie could always gruntle her father, when he was in a bad mood, by cuddling kittenlike in his lap.>

hagridden *adj* The rare verb *hagride* means to torment as if with a nightmare or evil spirit, especially female. *Hagridden* is the past participle of *hagride,* and means tormented, obsessed, overburdened: <hagridden by financial worries> <His wife took it personally when he said he was hagridden.>

maleficent *adj,* and related words. *Maleficent* is the antonym of *beneficent.* A maleficent person causes evil or harm; even if not successful, heshe at least tries to perform deeds that society in general deplores. The noun form is **maleficence.** The archaic **maliferous** (worth reviving) means "unhealthful in effect": <the maliferous stench of the decomposing bodies>.

minatory *adj* Latin *minari* means to threaten, and its descendant, *minatory,* means threatening, menacing: <minatory scowls> <a minatory cumulonimbus cloud>.

perfervid *adj* More fervid than ordinary; impassioned; zealous; excessively fervent: <the perfervid shouts of the political partisans>.

pringle *vi, vt* To tingle rather unpleasantly; to cause to tingle: <The rasp of fingernail on blackboard always pringled her spine.>

reboant *adj,* **reboation** *n* Latin *reboare* "to resound" is the source of these two words. A sound is reboant if it reverberates: <the cannon's reboant boom>. Reboation is an especially loud and perhaps prolonged reverberation: <The reboation of the drums filled the little valley, the sound bouncing back and forth from the steep slopes.>

reck *vi* An old-fashioned but still useful word meaning (1) to be apprehensive, to fear: <He recked little of the perils.> (2) to take heed of: <Barham, 1845: "Little

recked he of flowers—save cauliflowers."> (3) to matter: <W. Scott, 1828: " 'But what recks it?' said stout Sir Kenneth."> Oddly, *reck* tends to be used in expressions showing small rather than large extent: *recks little* but perhaps never *recks much.*

refulgent *adj* If something gives out a radiantly bright light, it can be described as refulgent: <the refulgent moon>.

risible *adj,* and related words. From Latin *ridēre* "to laugh," *risible* means pertaining to laughter, causing laughter, or inclined to laughter: <risible muscles> <risible appearance> <excessively risible students>. One's sense of humor or of the ridiculous can be called hiser **risibles:** <The dog's sad face after the rabbit escaped tickled my risibles.> **Risibility** is a tendency to laugh; laughter: <a man of slight risibility> <much risibility during the game>.

ruthful *adj* *Ruthless* is a familiar word, but its near-antonym, *ruthful,* is rare. *Ruth* is mercy, pity, compassion, and a person is ruthful if heshe shows these qualities. *Ruthful* may also mean sorrowful or regretful: <a ruthful look on her face>.

sangfroid *n* Literally "cold blood" in French, *sangfroid* in English means great calmness under strain, self-possession, almost cold-blooded refusal to react emotionally: <When the theater caught fire, his sangfroid was unbelievable.>

satispassion *n* The suffering of someone who repents something heshe has done is sometimes called *satispassion*—literally "suffering enough."

scabrous *adj* Something is physically scabrous if it feels gritty, rough, scaly: <as scabrous as a barnacled hull>. Abstractly, something is scabrous if it is unpleasant, repulsive: <scabrous magazines> <scabrous gossip> <scabrous manners>.

scunner *n* Occasionally, for no easily detectable reason, one feels antagonism toward someone or takes an inexplicable dislike for himer. Such an illogical, prejudicial, and hostile feeling is a scunner.

sensual *adj*, **sensuous** *adj* Often used interchangeably, but many writers treat *sensual* as a less favorable term, equivalent to *carnal* or *lewd*, and thus often suggestive of sexuality. It may also hint at worldly, irreligious enjoyment. *Sensuous* usually has no such connotations. It means "pertaining to the senses." So sensuous poetry, for instance, appeals to one or more of the five senses.

sough *n, vi* When the wind or a person soughs, the sound is that of a moan or a sigh. The noun means a deep sigh, a moaning or murmuring sound.

squeam *n* A squeam is what a squeamish person feels: <The sight of spiders, snakes, or blood always makes me full of squeams.>

sybaritic *adj* Sybaris was a wealthy ancient Greek city, though located in southern Italy. Its inhabitants, the Sybarites, were noted or notorious for luxurious, sensual life-styles. *Sybaritic* describes any comparable ways of living: <sybaritic people of Sodom and Gomorrah>.

thrum *n, vi, vt* To thrum a stringed instrument is to play it idly or monotonously—an alternative for *strum*. As a noun, *thrum* means a monotonous musical sound or any comparable sound. <the thrum of his fingers on the desk>.

thutter *vi* To thutter is to make a dull, repetitive sound: <The first raindrops thuttered on the roof.>

tintinnabulation *n* A word most often associated with Edgar Allan Poe: <"To the tintinnabulation that so musically wells / From the bells, bells, bells, bells, / Bells, bells, bells—">. It is, obviously, the ringing of bells, especially a chorus of small bells.

toothsome *adj* Originally, "pleasing to the taste," but now also pleasing to the eye; sexually appealing: <a toothsome blonde in a cutaway dress>.

transmundane *adj* Beyond or outside the world. Anything transmundane is likely to be mysterious, mystic, supernatural: <transmundane phenomena such as the voices of spirits>.

verdant or **verdurous** *adj* Green, especially the green of plants: <verdant lawns> <verdurous fields>. By extension, *verdant* means unsophisticated, inexperienced: <a half-dozen verdant stock clerks>.

whomp *n, vt,* **whomp up** *vt* A loud slapping or crashing noise may be a whomp: <heard the whomp of the enemy's artillery a few miles away>. To whomp an opponent (as in a sport) is to defeat decisively: <Chicago whomped the Lakers 112–70.> To whomp up may be to arouse: <time for you boys to whomp up an appetite> or to cook up or concoct: <whomped up a breakfast of ham and eggs and biscuits> <whomped up a big lie>.

Mastery Test

I. Write *a* if a word is primarily associated with seeing; *b*, hearing; *c*, taste; *d*, smell; *e*, feeling.

___ 1. redolent
___ 2. sapid
___ 3. tactile
___ 4. dulcet
___ 5. flump
___ 6. sonification
___ 7. tinnitus
___ 8. tenebrous
___ 9. stentorian
___ 10. vapid
___ 11. audile
___ 12. acerb
___ 13. osmatic
___ 14. optic
___ 15. sialagogue
___ 16. ululate
___ 17. effulgence
___ 18. gaudery
___ 19. eidetic
___ 20. nidor

II. Mark each statement *true* (T) or *false* (F).

___ 1. To *gruntle* a person is to cheer himer up.
___ 2. To *fleer* is to smile compassionately.
___ 3. *White noise* is, for example, the sound of curtains or sheets blowing in the wind.
___ 4. *Perfervid* language is quietly persuasive.
___ 5. A *maleficent* person causes harm or evil.
___ 6. To *pringle* is to tingle unpleasantly.
___ 7. *Dysphoria* is a feeling of sadness.
___ 8. A *risible* appearance may make people laugh.
___ 9. A *toothsome* morsel is one that sticks to the teeth.
___ 10. A *sough* is a sad book.

7
ON CHOPLOGIC, MISKNOWLEDGE, AND SOME TERTIUM QUIDS

Most of the words discussed in this chapter refer to flaws in reasoning. They will be familiar to anyone who has studied logic, and some of them will be known to persons whose study of English or speech has included argumentation. Other people may find them useful in analyzing their own processes of reasoning or those of others. An election year is an especially good time to observe both fallacies and straight reasoning, but almost any everyday conversation can also be analyzed.

Choplogic is involved, superficial, and illogical argumentation. Formerly (in a meaning worth reviving) it also meant a person who argues persistently but illogically. As an adjective *choplogic* means inclined to argue in an absurd fashion. <Such choplogic deserves no answer.> <Her choplogic husband was again attacking Congress for its inaction.>

One form of choplogic, often used by politicians, is the **argumentum ad hominem,** literally "argument against the man." For example, instead of talking about the point that is at issue, a speaker verbally attacks hiser opponent—pointing perhaps to flaws in hiser record or even in hiser personal life; as a variation, the speaker may discuss the praiseworthiness of hiser own record. An **argumentum ad captandum,** literally "argument for pleasing," is one intended to please the crowd by playing on their emotions, as Shakespeare's Mark Antony did in his funeral oration for Julius Caesar. An **argumentum ad ignorantiam** says that something is true because no one has proved it untrue; thus Mark Twain facetiously argued that elephants can climb trees—after all, no one has demonstrated that they can't.

Sometimes a debate may degenerate to something like "You're a liar!" "So are you!" The second part of this enlightening exchange is a **tu quoque,** an accusation that an adversary is guilty of the same crime or failing that the accuser has been charged with. The Latin means "You, too."

Indefinite proposition is a term in logic referring unspecifically (and usually falsely) to a group: <Poles and Swedes are stupid, as everyone knows.> It is thus a kind of generalization. As someone wisecracked long ago, "All generalizations are false, including this one."

The **exclusive proposition** is also often a hasty and untrue generalization. It is a statement to the effect that "What I am saying applies exclusively to one person, group, etc.": <Only my mother could make such delicious lemon pies.> <Only Congress can declare war.> As the examples show, the exclusive proposition may or may not be true and factual.

A fallacy is reasoning that is superficially convincing but actually incorrect or illogical. Fallacies may be classified as formal, material, and verbal. A **formal fallacy** is one in which the logical processes are wrong. For example, "All men are sinners, and all weaklings are sinners; therefore all men are weaklings" errs in not making a statement about all sinners. A **material fallacy** involves distorting the issue or just quietly assuming that the conclusion is true. For instance, "My wife has never lied to me." "How do you know?" "Because she has repeatedly told me so, and a truthful person doesn't lie." A **verbal fallacy** uses words improperly or ambiguously. A familiar example is "All fair things are honorable. This woman is fair. Therefore this woman is honorable." Here, *fair* has two meanings. Each of these three types of fallacies has a number of varieties.

Fallacies may also be classified in a different tripartite way. A **fallacy of accident** treats something accidental or coincidental as if it were essential and lastingly true; for instance, "This apple on the ground has a worm in it, so obviously the worm caused it to fall." A **fallacy of composition** assumes that what is true of one must be true of all others in the group; for example, "I don't understand how some people can watch TV for hours. I always get a headache after an hour or so of it." Its opposite is the **fallacy of division,** which assumes that what is true of a group is also true of each member. For instance, "I'm sure that Jones is a Democrat, for his county always goes heavily Democratic."

The **either . . . or fallacy** may be the most common of all. It says, "We must choose A or B," even though choice C, or C and D, or something between A and B may also be possible. For instance, the mountains and the seashore are not necessarily the only choices for a vacation. Another example: Although third-party candidates seldom do well in American politics, they sometimes hold saner positions than either of the major parties.

"Johnson got the most votes, so he won the election" and "He has a beautiful tenor voice, so he is probably an Italian" are examples of **enthymemes,** which are syllogisms with one part, usually the major premise, omitted. The full syllogism for the first example would be "The person who got the most votes won the election. Johnson got the most votes. Johnson won the election." Unless there are some unusual circumstances, this syllogism is valid. But the second enthymeme, when filled out, is "Men with beautiful tenor voices are probably Italian. He has a beautiful tenor voice. Therefore he is probably an Italian." Supplying the missing major premise of this enthymeme shows the conclusion to be rather ridiculous.

Some other examples of choplogic, as well as a few other terms related to reasoning, are in the following section.

Other Terms Pertaining to Reasoning

circumstantiate *vt* One circumstantiates a claim if heshe provides circumstantial evidence concerning it. Circumstantiating is less strong than substantiating, since to substantiate is to offer solid proof.

cut-and-try *adj* Cut-and-try techniques are experimental ones, not based on carefully thought-out theory or planning. No doubt the term arose because some seamstresses cut goods to approximate size and then pin them together to try the garment on. *Trial and error* is an equivalent term.

denial of the antecedent *n,* **affirmation of the consequent** *n* These are two related fallacies of reasoning. The first is illustrated by "If you bought this car, you would be sad, but you have not bought this car, so you are not sad." Notice that the "antecedent," the *if*-clause, is here denied. (And, of course, note that there are many possible causes of the lack of sadness, not just the fact of not buying the car.) The affirmation of the consequent takes this form: "If you bought this car, you would be sad, and you are sad, so you bought this car." Here the "consequent" (the part following the *if*-clause) is affirmed, but the conclusion does not inevitably follow.

empirical *adj* From Latin and Greek words for "experience," empirical reasoning is based on experience and experimentation, not on abstract thought or a hunch. If people who write instructions for assembling elaborate toys proceeded *empirically*, they would ask people not mechanically minded to try to follow them, and if they couldn't, the writers would revise and try again. And if the designer of a teapot that leaks around the lid had used *empiricism*, heshe would have made unnecessary some irate letters to the manufacturer.

excogitate *vt* To cogitate is to ponder over, meditate, or consider. To excogitate implies somewhat greater thoroughness and system, and often suggests rather specific results: <He excogitated his problem for hours, method-

ically arranging the arguments for and against the three possible solutions.>

intuitional *adj* Intuitional conclusions, or decisions based on intuition, are right part of the time but are not inevitably so. Although on occasion there may be no alternative to playing a hunch, careful thinking and a few tryouts will often bring better results. (See also *empirical.*)

misknowledge *n* A folk philosopher has defined *misknowledge* as "knowin' things to be true that ain't." Misknowledge of geography hampered exploration for centuries. The widely accepted Ptolemaic astronomy made it difficult for Galileo's counterevidence to get a hearing. Perhaps misknowledge has been a greater influence than ignorance in retarding the search for truth. Misknowledge is false knowledge and is a negative quality; ignorance is the absence of knowledge, and is neutral.

misologist *n,* **misology** *n* A misologist, one who believes in misology, dislikes discussion, argument, debate. Heshe may be a gentle person who is simply averse to conflict; perhaps many hermits became hermits because they were first misologists, and perhaps many husbands or wives disappeared for the same reason. But a misologist may also be a person of action, one who would prefer to plunge ahead, perhaps with both fists flying, rather than try to reach a conclusion through argument.

phrontistery *n* In Greek a *phrontistēs* is a deep thinker, an intellectual or at least one who pretends to be an intellectual. In English a phrontistery is the place where such a person reads, studies, meditates: <My boyhood phrontistery was a corner of the attic equipped with a chair and a meager supply of books.>

ratiocination *n* Cool, precise reasoning uninfluenced by emotion: <True, the social scientist needs the power of ratiocination, but since heshe is dealing with people, heshe cannot be completely cold and detached.>

simplism *n,* **simplistic** *adj* *Simplism,* "oversimplification," refers to the ignoring of complicating factors: <the simplism of attributing the 1930s depression to the stock

market crash>. *Simplistic* means characterized by simplism: <simplistic in his reasoning>.

sophistry *n* Reasoning that seems believable but that is really fallacious—often intentionally so.

stochastic *adj*, **stochastically** *adv* Greek *stochastikos* means proceeding by guesswork, but also means skilled in aiming. Today a stochastic procedure is one guided by guessing, although the guesses may be intelligent and informed, not necessarily random. *Stochastically* means in a stochastic manner: <Since several pieces of information were unavailable, he had to rely just on those he possessed and move stochastically toward a solution.>

supposal *n* The act or process of supposing: <That child is full of supposals—"Suppose this . . . Suppose that . . ." over and over.> It may also be used as a synonym of *supposition, hypothesis, conjecture, guess:* <The supposal was that inflation and economic depression could not coexist, but it was proved false.>

surgency *n* *Surgency*, a characteristic of personality, is an influence on reasoning ability, since it implies quickness, cleverness, and nimbleness of wit: <Jane Welsh was noted for her surgency, which often revealed itself in her letters to her future husband, Thomas Carlyle.>

tendentious *adj* A tendentious person is biased. Heshe attempts to promote a cause or a point of view: <As chairman of the badly split committee, Erskine tried to avoid any tendentious comments.>

tertium quid *n* Literally, "a third something"; a tertium quid is distinct from two other things but hard to name or classify: <neither fish nor fowl but a tertium quid> <In an either . . . or assertion, a defensible tertium quid may often be found.>

Mastery Test

Choose the best answer in each group.

___ 1. Y says, "You embezzled money." Z says, "So did you." Z's response illustrates (a) argumentum ad captandum (b) argumentum ad hominem (c) a formal fallacy (d) a tu quoque

___ 2. "After knowing Jacques for a year, I decided that you just can't trust Frenchmen." This statement illustrates (a) an exclusive proposition (b) a formal fallacy (c) a fallacy of composition (d) misknowledge

___ 3. One who uses intelligent guessing in reaching a conclusion is using (a) a stochastic procedure (b) choplogic (c) ratiocination (d) misology

___ 4. A person who argues in a biased fashion to promote a cause is (a) tendentious (b) a tertium quid (c) excogitating (d) phrontistery

___ 5. A syllogism lacking one part is (a) a cut-and-try (b) an enthymeme (c) a fallacy of division (d) an argumentum ad captandum

___ 6. "Our treasurer is probably dishonest. Nobody has proved that he wouldn't steal money if he had a chance." This statement illustrates (a) argumentum ad hominem (b) argumentum ad captandum (c) argumentum ad ignorantiam (d) denial of the antecedent

___ 7. Dislike of discussion or debate is (a) misology (b) phrontistery (c) sophistry (d) surgency

___ 8. Doctors for centuries believed that the best cure for many ailments was bleeding the patient. This erroneous belief illustrates (a) argumentum ad ignorantiam (b) material fallacy (c) a fallacy of accident (d) misknowledge

___ 9. Reasoning that appears convincing but that actually is flawed (often cleverly so) is known as (a) sophistry (b) tendentiousness (c) supposal (d) circumstantiation

___ 10. Reasoning that is based on experience and experimentation is (a) intuitional, (b) circumstantial, (c) empirical, (d) stochastic

8
DESCRIBING A FEW PEOPLE

It's probably not courteous to refer to your waddling, very short-legged friends as **duck-legged,** but it may be accurate. And there's the possibility that you may get slapped if you comment audibly on a young lady's **callipygian** (alternatively **callipygous**) attractiveness. You see, in Greek *kalli* means beautiful, and *-pygos* means buttocks. <Rubens delighted in painting rather hefty and decidedly callipygian damsels.>

Rubens's damsels may have been callipygian, but they certainly weren't **svelte** (also **svelt**). Svelte women are stylishly slender, lithe, and sleek, and tend also to be urbane, sophisticated: <his svelte wife, undressed in the latest fashion> <the svelte airs of a jet-setter>. Svelte people are generally a little too old and too blasé to be **dewy-eyed.** A dewy-eyed person (most likely a child or a young woman, apparently) is thought to be naive, credulous, and innocent. However, sometimes the adjective suggests that the credulity, etc., are faked, and that the dewy-eyed person may be engaged in some shrewd scheming.

The svelte person isn't a **rackabones,** either. A rackabones, most often a horse but sometimes another animal or a human being, is excessively thin; you can count every rib, as they say in the Ozarks. Sometimes the rackabones, or even the fatso, may be ill and **xanthous,** "yellow-skinned." The noun here is **xanthoderm.** An interesting color scheme is displayed by the xanthoderm with a **coppernose,** an unusually reddish, inflamed nose, such as often results from alcoholism or certain other diseases.

Speaking of noses, most persons don't have hair on top of them or on certain other parts of their bodies. Presence of hair in unusual places is **paratrichosis.** The English language is rich in its words for abnormal or excessive hairiness, a condition that may be called **pilosis, pilosism, or pilosity** —all from Latin *pilus* "hair."

Handedness, a generally innate preference for using one hand rather than the other, is described as **dextral** "right-handed" and **sinistral** "left-handed." However, these words may also mean on the right or on the left and inclined to the right or inclined to the left. A **dextro-sinistral** person is a naturally sinistral person who has been taught to write with hiser right hand: <Dextro-sinistral children, some psychologists say, encounter problems not ordinarily met with by others.>

The word *geriatrics,* "study of the physiology and pathology of old age," has become widely known in recent decades. Less well known is **gerontic,** "pertaining to old age," from Greek *geront, gerōn,* "old man" (but now not restricted to males). The search for an unobjectionable word for "old people" still goes on, since *senior citizens* is repulsive to many. I suggest as one possibility converting *gerontic* to noun use; people above a given age, say sixty-five, would be called *gerontics.* Another suggestion is *genarian*—the last syllable of *sexagenarian, septuagenarian, octogenarian,* and *nonagenarian.* But what I'd really like is spelling it *generian,* suggesting that these people *generated* much of what is good and bad in the world. *Generian* seems to me a respectful term, with desirable psychological and social overtones, and with none of the objections inherent in *old people, senior citizens, golden-agers,* and others.

There are several pretty good words to describe people's

manners of talking. Most of us know someone small, cheerful, probably (but not necessarily) a generian, and given to speaking in a **chirpy** manner. A **smarmy** person or remark, in contrast, is gushy, insinuating, or excessively flattering: <the smarmy conversation at her bridal shower> <The emperor preferred to be surrounded by smarmy courtiers.> Smarmy statements often come from **honeymouthed** or **honeylipped** people, who are sweet-talking and gently persuasive: <that honeymouthed temptress, Delilah>. The honeymouthed are seldom **spadish,** for they would think they were behaving **lumpishly** (stupidly, like a clod) if they bluntly called a spade a spade: <that rare person, a spadish politician>.

Some political partisans (and other kinds) are **rabulistic,** from Latin *rabula,* "brawling advocate." A rabulistic person talks noisily on behalf of a cause or a person. The word is pejorative, serving to criticize for pettifoggery or general obnoxiousness: <The candidate's rabulistic supporters antagonized many in the audience.> The rabulistic supporters were perhaps also **prevaricative** "having a tendency to lie": <Louise isn't a bad little girl, but she is a bit prevaricative.> But candidates and their adherents are often **rectitudinous,** a word used sarcastically to describe someone who assumes an air of extreme virtue: <*Westminster Gazette,* 1897: "notoriously and unctuously rectitudinous">.

A **tempersome** or **tempery** person has a quick temper, is easily irritated. Heshe might also be described as **splenetic.** Basically, *splenetic* means pertaining to the spleen, an organ that we hear about less frequently than the Elizabethans did. They associated it with hatred, spitefulness, anger, and unpleasant emotions in general. Even today, though, a sullen or bad-tempered person may be described as *splenetic.*

Splenetic people perhaps are more often than others **lowering** or **glowering.** (Rhyme this *low-* and *glow-* with *now.*) Both words mean scowling, frowning, dark, gloomy, threatening. "Lowering skies" has become almost a cliché, and good old-fashioned villains were glowering while they plotted their dastardly deeds. <Griffith-Jones, 1899: "Lowering influences in the environment">.

I like the picturesqueness of **astrut,** "puffed up; openly revealing pleasure about an accomplishment": <Head high, oblivious to the subrisive glances of his friends, he was astrut with joy over his victory.> **Subrisive,** in that example, is a good word for almost but not quite laughing; smiling broadly.

I'm sad that we sometimes need to apply **ahistoric** or **ahistorical** to human beings. Dogs and other animals are and are expected to be ahistorical; that is, they have no concern for or awareness of the history of their kind, and not much for even their own past and future; they are concerned almost exclusively with what is present or near-present. Unfortunately, some people are almost as ahistorical as dogs.

Other Ways to Talk About People

adonic *adj,* **adonize** *vt* Adonis, the beautiful youth loved by Aphrodite, has given his name to an herb, a medicine, and a verse form, as well as to the adjective *adonic,* "unusually handsome," and the verb *adonize,* "to make a man handsome": <If you persuade your husband to spend a few hours in our salon, we'll adonize him.>

akimbo *adj, adv* A local newspaper described a policeman "standing with his legs akimbo"—a difficult act, surely, since *akimbo* refers usually to placement of the hands on or near the hips, with the elbows projecting outward. Legs, however, may be akimbo when the knees, corresponding to the elbows, project outward, as in some yoga positions. But I still can't see how the cop *stood* with his legs akimbo unless he had ball bearings in his hips.

brownette *n* A person who has light brown hair, rather light skin, and (usually) blue, gray, or green eyes.

brown study *n* It's hard to say why a study, "a state of intense contemplation," should be called *brown* (or any other color), but when the contemplation is especially serious or perplexed, that's what it is: <He's in a brown study.>

Cassandran *adj* Cassandra, daughter of Priam, king of Troy, was able to foretell unhappy events, but her direful prophecies were never believed. The adjective *Cassandran* came from her name. <During the second Nixon administration, Cassandran journalists predicted the end of American democracy.>

cipherdom *n* The state of being a nobody, a nonentity: <Away from Washington, D.C., he felt relegated to cipherdom.>

dancy *adj* Suitable for dancing; inclined to dancing; lively: <dancy music> <a dancy young girl whose legs couldn't stay still>.

decrassify *vt* As is widely known, *crass* is an adjective meaning stupid, gross, insensitive, thickheaded, concerned only with the obvious and the worldly. To decrassify is to eliminate crassness from someone: <He thought he might decrassify parents by developing sensitivity in their children.>

élan *n* English has borrowed this French word and its meaning: vigor, dash, enthusiasm, high spirits, assurance, liveliness, imagination, and a bit of unpredictability: <Assuredly the president with the most élan was JFK.>

elflocks *n* "Let me comb out the elflocks," a mother says to her child. Hair matted, as after a night's sleep, is sometimes called by this attractive name.

empleomania *n* The Spanish gave us this valuable word for the mania for holding public office, which is a widespread illness afflicting both competent, honest and incompetent, dishonest persons.

gauche *adj,* **gaucherie** or **gaucheness** *n* The adjective for "awkward, tactless, socially crude" and its corresponding nouns seem slanderous of left-handed people. The French original means both "left" and "awkward." <an unforgivably gauche remark> <the gaucherie of interrupting his hostess>.

half-minded *adj* If one is half-minded to do something, hiser mind is half made up to do it. The same meaning is conveyed by "I *have half a mind* to do it."

hedgehoggy *adj* The European hedgehog, similar to the American porcupine, for defense rolls itself into a ball, leaving only forbidding prickly spines exposed. A person of forbidding appearance or manner is sometimes said to be *hedgehoggy*.

hipshot *adj* If one's hip is dislocated, one is said to be hipshot. Also, a pose favored by many female models, with one hip higher than the other, is a hipshot pose.

la-di-da, also spelled **la-de-da, la-di-dah, lah-di-dah** *adj, n, vi* Usually a term of mockery or contempt, *la-di-da* suggests pretentiousness, sham, exaggerated gentility or elegance, putting on airs, and sometimes effeminacy: <His la-di-da clothing made him unpopular.> <He's a real la-di-da.> As a verb, the word refers particularly to speaking affectedly: <She "clahssed" and "dahnced" and la-di-daed till we were sick of her>

ladify or **ladyfy** *vt* Less often now than formerly, mothers attempt to ladify their daughters—make ladies of them. A chief purpose of old-fashioned finishing schools was to ladify the girls who attended them. Today ladies—at least in the Victorian definition—are rare, so attempts at ladifying are relatively infrequent.

literal-minded *adj* When George Bush speaks of "a thousand points of light," the literal-minded person thinks of a thousand candles or fireflies. Heshe reads Dr. Seuss and says, "I don't see how that could happen."

minutiose *adj* A person who concerns himerself excessively with minute details may be described as *minutiose*.

mondain(e) *adj,* **mondaine** *n,* **demimondaine** *n* Anything or anyone very worldly, sophisticated, perhaps a bit blasé, may be described as *mondain* or *mondaine:* <the mondain jet-setters>. A woman with mondaine qualities is a mondaine: <Marie Duplessis, the peasant girl, in four years became a mondaine with her own Parisian salon.> True, Mlle. Duplessis was also a demimondaine, "a kept woman," literally a "woman of the half world, on the fringe of society."

moue *n* *She made a little moue*
When he told her, "I love you."

A moue is a small grimace, a brief pouting look: <Thackeray, 1850: "With a charming moue . . .">.

nakedize *vi* A person who goes naked nakedizes: <She often nakedizes while doing the housework.>

pixilated *adj* A pixie is a mischievous fairy, sprite, or person. Combine *pixie* with *titillated* and you get *pixilated*, "mischievous, amusingly tricky or unpredictable, whimsical, a bit eccentric": <my pixilated, prankish young cousin>. There's also a noun, *pixilation*.

pontifical *adj* Although some recent pontiffs (popes) have on occasion talked and acted like us ordinary folks, some of their predecessors probably contributed to the meaning of *pontifical:* pompous, stiff, or even pretentious.

prescience *n*, **prescient** *adj* Prescience is the ability to look ahead or to plan ahead, to show foresight; it is not a supernatural ability such as fortune-tellers claim to possess but a rational, respected, and respectable power of anticipation. *Prescient* means having foreknowledge, marked by foresight: <The chief reason why the British seemed so prescient in World War II was that they had cracked the Nazi military code.>

sardonicism *n* A person who is sardonic is scornful, disdainfully humorous. Sardonicism is scornful humor: <His sardonicism antagonized almost everyone he met.>

saturnine *adj* Astrologers have associated the planet Saturn with gloom and grief, and alchemists used *saturnine* to mean "leaden." Today's definitions are "gloomy, taciturn, sluggish": <a saturnine temperament> <a saturnine attempt at a smile>.

savoir faire *n* Literally, "knowing how to do." A person with savoir faire knows almost instinctively how to act appropriately in nearly any social situation: <the savoir faire of the best man who quietly slipped off his own wedding ring when the bridegroom dropped the one he was about to put on the bride's finger>.

savoir vivre *n* Literally, "knowing how to live." A person who has savoir vivre knows how to get the most out of life, especially how to live elegantly and in keeping with the dictates of fashionable society: <My uncle was a man with rare savoir vivre.>

sitting height *n* Because of different bodily proportions, some tall people when they are sitting look less tall than shorter people do. Sitting height is the measurement of the distance from the supporting surface to the top of the head: <Louise, five feet, seven inches, has a sitting height of thirty-six inches, but Ray, who is five feet, ten inches, has a sitting height of only thirty-five inches; so when they sit side by side, Louise looks taller.>

sniffy *adj* A person who is sniffy or acts sniffily doesn't necessarily sniff, but heshe is disdainful, haughty, supercilious: <a sniffy remark>.

stuporous or **stuporose** *adj* Both words mean in a state of stupor: <the stuporous condition of one under prolonged strain>.

supine *adj* If one lies in a supine position, heshe is on hiser back, face upward. Thus *supine* differs from *prone* "lying with face and belly down." *Recumbent* refers to reclining, regardless of position, as does *prostrate,* but the latter implies helplessness or submissiveness. *Supine* often suggests lethargy, indifference, or inertness.

tatterdemalion *adj, n* A tatterdemalion (person) is ragged, disheveled, sloppy in appearance. The word is sometimes extended to buildings or almost anything else that can be conceived of as worn and unattractive: <the tatterdemalion old schoolhouse> <the tatterdemalion fiscal policies of several inept administrations>.

telegenic *adj* A *photogenic* person looks especially attractive in pictures. The much younger sibling of that word, *telegenic,* means "especially attractive on television."

too-too *adj, adv* The idea of affectation is implicit in both the adverb and the adjective: <just too-too knowledgeable about imported wines> <He's really too-too, you know. Maybe he's just la-di-da.>

towny *adj,* **towniness** *n* A person is towny if heshe has qualities associated with towns rather than with the country or the city, and *towniness* is a noun that implies these qualities: <towny people that can't tell wheat from soybeans> <I think that my cousin's towniness is offensive.>

trepid *adj* *Intrepid,* "fearless," is familiar, but its antonym, *trepid,* "fearful, afraid," is unfairly discriminated against.

truculent *adj* Not related to trucks. Truculent language is hostile, often anger-provoking. Truculent behavior is fierce, unpleasant, challenging, even cruel. The ancestral word is Latin *trux*, "savage, pitiless." Noun forms are **truculence** and the less-used **truculency.**

walkative *adj* A useful coinage by a little boy, for "inclined to walk." After an hour of hiking with his parents, the three-year-old said, "I don't feel very walkative anymore"—obviously by analogy with *talkative.*

womanfully *adv* Many men work or struggle manfully, but it is commonly overlooked that many women also work or struggle womanfully (or personfully?).

youthy *adj* A middle-aged or elderly person who in dress, speech, and/or actions imitates much younger people is referred to, perhaps rather unkindly, as *youthy.*

zealotic *adj* A zealotic person is more zealous than a zealous person.

(in the) zone *adv phrase* Occasionally an athlete feels as though everything will go right for himer, and it does. Heshe gets over the high bar, can hardly miss the basket, allows no one to penetrate hiser part of the line. The athlete is in the zone, also called *in the groove.* Being in the zone means having for a while mental and physical coordination to do a task much better than usual. This applies to any task, not just athletic. Writers, actors, salespeople, executives, Wall Street types—anyone may sometimes experience the quickness, sureness, and joy of being in the zone.

Mastery Test

No right or wrong answers this time. Just tell which one in each of the following pairs you would probably like better. (The two are not necessarily antonymous or even in the same category.)

___ 1. a *splenetic* friend or a *chirpy* one
___ 2. a *prevaricative* person or a *tempersome* one
___ 3. a *coppernose* or a *tatterdermalion*

____ 4. a *dextral* person or a *sinistral* one
____ 5. a *honeymouthed* temptress or her *glowering* father
____ 6. one who is *astrut* or one who is *dancy*
____ 7. a man who is *hedgehoggy* or one who is *la-di-da*
____ 8. an *ahistorical* person or one who is in a *brown study*
____ 9. a woman who is *duck-legged* or one who is *callipygian*
____ 10. a woman who is *svelte* or one who is a *rackabones*
____ 11. a *subrisive* glance or a *sniffy* remark
____ 12. a *mondaine* or a *demimondaine*
____ 13. one who is *youthy* or one who is *gerontic*
____ 14. a *rectitudinous* person or one who *nakedizes*
____ 15. a *rabulistic* group or a *smarmy* group
____ 16. a *truculent* person or a *stuporose* one
____ 17. a *telegenic* person or a *towny* one
____ 18. a *winsome* girl or a *gauche* one
____ 19. *saturnine* friends or *pontifical* friends
____ 20. a *pixilated* person or a *walkative* one

9
MORE WAYS TO TALK ABOUT PEOPLE

When a person refers to himerself more than is normal, especially if boasting, heshe is **egotizing:** <He often egotized, saying, for instance, "I hold a record. Nobody else on our team ever made as long a run as *I* did."> Very often **lippiness** is a characteristic of one who egotizes. It is excessive talkativeness, especially impudent, impertinent language. Perhaps **snidery** is another of the lippy one's qualities. This word is based on *snide*, "slyly critical," and refers to the practice of indulging in snide remarks: <His snidery cost him many friends.>

We'll glance here at a number of such unpleasant characteristics that some people have, and then in the alphabetical list turn to some that are more desirable.

A **sociopathic** person regularly displays asocial or antisocial behavior: <Sociopathic acts can be explained only partially on the basis of early childhood experiences.> Often such a person illustrates **parvanimity,** the opposite of *magnanimity;* for instance, heshe is selfish, ungracious, ignoble, and petty: <Almost everything he did illustrated his parvanimity: taking the most comfortable chair, ridiculing the ac-

cents of the servants, giving only grudging credit to anyone else's accomplishments.> **Despisal** may be another characteristic of a **sociopath.** Obviously *despisal* is the noun form of *despise* and refers to the act of despising. The sociopath is also likely to be more **complaintive** than most folks—excessively inclined to complain, or showing dissatisfaction by a whining voice or other indicator <complaintive sighs>.

Some people deceive themselves in one way or another. They may, for instance, illustrate **ostrichism,** a word that derives from the calumnious assertion that ostriches hide their heads in the sand when in danger. Ostrichism is self-delusion, a refusal to admit the existence of a threat, or a refusal to cope with it. **Podsnappery** is somewhat similar. In Dickens's *Our Mutual Friend,* Mr. Podsnap is a complacent man who will not admit anything unpleasant. Dickens says of him, "He never could make out why everybody was not quite satisfied, and he felt that he set a brilliant social example in being particularly well satisfied with most things, and, above all other things, with himself." Such a tendency, in commemoration of Mr. Podsnap, is now known as *podsnappery* (sometimes capitalized).

Dionysus was the Greek god of wine, called Bacchus in Rome. **Dionysian** refers to worship of him, but more generally to drunken, frenzied, orgiastic celebrations, parties, etc.: <His few months at Oxford were spent in Dionysian revelry.> **Ebriosity** is obviously related to *inebriation* but is more similar in meaning to *alcoholism.* Whereas *inebriation* often means just a temporary state of intoxication, *ebriosity* refers to it as habitual: <His ebriosity seldom allowed him to keep a job more than a week.>

A drunk often becomes **robustious.** *Robust* means strong, healthy, sound, firm, full-bodied, or (sometimes) rude or rough. *Robustious* is similar but generally stresses rudeness, roughness, boisterousness: <robustious living> <robustious jokes that in those days were expected to make ladies cover their ears and look shocked>. The alcoholic sometimes attempts a reform, but often becomes a **recidivist,** a backslider. This term, along with its other forms **recidivism** or **recidivation** and **recidivate,** also applies to backsliding into crime, or, more rarely, into illness, especially mental illness.

More Things to Say About People

beamish *adj* A delightful word, I think, to describe people or faces bright with good cheer, forthrightness, optimism, or the like.

bearwalker *n* The much-publicized werewolf is a person who assertedly takes on the appearance and the undesirable attributes of a wolf. Hiser less famous ursine cousin, the bearwalker, is an evil person who is said to assume the shape of a bear before going about hiser nefarious tasks.

birkie *n* Some Scottish words have no precise equivalents south of the border. English needs a word for a lively, engaging, intelligent, clean-cut, confident person—in order to eliminate that string of adjectives. So why not adopt the Scottish *birkie,* which has that meaning?

bourgeoisify *vt* To instill middle-class beliefs, values, and desires. <If big business can bourgeoisify almost everyone, it can still more readily manufacture products and media offerings from the same matrixes, for everyone will want to be the same and have the same as everyone else.> The noun form is the awkward **bourgeoisification.**

breeder document *n* A document such as someone else's birth certificate, driver's license, or even credit card that, in the hands of an unscrupulous person, can "breed" (make possible) the issuance of false documents such as passports or additional credit cards.

categorically needy *n* Governmentese for needy people who fall into one or another category and thus may be eligible for public assistance.

childsnatching *n* Kidnapping of a child by hiser father or mother, usually in connection with the breakup of a marriage.

clean-run *adj* "He's a clean-run chap," say some Britishers, meaning that he is healthy, vigorous, and generally attractive. The British term, though similar to *clean-cut,* may be worth importing: <a clean-run girl, the sort you like to think of as a mother of the generation to come>.

commonsensible or **commonsensical** *adj* Common

sense has been described as one of the least common possessions. But the few persons who have it, as well as the ideas or solutions they conceive, may be called either *commonsensible* or *commonsensical.*

cose *vi* To be cozy; to make oneself cozy: <Dad cosed in his favorite chair.>

crotchet *n* Originally the same word as *crochet,* "hook," a crotchet is something in a person's habits or actions or character that does not follow a straight line; it is a peculiarity, a whim, an idiosyncrasy: <The crotchets of the old, though often annoying, are more easily forgiven than similar oddities in the young.>

dégagé *adj* This French word is sometimes approximately an antonym for *decorous.* It means unconcerned about propriety and about appearances in general, carefree, completely at ease, not at all stiff: <Women admired his dégagé air, although in reality he was a serious young man.>

demiworld *n* The underworld is the criminal element of society. Above it is the demiworld, people whose ethics and behavior are not ordinarily considered illegal but are almost so. The English word may have been influenced by French *demimonde,* the world of prostitutes and others whose activities are in some places treated as criminal: <Unethical businesspeople, such as some Wall Street profiteers, are not usually classed within the demiworld but perhaps should be.>

disingenuous *adj* Ingenuous is a familiar word meaning simple and frank in a childlike way. *Disingenuous* can be its antonym, "not ingenuous," but it has also taken on a more pejorative meaning: artful, scheming, deceptive, pretending frankness: <People who did not know her well never realized that her smiles were disingenuous.>

dry grins *n* When you smile a nervous or feeble little smile because you are embarrassed and don't know what else to do, you have a case of the dry grins.

fiver *n* A person who gives at least 5 percent of hiser income to charity and/or five hours a week to voluntary community service.

fustle *vi* This British dialect word is a blend of *fuss* and *bustle*, and means just that: to fuss and bustle about.

grazer *n* Informal for a snacker who customarily eats many small amounts throughout the day rather than three regular meals.

habitude *n* One's habitude is the total of hiser habits, the inclinations or behavior or ways of doing things, that over a period of time have become customary to himer: <his indolent habitude> <the born housewife's habitude of keeping everything in its place>.

hubris *n*, **sophrosyne** *n* Hubris is great self-confidence, amounting often to arrogance. Sophrosyne is almost its opposite: self-control, temperance, prudence, modesty.

iconoclast *n* Literally, a breaker of images—religious or other—but now more likely to refer to one who attacks widely held and respected beliefs and institutions: <Some iconoclasts are mere troublemakers, but others, such as Socrates and Thorstein Veblen, may serve society well.>

incent *vt* A recent back formation from *incentive:* <The store owner incented employees by promising to divide among them one half of the net profits.>

kempt *adj* It has been stated incorrectly that *unkempt* has no positive form, but *Webster 3* records *kempt*, defining it as "neatly kept: TRIM." Etymologically the word means combed, a participial form of Middle English *kemben*, "to comb." John Wyclif, translator of the Bible in 1380, distrusted kempt men: "Yif a man haue a kempt head thanne he is a lecherous man."

longanimity *n*, **longanimous** *adj* Latin *longus*, "long," and *animus*, "soul, mind, or spirit," combine in these two words. One who is "long of spirit" is patient and forbearing, suffering without complaint: <Blount, 1656: "Longanimity is an untired confidence of mind in expecting the good things of the life to come."> <J. R. Lowell, 1861: "The present Yankee, full of shifts . . . longanimous, good at patching">.

mestiza *fem n*, **mestizo** *masc n* Spanish and now English for a woman or a man of racially mixed ancestry:

<Latin America and the Philippines have millions of mestizas and mestizos.>

Métis *n* In Canada, a person born to an American Indian (usually female) and a white (usually French male) person. Uncapitalized (both in Canada and elsewhere), the word means anyone of mixed ancestry.

minauderie *n* Derived from a French word for simper, and related to English *mien*, "appearance," *minauderie* (generally pluralized) means coquettish airs or actions: <Feminists consider minauderies demeaning to their sex, but seem not to have eliminated them.>

misgive *vi, vt* Although the noun (or gerund) *misgiving* is widely used, the verb on which it is based is relatively rare. To misgive is to make or be apprehensive: <Her conscience misgave her.> <You have nothing to misgive about.>

multipotent *adj* A multipotent person or object (such as a medicine) has the power to do many things: <My grandfather—sailor, farmer, artist, musician, teacher, and politician—was the most multipotent person I have known.>

narcissistic personality *n* Named for the mythological youth Narcissus, who fell in love with his own reflection, a narcissistic personality is recognized by psychiatrists as extreme self-centeredness, ceaseless search for admiration, and troubled relations with other people.

nebbish *n* Slang, from Yiddish for "pitiful, unfortunate." A nebbish is usually timid, ineffectual, and unlucky.

nephalism *n*, **nephalist** *n* It is said that *teetotaler* originated with a nondrinker who stuttered "I'm a t-t-total abstainer." *Nephalist*, from Greek *nēphein*, "to drink no wine," is a more formal word for a teetotaler, and hiser total abstinence from alcoholic drinks is *nephalism*. (If you tell someone at a party that you are a nephalist, heshe will probably think you are a convert to some new religion.)

obfirm *vt* This obsolete verb should be revived, since we now have no single verb meaning to make firm (in a bad sense), to make obdurate (an opinion, decision, or activity): <J. King, 1597: "an obstinate, obfirmed minde

against the commandement of God"> <His year in prison obfirmed him in criminality.>

oblivial *adj* A person is *oblivious* if heshe is unaware of something, without conscious knowledge of it: <oblivious to his danger>. In contrast, someone or something that causes such unawareness is *oblivial:* <a severe, oblivial blow on the skull>.

odd man out *n* Originally a device to select or eliminate someone—for example, by coin-flipping—an odd man out today is most likely someone who because of circumstances or hiser own choice does not participate actively in what others are doing: <At cocktail parties he was always an odd man out, for he was frankly bored by trivial conversations.>

panache *n* Originally a feathery ornament on a helmet, *panache* was gradually extended to mean flamboyance, swagger, a swashbuckling air: <Douglas Fairbanks, Sr., played the role of the desert chieftain with his usual panache.>

passivism *n* An inactive, acceptive, nonrebellious attitude: <Americans' passivism in the face of all sorts of abuse by government, big business, and big labor seems to be increasing.>

pettifogger *n* A colorful name for a bickering, quibbling person who overemphasizes trifles. Heshe may also be an especially quibblesome lawyer, possibly one who is not only petty but also shifty and unethical. The verb **pettifog** is a synonym of *quibble, bicker,* or perhaps *temporize:* <The mind of a pettifogger may be as small as hiser concerns.>

proactive *adj* Many people, companies, or governments wait for something to happen and then *react*—take whatever action seems appropriate. *Proactive* people or groups, in contrast, try to anticipate events, especially potentially harmful ones, and to take steps to avert them or reduce their impact. <Proactive measures by the government in the 1980s could have prevented huge taxpayer losses caused by housing, banking, and savings and loan bungling.>

psychic income *n* Usually one receives money as a reward or payment for hiser work, but psychic income is the intangible reward often received in addition or instead; it may be, for instance, pleasant companionship, prestige, opportunity to travel, pleasure in helping others, or naturally beautiful surroundings: <When Gardner was in political office, his chief psychic income may have been the pleasure of power and the satisfaction of service.>

reverse snob *n* A snob looks down on most people and sees himerself as superior—usually more "cultured" than they are. A reverse snob, in contrast, is excessively proud of hiser "commonness," elevating it while disparaging those who have more education, ability, or interest in the arts. Heshe puts on airs and condemns those who heshe says put on airs.

supererogation *n,* **supererogatory** *adj* A supererogation is an act beyond the call of duty or obligation, or an instance of doing more than necessary or perhaps even desirable: <The pope praised the supererogation of the bishop who had risked his own life to bring aid to the village.> <As a final supererogation he took a full day from his work to take care of his wife when she was only pretending to be ill.> *Supererogatory* means beyond the call of duty, obligation, or necessity: <supererogatory service>.

systematist *n* Some people have more orderly minds than others, or at least have become adept at attaining orderliness. A systematist is one such person, interested in and efficient at classifying, systematizing, and bringing or restoring order to a tangle.

vulgarian *n* A person fond of vulgar language and behavior even though, often because of background, heshe would be expected to avoid vulgarisms.

Walter Mitty *n* An example of antonomasia (see chapter 10). In James Thurber's "The Secret Life of Walter Mitty," the humdrum, unexciting, henpecked Mitty spends most of his time imagining that he is a world-famous surgeon, pilot, or other glamorous figure: <Today many Walter Mittys are flying to amazing, previously unknown parts of the universe or even to other universes.>

wiseacre *n* A know-it-all who, as another wiseacre might say, "deep down is very shallow." In a different sense, a wiseacre is a wisecracking "wise guy," a smart aleck.

xenophile *n,* **xenophobe** *n,* and related words. A xenophile likes and is attracted to foreigners and their cultures. A xenophobe dislikes or fears them. Related nouns are **xenophilia** and **xenophobia.**

zoomers *n* Based on the verb *resume,* this informal term refers to the several million people who had dropped out of college but have now returned. According to the *Washington Post,* slightly over half of these students are aged twenty-five to thirty-four, some are midcareer adults seeking better-paying jobs, and others are older adults driven by curiosity and an eagerness for mental enrichment.

Mastery Test

Decide whether each statement is true (T) or false (F).

___ 1. A person illustrating *parvanimity* is likely to be petty.
___ 2. A *birkie* is an evil person who acts like a bear.
___ 3. A *recidivist* is usually successful in leading a good life.
___ 4. A person who is *dégagé* tends to be stiff and formal.
___ 5. Most people like to *cose* occasionally.
___ 6. A *disingenuous* person is likely to do more pretending and scheming than a naive person.
___ 7. A person with *sophrosyne* is likely to have self-control and modesty.
___ 8. A *nephalist* drinks nothing alcoholic.
___ 9. A person known for *ebriosity* drinks nothing alcoholic.
___ 10. A person with *Dionysian* inclinations probably drinks nothing alcoholic.
___ 11. A coquettish girl displays *minauderies.*
___ 12. *Panache* is delicious as a dessert.

____ 13. *Psychic income* may be more satisfying than a million a year.
____ 14. A person who performs *supererogatory* acts is likely to be unselfish.
____ 15. *Podsnappery* and *complacency* are somewhat alike in meaning.
____ 16. *Crotchet* is a word now used as an approximate synonym of *knit.*
____ 17. *Longanimity* refers to long life.
____ 18. To *obfirm* is to be persistent, as, for instance, in raising money for charity.
____ 19. A *sociopath* is a person who is antisocial or asocial in behavior.
____ 20. A very cheerful person is sometimes *beamish.*
____ 21. A *Walter Mitty* is a truly heroic person.
____ 22. A *nebbish* is a young professional golfer.
____ 23. A *fiver* is likely to be considerate of others.
____ 24. *Grazers* eat frequently.
____ 25. Most politicians are avowed *iconoclasts.*

10
PEOPLE'S NAMES FOR NAMES

Many people have an interest in the origin of personal names or place-names—enough, in fact, that George R. Stewart's *Names on the Land* was once a Book-of-the-Month Club choice. (His later *American Place-Names*, in dictionary format, is more inclusive and more scholarly.) Kelsie Harder's *Illustrated Dictionary of Place Names: United States and Canada* is also excellent. There are a number of books about personal names. I especially like Elsdon Smith's *New Dictionary of Family Names*, and I have proprietary interest in my *Family Names: How Our Surnames Came to America* and *All Those Wonderful Names*.

The Greek *onoma*, "name," is the source of most of our words about names. **Onomastics** (also called **onomatology**) is the study of proper names: <From my first lesson in onomastics I learned that *Johnson* and *Ivanovich* are the same name.> *Onomastics* may also signify the study of the etymologies and forms of words in a particular field, or the system used by speakers of a language in forming proper names: <The onomastics of Spanish and of Chinese fascinated her.>

An **onomatist** or **onomatologist** is a student of names. An **onomastician** invents names—for instance, attractive names for commercial products or new companies: <An onomastician might have chosen a better name than *Edsel*.> An **onomasticon** is a collection such as an onomatist might make. **Onomastic** means pertaining to a name or names: <The onomastic significance of several mythological names has never been firmly established.> **Onomasiology** is the study of a group of related words: <the onomasiology of the place-names in our valley> <His dissertation was on onomasiology, and dealt with miners' names and nicknames for their tools and equipment.> **Onomancy** is divination based on the letters in a name: <Through onomancy seers determined that Gudrun would come to a tragic end.>

A **euonym** is a name that one considers especially appropriate for a person, place, or thing. Thus the child who said "*Pig* is a good name for that animal because it is so dirty" had already developed a belief in euonyms. <*Devil's Delight* is a euonym; only the devil could be happy in a place that gets so hot.> **Euonymous** means "suitably named": <my euonymous sister, Joy>. (The noun *euonymus*, applied to various trees, shrubs, and vines, is from the same source, Greek *euonumos* "of good name.")

A **patronym** or **patronymic** is a name usually based on the name of one's father or grandfather; *Robertson, MacDonald, O'Brien,* and thousands of other surnames have affixes meaning "son or grandson of." A **matronym** or **matronymic** (also **metronymic**) is based on the mother's name—most often the given name; thus Dorothy may have a daughter or a granddaughter with the matronymic *Dorothy*. A few surnames may also be matronymics, although these are rare in English, but ordinary in Spanish. When a son or daughter becomes well known, there may be a **teknonymic,** the name of the offspring used in identifying the parent, usually in phrases like *Laërtes, father of Odysseus.*

If your name is, say, *Wattle*, and for a pseudonym you spell your name backward, *Elttaw*, you are using an **ananym.**

(One of the meanings of *ana-* is "backward.") Unfortunately, **anonym,** very different in meaning, is similar in pronunciation. An anonym may be (a) a person who chooses to be anonymous, (b) a person whose name is unknown, (c) a book or other work produced anonymously, (d) an idea for which no word exists.

Something or someone having many names is **polyonymous:** <a polyonymous criminal>. The use of a number of names for the same thing is **polyonymy:** <A thesaurus demonstrates that polyonymy is much more common than one would suspect.> <Polyonymy makes some Russian novels difficult to read; it seems that the same character may be called a dozen different things.>

When Mary Ann Evans adopted a man's name, George Eliot, for her writings, she was engaging in **pseudandry,** "unauthorized use of a man's name by a woman." And when Huck Finn, dressed as a girl, said that his name was Sarah Williams, he was engaging in **pseudogyny,** "unauthorized use of a woman's name by a male." (*Andr-*, "man," and *gyn-*, "woman," are more familiar in *polyandry,* "having several husbands," and *polygyny,* "having several wives.")

An **allonym** is a special kind of pseudonym—a name of another person, taken over by an author, often with the intent to deceive. Thus if your name is Henry Wright and you publish a book or an article under the name John Updike or even Samuel Johnson, the assumed name is your allonym. (If it were not the name of a real person, it would be only a *pseudonym.*) The **allonymous** work itself may also be called an *allonym.*

An **eponym** is a person for whom something is named or believed to be named. Thus *Romulus* is the eponym of Rome, Dr. Richard *Bright* the eponym of Bright's disease, and a wolf the eponym of various American Indians or groups of Indians. **Eponymous** (also **eponymic**) means having the same name as one's eponym, or being an eponym: <the tribe's eponymous ancestor, the fox>.

Many of us like names—their sounds, their meanings, their histories, and so on. Perhaps there should be a word —say, *onomatophilia*—for the love of names or of words in general. Unfortunately, there is only a stronger word—

onomatomania—which goes beyond love to obsession, to an uncontrollable passion for words, and which in some cases may even degenerate into babbling repetition of words or nonsense sounds.

More Words for the Budding Onomatist

anthroponymy *n* Greek *anthrōpos*, "human being," has been adopted by English in many words, most notably *anthropology*, "the study of human beings." It combines with *nym*, "name," in *anthroponymy*, "the study of human names, especially given names."

antonomasia *n* If you call a man a Romeo or a Scrooge, or a woman a Juliet or a Portia, you are illustrating one meaning of *antonomasia*, from Greek *antonomazein*, "to name instead." Slightly different is addressing an official as "Your Honor" or "Mr. President." A fiction writer employs antonomasia when heshe calls someone by a characterizing name: <Judge Lawless> <Christian (in Bunyan's *Pilgrim's Progress*)>. Finally, the making of a common noun or verb from a proper noun is also antonomasia; *derrick* was once the name of a hangman, and *fletcherize*, "to chew food very thoroughly," was named for a Dr. Fletcher.

augmentative *n* In onomastics, the opposite of a diminutive. In Italian, for instance, *-elli*, *-illi*, or *-illo*, when appended to a name, is a diminutive, meaning "little," and *-one* is an augmentative, meaning "big." An Italian mother may distinguish her little son, Pietro, from his father, also Pietro, by calling them respectively Petrelli and Petrone.

cryptonym *n* A cryptonym is a pseudonym that is kept secret from all but one or a few persons: a code name. <Rogers was assigned the cryptonym "George Secrest.">

day name *n* In some African tribes, in what may be an obsolescent custom, a newborn child has often been named for the day of birth. *RHD* gives these examples of male and female names: Quashee, Washeba (Sunday);

Cudjo, Juba (Monday); Cubbana, Beneba (Tuesday); Quaco, Cuba (Wednesday); Quao, Abba (Thursday); Cuffee, Pheba (Friday); Quamin, Mimba (Saturday).

hydronymy *n* The study of the names of bodies of water —what they are and how they came to be.

hyponym *n* The name of one kind of item in a larger class is a hyponym. (*Hypo-* means "lower, smaller.") Thus *dictionary* or *novel* is a hyponym of *book*.

numeronym *n* Novelist Eric Kraft is credited with coining *numeronym*, c. 1989. It is a telephone number that spells a word, usually as a slogan or an ad. An all-news radio or TV station, for instance, could have the numeronym ALL-NEWS (equivalent to 255-6397).

paraph *n* In signing their names some people add a more or less elaborate flourish, like that of John Hancock when he signed the Declaration of Independence. Such a flourish is a paraph.

prêt-nom *n* From French words for "to lend a name," a prêt-nom is a person who allows another to use hiser name: <"I am Robert Gray," he told the guard, as his prêt-nom, the real Robert Gray, had instructed him.>

surnominal *adj* Pertaining to a surname: <variant surnominal spellings, as *Gerhard, Gerhart, Gerhardt, Gearhart*>.

tautonym *n* In scientific naming, the generic and specific names are sometimes the same, the combination being known as a tautonym. Thus one sort of euonymus shrub is known by the tautonym *Elatis elatis*.

theophoric *adj* A person who has the name of a god is theophoric: <The infant's parents named her *Minerva*, obviously theophoric and, as it turned out, prophetic.>

toponymy or **toponomy** *n*, and related words. Toponymy is the study of place-names. A place-name is a **toponym.** One who specializes in the study of place-names is a **toponymist.** (*Top-* or *topo-* is from a Greek word for place or locality.)

within-named *adj* A stiff, usually legal term for "named elsewhere in this document."

Mastery Test

Fill in the blanks.

An ________________ (student of names) decided that his wife's maiden name, Happy Day, was a delightful ________________ (appropriate name). His own name, Keith Jacobson, was obviously a ________________ (name based on one's father's name). As a boy he had sometimes signed *Nosbocaj*, an ________________ (name spelled backward). Once, wanting to be an ________ (unidentified person), he did not sign at all. He told Happy that she was guilty of ________________ (unauthorized use of a man's name) when she signed a story "Kevin Marx." If she had signed "Karl Marx," she would have been using an ________________ (borrowed name of a real person). She did not share his interest in ____________ (study of human names, especially first names) or in _____ (study of place-names). ________________ (Pertaining to surnames) variants interested her much more than variants in first names. In signing her own name she often drew an elaborate ________________ (flourish) beneath it. Once she correctly informed her husband that Robinson Crusoe's Friday had a sort of ________ ________ and that the telephone number 367-7368 (FOR-RENT) is called a ________________.

11

OF NEEDMENTS AND TRUMPERY

Most of us occasionally get discouraged about the conditions in which we must live, and complain about the "rat race" or about the **squirrel cage** in which we find ourselves. An actual squirrel cage consists of a revolving horizontal cylinder made usually of heavy screen; when a squirrel or any small animal inside the cage attempts to climb, the cylinder revolves. Figuratively, anything that is comparable to this frustrating prison in unproductive repetition is a squirrel cage: <what he considered to be the squirrel cage of his office work>.

Being in a squirrel cage can give one a sense of **ill-being,** the seldom-used antonym of *well-being.* It implies too little prosperity, maybe lack of good familial and social relations, perhaps ill health, or just a general unease. A feeling of ill-being can be accentuated by any of a number of large or small annoyances. For instance, one's family may be crowded into a small apartment. They are **flatites,** as Australians say—a briefer and uglier term than American *apartment-dwellers.* Maybe one or two persons in the family are afflicted by a disease that flourishes in twentieth-century America—**tele-**

phonitis, which is symptomized by an urgent, even insatiable desire to listen to and talk into a telephone for long periods of time. And there are certainly occasional very stormy times, which the British call **gale days,** when the rent or the mortgage payment or the income tax return is due. And there are frequent moments when one longs for the return of what one conceives to be the "good old days," when life was simpler, people were more friendly, and food tasted better. In today's supermarkets one finds, for instance, bacon almost always machine-sliced and wrapped in small packages, but in the good old days people kept it in their kitchens or smokehouses as a **gammon** or **flitch**—a whole side of bacon, weighing maybe ten to twenty pounds, smoked for days over burning hickory chips or logs and not just chemically injected.

There aren't, perhaps, as many times of real **bellycheer** today as there once were. Dictionaries, in fact, label the word "obsolete." It was a vigorous word in those long-ago years when people had prodigious appetites and the meat and drink to satisfy them (although by no means everyone, even then, was comfortably off). It could refer either to the items of food themselves: <the rich bellycheer of my grandfather's table> or to the process of gratification: <Thomas Lupton, 1580: "gave himself to nothing but drincking . . . and bellycheere">. As a verb it meant to feast luxuriously: <Nicolas Udall, 1549: "Riotous bankettyng, pottecompanyoning, and belychearynge">. Can't we revive the word for at least those occasions when, as people used to say. "the festive board groans"?

And those occasions do still exist, at least in millions of fortunate homes.

The already prepared **convenience foods** require comparatively little time to cook—a good thing, too, because both partners must often work forty hours a week to pay for comforts that the family couldn't otherwise have. Before a meal today there may be cocktails, and with the meal may come proof that **enology** still flourishes (spelled **oenology** by the conservative and the pompous); it is the science—or is it an art?—of wine-making, from Greek *oinos*, "wine." And more than likely, as has been true for millenniums, the family still follows the **commensal** custom: eating together—a custom that still helps to keep many families intact. As a noun, *commensal* means one who sits at the same table. The word is from Latin *mensa*, "table."

Sometimes there's a party. An old noun, **foy,** would still be useful today for certain kinds of parties, especially for leavetaking. Latin *via* means way, road. The French borrowed it as *voie*, "way, journey," and the Dutch a few hundred years ago took it over from the French as *voye* or *foye*, which they defined not only as way or journey but also as a going-away party. The word later became Dutch *fooi*, "a dinner that a farmer gives his hired hands before they leave after the harvest." The Scottish got the word from the Dutch, retaining the same meaning but adding a new one: a party before a marriage. We could use *foy* as a short, inclusive substitute for going-away party, pre-marital party, bachelor dinner, bridal shower, and the like.

In some families there are still quiet evenings, too, with the TV turned off or down and maybe with the family just reading and talking or perhaps with a neighbor family in for simple, old-fashioned treats like popcorn or caramel apples. The house or apartment may have available for such an evening an **inglenook,** a word that I consider as pleasant as the thing itself. An **ingle** may be a fireplace, or lacking that, any comfortable corner. The inglenook or **ingle recess** may be the fireside, a corner close to the chimney, any comfortable area for calm relaxation, or—seldom seen today—a pair of high-backed benches sometimes placed facing each other and at right angles to a fireplace.

Even the people with no inglenooks—at least nearly all in America and a high proportion in the rest of the world—are still fortunate enough to have what used to be called the **needments,** "that which is needed." The word may refer to the basic essentials of food, clothing, and shelter, or to the small personal items, such as toothbrushes and combs, needed for comfort. And with living conditions as they are in America today, even during periods labeled "recession," much more money is spent on **need-nots** than on needments.

The words that follow are a collage providing a few more

glimpses of living conditions as reflected in words that most of us seldom use.

More Words About the Ways We Live

blinky *adj* "The milk isn't sour, but it's blinky," my mother used to say, and we knew that the milk was just on the edge of sourness. Since then I've learned that some folks use *blinky* also to describe beer that has been opened for a while. Though labeled "dialectal," *blinky* is a useful word for drinkers of milk or beer to know.

brightwork *n* The chrome or other polished metal on your car, boat, refrigerator, etc., is brightwork. So is the varnished (not painted) wood on a ship.

brimmer *n* When your glass or cup is brimful, you have a brimmer.

chevon *n* *Beef, pork, veal, mutton,* and *venison* are all familiar words. But what does one call meat of a goat? The lack of such a word has only recently been met with *chevon,* from French *chèvre,* "goat," plus the ending of *mutton.*

conurbation *n* An aggregation or string of urban areas, like that extending north and west from New York City, is a conurbation—literally "with cities": <Conurbations are more and more typical of human living.> <The conurbation extending from above *Bos*ton through *N*ew *Y*ork on to and beyond *Wash*ington, D.C., has been nicknamed **Bosnywash.**> (A *megalopolis,* in contrast, is made up of several nearby cities and their suburban areas.)

cord (of wood) *n* The term cord of wood is familiar to most fireplace owners, but many of them do not know exactly what a cord is and hence may be cheated by unscrupulous dealers who use *cord* to mean anything from a few logs to a small truckload. A cord actually should contain 128 cubic feet, say, a pile four by four by eight feet—a considerable amount.

exurb *n,* and related words. Outside the city lie the suburbs, and beyond the suburbs lie the exurbs, also called **exurbia** (by analogy with *suburbia).* People who live in the exurbs are **exurbanites.**

gewgaw or **geegaw** *n* A piece of trashy jewelry or any other small, showy, and nearly worthless object. By extension, anything whether real or abstract may be a gewgaw if it is small and not worth much: <Unfortunately, many people today consider poetry a mere gewgaw.>

grist *n* "Grist for the mill" is a familiar phrase, but many students don't know what grist is. The word is related to Old English *grindan,* "to grind." Grist is the unprocessed wheat or other grain brought to a mill for grinding. Now, though, the meaning is much broader, encompassing any raw materials (or even *im*materials) that will be altered for use: <Their own childhood experiences provide grist for many authors.>

gut-hammer *n* In a logging camp one of the most welcome sounds is that of the gut-hammer, a large steel triangle that Cookie strikes to call lumberjacks to their meals.

lead-in groove *n* When you put on a phonograph record, a blank spiral called a *lead-in groove* leads the needle to the beginning of the recording.

Oslo breakfast or **Oslo meal** *n* Maybe it will never replace America's coffee break, but an Oslo meal is more nutritious. It is a midmorning or midafternoon snack of health foods such as raw fruits and vegetables, milk, cheese, and whole wheat bread.

pass-through *n* A wall opening between two rooms (generally the kitchen and the dining room) through which dishes, food, etc., may be passed.

peak-fresh *adj* Fruit or vegetables that have reached but not gone beyond the ideal stage of ripeness are described as *peak-fresh.*

penturbia *n* Professor Jack Lessinger of the University of Washington coined this word for what he considers the fifth major migration since the American Revolution. It means a mixture of small cities and towns and a scattering of industrial and commercial districts, all seemingly strewn about the countryside in areas of farms and forests. Earlier migration to cities and suburbs, says Lessinger, has slowed; migration now is more and more toward penturbia.

pophole *n* If you have cut a small hole in a door or a wall for your dog, cat, or other pet to pop through, you have made a pophole.

runcible spoon *n* Edward Lear's owl and pussycat (an odd miscegenation) "lived on mince, and slices of quince, / Which they ate with a runcible spoon." In Lear's poem the term was nonsensical, but man's ingenuity is so great that a real runcible spoon was invented, although it turned out to be a small fork with three wide, curved prongs and a sharp edge. It's most likely to be found in a pickle dish.

sewing bird *n* Our ingenious grandmothers, sometimes needing something to hold up an end of material being sewed, devised a clamp shaped like a bird that they fastened to a table edge. When they lifted the bird's tail, its beak would grasp and hold a piece of cloth.

singspiration *n* A religious song service, as in a revival meeting, in which most of the songs are hymns, which may be followed by a short sermon.

squaw wood *n* Sometimes a tree may have low-hanging dead branches. Since squaws could rather easily gather these for firewood, the term *squaw wood* was and is occasionally used for such branches: <"Get some squaw wood," the camper told his children.>

table book *n* Table—or coffeetable—books are intended less for perusal than for display. (Conspicuous consumption, Thorstein Veblen would have called their use.)

tidy *n* Any of several household items designed to aid and encourage tidiness, as a small drain pan kept in the sink to hold potato peels and the like, a cloth protector of the arms or headrest of a chair or sofa, or a receptacle for holding thread or other small articles.

totlot *n* A lot, usually with playground equipment, where small children may play together; often the outdoor part of a nursery school.

trumpery *adj, n* Trumpery consists of small household articles or other articles of comparatively little worth; by extension it may be stories, songs, TV programs, conversation, or anything else considered to be of little value: <One person's trumpery may be another's addiction.> As an adjective it means of little worth or quality; fraudulent: <the trumpery jewelry sold at many five-and-tens>.

village economy *n* Economic historians tell us that our early ancestors were hunters. Their descendants were farmers. Then came the villagers, who lived in small communities and bartered with one another and with neighboring villages and with the surrounding farms. Theirs was a village economy, which differed from the present industrial economy that tends to be urban and that depends on division of labor into tiny segments.

villageous *adj*, **villagey** or **villagy** *adj*, **villagism** *n* *Villageous* means pertaining to a village or villages: <villageous preoccupation with birth, courtship, and death>. *Villagey* is a somewhat contemptuous equivalent: <Don't act so villagey!> A *villagism* is a word, pronunciation, or phrase that is considered characteristic of villageous or rural speech but not of urban speech.

Mastery Test

Match each term at the left with the best definition in its group of ten.

___	1. chevon	a.	small, nearly worthless object
___	2. squirrel cage	b.	going-away party
___	3. telephonitis	c.	what teens especially are accused of having
___	4. enology	d.	goat meat
___	5. foy	e.	hole for your dog
___	6. blinky	f.	almost sour
___	7. gewgaw	g.	wine-making
___	8. pass-through	h.	place of boring work

___	9. pophole	i. elegantly printed item for display
___	10. table book	j. hole in the wall
___	11. totlot	k. expression perhaps not heard in the city
___	12. villagism	l. time of financial strain
___	13. flatite	m. eating together
___	14. gale day	n. place twice-removed from the city
___	15. Bosnywash	o. maybe you, if you live in a city
___	16. bellycheer	p. pleasant spot for a family evening
___	17. commensal	q. things of little value
___	18. inglenook	r. much to eat and drink
___	19. exurbia	s. place inhabited especially by children
___	20. trumpery	t. settled area including three eastern cities

12
FROM YOUR HEAD TO YOUR MINIMUS

Most of the thousands of entries in medical dictionaries are too specialized or technical for inclusion here, even if I understood what they mean. But I've picked out a few dozen that may on occasion prove useful—say, in talking with hypochondriacal people or with friends in or just out of a hospital.

"Now blessings light on him who first invented sleep," said Cervantes. Doctors didn't invent sleep, but they can induce it through the use of **somniferous,** "sleep-inducing" drugs. The drowsy, often restless or fretful period before one goes to sleep is described as **hypnogogic:** <the hypnogogic hours when he worried about tomorrow's court appearance>. In contrast, the half-awake time when one is struggling for complete consciousness—say, the time after the alarm rings—is described as **hypnopompic:** <the hynopompic minute when either sleep or wakefulness can win>.

Narcolepsy is an ailment that results in occasional attacks of heavy sleep. Some drugs produce a stuporous condition called **narcoma. Narcosis** is an even deeper state of unconsciousness, also drug-induced. Again under the influence of drugs, although sometimes because of disorders such as epilepsy or schizophrenia, one may enter a dreamy condition, an unawareness of reality, called a **twilight state.**

Hypersomnia, "sleeping too much," is the opposite of insomnia. It should not be confused with sleeping sickness, since **hypersomniacs** do have enough waking hours and energy to perform most or all of their normal tasks. It is a bit confusing, perhaps, that *hypersomnia* may also mean sleeping too deeply, as if drugged.

If you unknowingly grind your teeth when you are asleep or in a time of stress, you are exhibiting **bruxism** (from a Greek verb for "to gnash the teeth"). And if you feel numb when you wake up, you are experiencing **narcohypnia,** which should not be confused with **narcohypnosis,** a hypnotic state induced by drugs, used by some psychotherapists.

When your doctor examines you, heshe is almost sure to tap you here and there, as, for instance, when heshe checks your reflexes by tapping your knee with a little rubber hammer. To tap is to **percuss,** which is the verb form of *percussion.* "The doctor took his little flashlight and looked at my throat," you say to a friend. The "little flashlight" is a **cavascope**—a device for illuminating various bodily cavities. When the doctor listens to your chest and hears an abnormal sound, it is a **rale,** from the French *râler* "to make a rattling sound in the throat." To detect abnormalities in the functioning of the brain, a qualified doctor may attach electrodes to the scalp; these are connected to an **encephalophone,** a humming instrument that changes pitch according to the brain waves transmitted through it. *Encephalo* comes from the Greek word for brain and occurs in some twenty or more words in English, including **encephalitis,** "an inflammation of the brain."

Anything from the brain (and the scalp and hair above it) down to the **minimus** (which is your smallest finger or toe) may have its own defects or ailments. For instance:

> The source of any man's neurosis
> Is finding that he has **psilosis.**

(Psilosis is the losing of hair.) And occasionally, perhaps because of a burn or friction, one may have **blebs,** "small blisters." The word is also used for a bubble in glass or some other formerly fluid substance: <Desaguliers, 1716: "The Lens ought to be . . . without Veins or Blebs."> To **desquamate** is to peel off (as skin) in the form of scales: <After the fever he desquamated for a week.> One frontier for medical researchers concerned with the elderly is **elastosis,** the loss of skin elasticity caused by degeneration of tissues: <Elastosis results in wrinkled, flabby, lifeless-looking skin.> If you are afflicted with **phonasthesia,** your voice is weak or you are hoarse. **Paresis** is partial or slight paralysis: <"With care," said the doctor, "you can overcome the paresis."> **Myopathy** is a disease of the muscles or muscle tissues.

Dreaded especially by the elderly is the possibility of an **embolus,** an abnormality such as an air bubble or a blood clot circulating in the blood stream and capable of causing a stroke. The embolus is popularly called an **embolism,** but technically **embolism** refers to the act of obstructing the blood stream rather than the obstruction itself. To **embolize** is to lodge in and obstruct a blood vessel or an organ. The condition of being embolized is **embolization.** An embolus may be removed or broken up in various ways, one of the older being a surgical procedure called **embolectomy.**

Most disorders, of course, are much less serious than paresis or embolization. Often one just feels **all-overish,** as some British people say; that is, one is slightly indisposed physically, with no very specific symptoms, or one may be only vaguely ill at ease or apprehensive about one-knows-not-what. Some Americans say they have the **collywobbles** when they have an intestinal disturbance, perhaps with mild diarrhea—a disturbance that does not appear to be severe enough for a more sedate name. Probably the word comes from *cholera* and *wobble,* with some influence of *colic.* A person who has no known or specific ailment but nevertheless feels tired and perhaps listless and lustless may be said to be in a state of **subhealth.** In ascending order, one may be in nonhealth, subhealth, or health. It is certainly easy to understand why "To your health" or an equivalent expression is the toast most widely used around the world.

Other Medical Words

ablactation *n* The act of taking milk away from: <Ablactation was a long and difficult process for both mother and child.> Thus *ablactation* may be a synonym for *weaning*, but the latter has been extended to refer not only to milk but also to salt, alcohol, or almost anything else to which one has been accustomed: <J. Swift: "to wean us gradually from our fondness of life">. If you want to refer solely to deprivation of milk, *ablactation* will do the job.

afterpain *n* Although most mothers remember the afterpains caused by the contraction of the uterus after giving birth, less often referred to is the afterpain that comes, following a period of comfort, after an operation or other cause of pain. The sequence is operation, comfort, afterpain. The aftershock such as sometimes belatedly follows an accident or near-accident is probably related.

anile *adj*, **anility** *n* As everyone knows, *senile* and *senility* refer to old age. *Anile* and *anility* refer specifically to feeble, elderly women: <her anile remarks concerning her first husband, who died sixty years ago> <Even at age ninety, Alice Roosevelt Longworth showed few signs of anility.>

arrhythmia *n*, and related words. Physicians who note any pronounced irregularity in the force or rhythm of the heartbeat refer to the condition as *arrhythmia*. The adjectival forms are **arrhythmic** and **arrhythmical** (both sometimes spelled without the first *h*). The meanings of the adjectives, though, have been expanded to refer to lack of rhythm of any sort, not just in the heartbeat: <Much modern music is arrhythmic.>

bimana *n*, **bimanal** *adj*, **bimanual** *adj*, **quadrumana** *n* Man is the only true bimana, a creature with hands unlike the feet. Other primates are quadrumana: their feet are shaped like hands. *Bimanal*, the adjective formed from *bimana*, means having two hands. And *bimanual*, most familiar of these words, means requiring the use of two hands: <Young lovers sometimes forget that an automobile is intended for bimanual operation.>

borborygmus *n*, **borborygmic** *adj* Greek *borborygmos* is a noun meaning rumbling. In English, the rumbling caused by gas in the intestines is called *borborygmus* (plural *borborygmi* or *borborygmies*), and the adjective for "pertaining to intestinal rumbling" is *borborygmic.*

callosity *n* A callous or callus is a thick, hardened piece of skin. *Callosity* may refer to this abnormal hardness, or metaphorically to emotional "hardness" or insensitivity: <The callosity of her treatment of the children was unbelievable.>

caries *n* Best known as a synonym of *tooth decay, caries* can be traced back to Sanskrit for "he breaks, crushes." It refers specifically to the process responsible for destroying tooth tissue, or, more generally, to the ulceration and destruction of other bone formations: <caries of the fibula>.

cavitation *n* Cavitation is the forming of cavities, as in the teeth or lungs or in inanimate solids or liquids: <His pulmonary cavitation has reached a dangerous stage.>

cellulitis *n* In some people (women more often than men) excess deposits of fat may occur, especially in the thighs and buttocks. It is called *cellulite,* and if it becomes inflamed, the condition is known as *cellulitis.*

cephalic index *n* If you want to know whether you are broad-headed or long-headed, have someone measure the greatest breadth of your cranium and the greatest front-to-back length. Multiply the ratio by 100. For example, breadth = 6.125″; length = 7.25″. Divide 6.125 by 7.25 and get a ratio of .845. Multiply by 100. Your cephalic index is 84.5, definitely broad-headed (more than 81, technically *brachycephalic*). With an index below 75, you would be long-headed (*dolichocephalic*). Good hatmakers, hard to find, make hat sizes to conform to heads of different sizes.

ciliary *adj* A *cilium* (plural *cilia*) is an eyelash, and *ciliary* means pertaining to eyelashes or other hairlike processes. The *supercilium* is the eyebrow, whose sometimes scornful liftings gave us *supercilious*.

crymotherapy or **cryotherapy** *n*, **thermotherapy** *n* In the International Scientific Vocabulary (ISV) *crymo-* or *cryo-* means cold and *thermo-* means hot. Medical treatment that involves freezing, cold baths, and the like is crymotherapy; that which involves application of heat is thermotherapy.

cryptogenic *adj*, **phanerogenic** *adj* A disease of unknown or obscure origin is described by doctors as *cryptogenic;* antonymously, a disease of obvious origin is *phanerogenic.* (*Crypto-*, as in *cryptography*, means hidden, and *phaneros* is Greek for visible.)

demulcent *adj,n* A demulcent substance, such as acacia, soothes the throat. The ancestral Latin word *demulcēre* means to caress, to soothe. <The demulcent quickly eased but did not eliminate the child's discomfort.>

dentulous *adj*, **edentulous** *adj* A dentulous animal or person has teeth. An edentulous one does not: <as edentulous as the proverbial hen>. *Dentate* and *edentate* correspond in meaning to these two words. *Edentulate* is also sometimes used.

dermatograph *n* A surgeon may make markings on the skin, so as to sketch externally the outlines of an internal organ. The instrument heshe uses is called a dermatograph. The term may also mean a kind of crayon useful in testing for allergies.

dermatosis *n*, and related words. Any disease of the skin is dermatosis, also called **dermatopathia** or **dermatopathy.** A skin disease caused by a fungus is **dermatomycosis.**

dol *n* Intensity of pain is measured in tenths, from one dol for barely perceptible pain to ten dols for pain so severe that any added stimulus does not increase the feeling: <"I've got an eight-dol headache," she said.> The source of the word is the same as that of *dolor* and *dolorous*.

efferent *adj*, **afferent** *adj*, **effector** *n* You touch a moderately hot dish. A receptor in your fingertips detects that fact, and sensory, or *afferent*, nerve fibers carry the message to your central nervous system. *Afferent* comes from Latin *ad*, "to," and *ferre*, "carry." In the central system, motor, or *efferent*, nerve fibers carry the return message out to your fingertips. *Efferent* comes from Latin *ex*, "out," and *ferre*. The message goes to your *effectors* (which are organs making your muscles act), telling them that the dish is uncomfortably warm and that it would be judicious to move your fingers. The entire communication and resulting action require but a fraction of a second.

egest *v*, and related words. To **ingest** is to take substances such as food and drink into the body, especially through the mouth; the process is **ingestion** and what is taken in is **ingesta,** a rather useful word that can cover not only the ordinary but also all the weird things that we sometimes put into our mouths (like truffles, fish eggs, birds' nests, and commercial soft drinks). Most of what comes in also goes out—whether through skin, lungs, kidneys, or bowels—and at that time becomes **egesta** (from Latin for to carry out). The process, whichever kind it is, is **egestion,** and a five-letter word that encompasses *sweat*, *exhale*, and a couple of four-letter verbs is **egest** (which most often refers to excreting from the digestive tract).

heliotherapy *n* Although excessive exposure to sunlight may be harmful, the sun's rays in moderate quantities may be therapeutic. The use of sunlight (or artificially produced ultraviolet or infrared rays) for healing purposes is heliotherapy.

heterodont *adj*, *n*, **homodont** *adj*, *n* An animal that has different kinds of teeth (incisors, canines, and molars) is a heterodont: <Man is a heterodont animal.> An animal whose teeth are all of one kind is a homodont.

hypesthesia *n* "There's no feeling in my fingers," a patient tells the doctor. Reduction or lack of tactile sensitivity is hypesthesia.

laterality *n*, **dextrality** *n*, **sinistrality** *n* The tendency of an individual to use one side of hiser body more than another is known as laterality—for example, the preference for using one hand rather than the other. If we favor the right side, we illustrate dextrality; if the left, sinistrality: <Her degree of sinistrality was high; she wrote with her left hand and she kicked her dog with her left foot.>

maxilla *n,* **maxillary** *adj* Maxillae or maxillas are jaws or jawbones. *Maxillary* means "pertaining to a jaw or jawbone."

medius *n* Fingers (usually the thumb is excluded) are, in order, forefinger, medius, third finger, and minimus. Toes are big toe, second toe, middle toe, fourth toe, and minimus.

mons pubis *n* The small, slightly rounded mass of fatty tissue above the pubic bones. The literal meaning is "pubic area higher than its surroundings." Specifically in the human female it is also called *mons veneris,* translated as "mount of Venus."

pandemic *adj,* **endemic** *adj* A disease is *epidemic* if it afflicts many people in a given area, *endemic* if it is constantly present in an area, and *pandemic* if it is very widespread at a given time and affects an unusually high proportion of the people: <pandemic influenza racing across Europe>.

physianthropy *n* A study of human beings emphasizing the human constitution, the diseases to which people are prey, and their remedies.

synergism *n* The cooperative action of two or more drugs, organs, or organisms, which working together are more effective than either alone.

Mastery Test

Fill in the missing letters.

1. e_________s	having no teeth
2. d__	a measurement of pain
3. h___________y	treatment by sunlight
4. s________m	cooperative action by two drugs

5. s_________s — sleep-inducing
6. h_________a — excessive sleeping
7. b_____m — gnashing the teeth
8. m_____s — your smallest toe
9. e_______s — loss of dermal elasticity
10. e_____s — bubble or clot in the blood stream
11. c__________s — slight intestinal disorder
12. s_______h — between health and unhealth
13. a_________n — five-dollar word for *weaning*
14. a___e — pertaining to a very old woman
15. b______l — requiring the use of two hands
16. d_______t — throat-soothing
17. d________s — any disease of the skin
18. i____t — to eat or drink
19. a______t — carrying to the brain
20. l________y — tendency to use one side of the body
21. n______s — drug-induced unconsciousness
22. p_____s — to examine by tapping
23. e__________s — inflammation of the brain
24. p______s — loss of hair
25. a_______n — delayed pain
26. a________c — irregular, uneven (said of a heartbeat)
27. c________s — inflamed fat
28. c__________y — frigid treatment
29. t___________y — hot treatment
30. c______c i___x — way to classify a head

13
PHILOSOPHY: THE CONTRADICTORY GUIDE

Norman Cousins wrote: "After several hundred thousand years of existence on this planet, the human species is still bedeviled by unanswered questions that make life less rewarding than it ought to be. The most important of these questions have to do less with technology than with behavior and philosophy." He went on to say that conceivably creatures in other worlds have answered some of these questions and that we would be justified in spending large sums of money to try to ascertain by microwaves whether that is true: ". . . if there are places in the universe where people make genuine sense of their existence as a species and where they comprehend the delicate connections between individual and collective existence, all the treasures on earth would be a small price to pay for the clues."

In a few words, Cousins here defined the basic purpose of philosophy: to "make genuine sense of . . . existence." So far, though, earthbound philosophers have come out with highly divergent views, often complete contradictions. Perhaps someday, in a still-to-be-found homegrown philosophy or in one imported from another galaxy, we may find a guide that will serve us in understanding ourselves and others, in eschewing selfishness, in solving disagreements without recourse to battle. Perhaps someday. But not yet, for the philosophers do still disagree with one another as much as any other people do.

Consider, for example, the **determinists** and the **indeterminists.** In general **determinism** holds that forces outside each person determine hiser actions and fate. **Indeterminism,** in contrast, says that little or nothing in human life is completely predetermined or outside the human power to influence. The determinist sees a mechanistic universe consisting of and controlled by physical forces; the indeterminist sees a universe that any person may change a little through hiser own powers of decision and action.

Or consider the **deteriorist** and the **meliorist. Deteriorism,** a form of pessimism, is the belief that everything is going to the bad and that nothing can be done about it. **Meliorism,** a form of optimism, grants that this isn't the best of all possible worlds but says that things are gradually getting better and that people can help in the process.

The **modernist,** too, believes that what exists today is superior to what existed in the past. In the arts, heshe applauds new modes and shapes of expression; in religion, heshe tries to dismiss beliefs that seem no longer valid, replacing them with others heshe considers more compatible with scientific findings; in government, heshe argues that modern democracy, despite its weaknesses, is superior to Roman monarchy or even to Athenian democracy, which served well only a small proportion of the people.

The **futurist** believes that the goal of existence is to create a better future. But the **survivalist** disagrees. Perhaps **survivalism** is a counsel of desperation, since its exponents argue that survival is or should be the chief goal of an individual, group, or nation, and thus in effect denies the likelihood of progress and the rights of anyone else who stands in the way of one's own survival. A hungry survivalist will snatch bread from hiser own child, but a hungry futurist will steal bread from the elderly and give it to a child.

Even philosophers who wear the same general label differ markedly among themselves. Hedonists, for example, believe that happiness is the goal of life. But note how different the major varieties of hedonism are:

egoistic hedonism The goal is one's own happiness.
epicurism The goal is sensual gratification, especially as derived from food, drink, and easy living. (This is actually a misinterpretation of Epicurus, who stressed simple pleasures, friendship, and intellectual gratification.)
eudaemonism The goal is happiness and well-being attained through reason.
universalistic hedonism The goal is the greatest happiness of the greatest number. Also known as **multitudinism,** which says that the interests and well-being of the multitude are more important than those of the individual.

Words related to *hedonism* and *hedonist* are **hedonic, hedonics,** and **hedonistic.**

Energism, facing the question of whether one should seek pleasure as life's goal, answers, "Not necessarily, and not directly." **Energists** believe that the greatest good lies in using all one's physical and mental faculties efficiently. If one does that, they say, contentment will follow and one will make a satisfying (and incidentally happiness-producing) contribution to hiser little corner of the universe.

And so it goes, through uncounted schools and coteries of philosophers and the variations wrought by the progeny of each. Yet the search must continue until solutions—beliefs—are found that most human beings can accept and live with and if necessary die for.

That search is basically concerned with the questions that **eschatology** asks—such things as "Why is there a world? Why a universe? Why are people here? What is their role in the eternal scheme of things?" And the search is concerned with the values that **axiology** asks about: "What are the relative values of truth and deceit? of any two things? What is the beautiful and what is the ugly and what is the worth of each? What in general is worthwhile and what is worthless, to the individual and to humankind?"

Other Philosophical Terms

agathism *n*, **agathist** *n* Agathism is an extreme form of optimism that holds that all things tend finally toward good. Thus war and cancer, an agathist believes, are good things because they prevent overpopulation. But opposition to war and cancer is also good because it gives the individual what heshe considers a constructive cause.

bioethics *n* Among the many concerns of bioethics are questions about abortion, euthanasia, bioengineering, transplants, physician-patient relationships, use of animals in research and medicine—any questions, in fact, that have ethical implications for biological and medical activities. The word dates only from 1970–75, but bioethical discussions now receive much public attention.

chapter of accidents *n* This refers not to part of a book but to any series of unpredictable events such as greatly influences the life of each of us. For example, part of the chapter of accidents in your own life may be that your teenage grandmother-to-be happened to visit a teenage girlfriend, and your grandfather-to-be happened to come past on the near side of the street. If the visit hadn't occurred at that time, or if the boy had been on the other side of the street, you might not exist.

concause *n* It is a truism that nothing is as simple as it seems. For instance, there is seldom a single cause for any effect, but rather a group of interrelated, perhaps inseparable causes. Each cause working with others in a group is a concause: <A concause of the Civil War was the difference of industrial development of North and South.>

dharma *n* In the ancestral Sanskrit this word meant that which is established; the various modern meanings in Oriental religions derive from this. In Hinduism, specifically, dharma is regarded as the body of universal laws from which no one can escape, and also what one needs to do to live in harmony with these laws—the social, caste, or religious customs it is one's duty to obey. <It

is the dharma of water both to sustain and to drown.> <Our dharma forbids murder and theft.>

dogma *n,* **dogmatic** *adj* Beliefs and tenets prescribed usually by a church but sometimes by a political or other organization constitute dogma. A person who is dogmatic holds strictly to such dogmas or to other beliefs or opinions and is unwilling to accept different ones.

egocentric predicament *n* Some philosophers claim that all we can know is what is in our own minds. Therefore we cannot get beyond ourselves, beyond our own mentalities. This unhappy state of affairs, whether we believe in it or not, is the egocentric predicament.

élan vital *n* French philosopher Henri Bergson hypothesized that there is a source other than physical and chemical action that exists within each organism and causes its growth and development. This force he called *élan vital.*

ephectic *adj* From a Greek verb meaning to hold back, *ephectic* means reserving judgment. It is used primarily with reference to the group of ancient philosophers called Skeptics. But the term deserves broader application to describe the attitude of deferring judgment or to describe people who defer judgment or decision: <He is a very ephectic corporation president: He waits for all available evidence before making a decision.>

existentialism *n* Existentialists believe that the universe is indifferent to human beings and that each person must make hiser own decisions and be responsible for hiser own acts. No code of conduct can cover every person and every situation.

geocentric *adj,* and related words. *-Centric* is a combining form that means "having as the center." So *geocentric* means having the earth as the center. Most of us are necessarily geocentric in our thinking: Anything in the universe we are forced to regard in relation to what we know of earth and earthly things. However, a solar system is **heliocentric,** "having the sun as the center." An **anthropocentric** person believes that humans are the center of the universe, the measuring rod for everything.

Homocentric may mean "man-centered," too, but also "having the same center." **Polycentric** means "having many centers": <the polycentric culture of the United States>. Many of the *-centric* words exist also as other parts of speech, such as **anthropocentrism** "the belief that humans are the center of the universe."

gymnosophist *n,* and related words. In Greek *gymnos* means "naked" and *sophistēs* "philosopher." The name *gymnosophists* was once attached to a sect of Hindu philosophers who lived ascetic lives spent chiefly in meditating in the nude. Today some erudite nudists call themselves gymnosophists whether or not they are ascetic and meditative; their belief in nudism is dignified as **gymnosophy,** and they may learnedly discuss their **gymnosophical** ideas concerning themselves and their long-dead Hindu philosopher-friends.

homiletic *adj* Like a sermon, sermonizing: <his homiletic remarks> <Fathers are reputed to be more homiletic than mothers.>

instrumentalism *n* Pragmatists believe that ideas have value not in themselves but only as guides to action; an idea is valid if the action it generates is successful. This belief is called *instrumentalism.*

knowability *n* Although the sum total of human knowledge is said to double every five to ten years, many old or not-so-old questions remain unanswered and perhaps will never be answered. *Knowability* refers to capability of being known. We may speak with some certainty about the knowability of the precise structure of the atom, but with less certainty about the knowability of the processes of original creation.

latitudinarian *adj, n* Edward Phillips in his dictionary of 1696 wrote: "*Latitudinarians* in Religion, are those who profess a Freedom, and as it were a greater Latitude than usual in their Principles and Doctrine. It is also vulgarly applied to such as take a more than ordinary Liberty in their Lives and Conversations." Phillips's explanation is still good, except that *vulgarly* would now be omitted. The term even yet is most often used to refer to tolerance concerning variations in religious belief. Latitudinarian standards of conduct tend now to be called *permissive*.

mystagogue *n*, **mystagogic** *adj* A mystagogue is one who teaches or otherwise publicizes mystical doctrines.

mythogenesis or **mythopoeia** *n* The act of creating myths. Myths are imaginative, usually narrative explanations of common events; for example, explaining storms at sea in terms of the wrath of Neptune, explaining the apparent movement of the sun in terms of the driver of a sun chariot, or explaining an American business success in terms of Horatio Alger.

nada *n* A favorite word of Ernest Hemingway, *nada* is Spanish for "nothing" and means nothingness, a state of nonexistence: <Why struggle? Everything is nada.>

negativism *n* One sort of negativism is illustrated by the child who refuses to do what heshe is asked or who tends to do exactly what heshe is told not to do. Another sort is illustrated by the skeptic who habitually expresses doubt or disbelief about what others are affirming.

nihilism *n* From Latin *nihil*, "nothing." Nihilists are skeptical about everything, even about whether they or anything else exists. Rejecting all established institutions and laws, they may sometimes turn to terrorism, assassination, and anarchy, as some nineteenth-century Russian groups did.

overworld *n* The overworld, contrasted with the underworld, is the social level consisting of virtuous, respectable people. More rarely it is the world of the supernatural.

Panglossian *adj* In Voltaire's satiric *Candide*, Dr. Pangloss stresses the view that everything is for the best in this best of all possible worlds—a view that Candide naively shares despite the parade of horrible incidents that befall him and his beloved. Such an excessively optimistic view is described as Panglossian.

perspectivism *n* The philosophical belief that there is no reality per se but that every being must experience reality from hiser own point of view at a given moment. For instance, a runner's slide into second base does not seem exactly the same to everyone, and if the slide happened a moment or two earlier or later, it would appear slightly different to the same observer. <Some of the beliefs of general semanticists are based on perspectivism; they might write, for example, American politics$_{1964}$ or American politics$_{1990}$ to suggest that political beliefs and processes do not remain constant.>

probabilism *n* Ancient Greek philosophers called Skeptics believed in probabilism: that one cannot be certain about anything but must make decisions on the basis of what seems most probable.

progressionist *n* A progressionist is an optimist who believes that humanity is continuously making progress toward a better state. Heshe is thus similar to the meliorist and the modernist.

pseudodoxy *n* Pseudodoxy may be either a false opinion or the holding of false opinions: <the pseudodoxy that one number is luckier than another> <Legislative progress is often hampered by pseudodoxies.>

selectionist *n* A person who believes that natural selection, "the survival of the fittest," is a basic, essential part of evolution.

shu *n* Shu, in the teachings of Confucius, is the Chinese equivalent of the golden rule, recommending that in all actions there should be consideration of others.

tao *n* An important concept for about twenty-six hundred years in the Chinese philosophy called Taoism, tao is the first principle of the universe, the almost unimaginable source of all that is and is not. In Confucianism, though, it is the heart of a moral code, differentiating right from wrong and pointing the way to virtuous conduct.

teleology *n* A teleologist believes that there is purpose or design in everything that exists or occurs. One group of eighteenth-century teleologists thought that everything was arranged for the good of humankind, going so far as to say that fleas are dark to make them more visible on white stockings.

tychism *n*, **uniformitarianism** *n* Tychism holds that chance operates in the universe, but uniformitarianism argues that everything is the result of universally applied principles. So tychism says, for instance, that some evolutionary variations happen only by accident, but uniformitarianism says that there are no accidents.

ultraism *n* Advocacy of extreme measures, or an example of extreme measures: <His ultraism alienated even his most radical friends.>

world soul *n* A believer in a personal soul may believe also in some spiritual being or force that is related to the world as the human soul supposedly is to the body.

wu wei *n* Wu wei is letting nature takes its course, working in harmony with natural laws rather than at cross-purposes to them. Following this principle, believers in wu wei object to more than minimal regulation by government. They also favor nonviolence and a minimum of argument.

Mastery Test

Complete each statement.

1. If I believe that everything in my life is determined by outside forces, I am a d__________t.
2. If I believe that things are getting worse all the time, I am a d__________t.
3. If I believe that my major purpose in life should be to make myself happy, I believe in e_______c hedonism.
4. If I believe that the goal of life is happiness for as many people as possible, I believe in u______________c hedonism.
5. If I believe that it is especially important to use my mental and physical powers as well as I can, I am an e_______t.
6. If my philosophy is especially concerned with values, it may be called a_______y.
7. If I try to follow the golden rule, a Confucianist would say that I believe in s___.

8. If I believe that chance operates in the universe, I believe in t_____m.
9. If I believe that many unforeseeable events influence people's lives, I might sometimes talk about the c_____r of a_______s.
10. If I am a Hindu, I may believe in a body of universal laws called d____a.
11. If I am highly permissive and acceptive of varied beliefs, I may be called l____________n.
12. If I try to spread mystical doctrines, I am a m________e.
13. If I constantly express doubt and disbelief, my words reflect my n________m.
14. If I agree with Candide, my philosophy is P_________n.
15. If I believe that all things tend at last toward good, I am an a______t.
16. If I tend to defer judgment, I may be described as e______c.
17. If I believe that human beings are central to the universe, I am an a_____________c person.
18. If I hold a false opinion, it may also be called a p________y.
19. If I believe in survival of the fittest, I am a s___________t.
20. If I advocate extreme measures, I am illustrating u______m.
21. If I believe that everything has a purpose or design. I believe in t_______y.
22. If I am skeptical about everything, I am a n______t.
23. If I follow prescribed beliefs or tenets, I am d______c.
24. If I often consider problems of abortion, mistreatment of animals, or euthanasia, I am concerned about b_______s.

14
MANY GODS FOR MANY PEOPLE

Historians of religion disagree about whether primitive people were **polytheistic,** "worshiping many gods," or **monotheistic,** "worshiping a single god." The answer appears to be that both **polytheism** and **monotheism** existed, perhaps simultaneously or perhaps at different times. There is some evidence, for instance, that neighboring communities worshiped a different god or different gods, so that a given area might be polytheistic even though each community or tribe might have been monotheistic.

There is evidence, too, that the objects of worship took many forms. Believers in **animism** felt that every living thing—trees and animals especially—contained a spirit or soul deserving of veneration. The sun, according to believers in what we call **heliolatry,** was the deity or at least the chief deity, but believers in **pyrolatry** opted for fire. Water has always been so important to people that the existence of **hydrolatry** is not surprising; even the relatively sophisticated ancient Greeks and Romans personified the oceans as a god, Poseidon or Neptune, and believed also that there were localized supernatural beings, the **naiads** in springs, lakes, and streams (as well as **dryads** in forests, **hamadryads** in individual trees).

The name **theriomorphism** (from Greek *thērion*, "wild beast") is given to the belief that deities exist in animal form. **Theriolatry** is the worship of animals or of gods in **theriomorphic** form. In some primitive societies, theriolatry or **zoolatry** involved worship of a tribal totem—such as a wolf—in animal form. (In modern society, *zoolatry* generally means only excessive love of pets or other animals: <After Fido died, she vowed that she would never again succumb to zoolatry.> A **zoolatrous** person is a **zoolater** and may also be described as **zoophilous,** "animal-loving.") **Totemism** is a belief in totems, or adherence to the customs or rituals or patterns of social organization that are to be found in a **totemic** culture.

Ditheism is a belief in two gods, usually one good and one evil, as in Manicheism, an ancient religion of Persia; Christians holding the belief that God and the devil are in constant and fairly equal combat are in a sense **ditheists. Tritheism,** of course, is a belief in three gods; specifically, according to leading dictionaries, one who believes that the Father, the Son, and the Holy Spirit are three distinct Gods is a **tritheist. Tetratheism,** although it may mean belief in four gods, is usually defined as belief in the Father, the Son, the Holy Spirit, and a divine essence underlying and responsible for the Trinity; when this divine essence is counted as part of the Godhead, four "Gods" are worshiped.

The devil has not lacked his own adherents. Dealings with the devil, belief in devils or a devil, and worship of the devil are all included under **diabolism.** A **diabolist,** also called a **diabolonian,** is one who practices diabolism, sometimes including savage sexual rites. To **diabolize** is to add something diabolical or to subject a person or thing to the devil's influence. **Diabology** is the study of devils or a devil.

Other Words Pertaining to Religion

antinomian *n* A person who believes that God's grace has freed devout Christians from observance of the laws of Moses and of the secular community. Some early believers in antinomianism considered it a justification for licentiousness, but most later antinomians—present in many sects—disagreed.

bat mitzvah *n* The more widely known *bar mitzvah* is the solemn ceremony to admit thirteen-year-old Jewish boys, who have been given specified instruction, as adult members of the Jewish religious community. A *bat* (or *bath* or *bas*) *mitzvah* is a similar ceremony for twelve- or thirteen-year-old girls.

creationism *n*, **creationist** *n* In contrast to evolutionism or Darwinism, which holds that new species develop through gradual changes in older ones, the doctrine of creationism holds that matter and the various species of living creatures were created out of nothing by an omnipotent god. A person adhering to such a belief is a creationist.

crisis theology *n* Probably almost everyone is bothered by contradictions in human existence, such as a love-hate relationship between parent and child, or the imposition of more severe penalties for small crimes than for large ones. Karl Barth and other believers in crisis theology stressed the need for faith and divine assistance in overcoming the crises that may arise from such contradictions.

demonist *n* A demonist believes in demons or studies demons and demonology, also called *demonism*. <As a demonist, she was certain that a real Satan exists and is aided by a host of horned and long-tailed assistants as well as by countless witches and other low-powered aides.>

demythologize *vi, vt* Many religious and other writings consist of stories intended to dramatize messages or lessons. A person who attempts to separate such a story from its underlying significance is said to be demythologizing: <He claimed to be devoting his life to demythologizing the book of Genesis.>

double predestination *n* A belief that God has predetermined not only who will be saved but also who will be damned for all eternity. No matter what you do on earth, double predestination decrees, your abode after death has been decided. Believers may find no reason to be "good."

earth mother *n* (sometimes capitalized) (1) The fertile earth, like a fertile woman, is the source of life and therefore is to be venerated. (2) The Earth Mother is a female spirit, worthy of worship. In an age that continues to abuse and desecrate the earth, a return to something like those beliefs, some people say, is essential for survival.

ecclesiolatry *n*, **religiosity** *n*, **piosity** *n* Ecclesiolatry is worship of a church as an institution, or excessive reverence for churches—in contrast to a high degree of religious devotion. *Religiosity*, too, has a negative connotation, referring to an excess of religiousness, especially excessive attention to religious forms and formalities rather than to the deeper significance of religion; it sometimes implies hypocrisy or self-deceit, as in a person who believes heshe is religious because heshe attends church regularly and puts money into the collection plate. *Piosity*, also unfavorable, refers to a display of reverence that often is not genuinely felt.

ecumenical *adj* An ecumenical movement in religion represents an attempt by two or more churches or denominations to find ways to cooperate or even unite. Outside religion, the term refers to mixed styles or parts. <The new office building is a weirdly ecumenical blend of at least three quite different architectural styles.>

eisegesis *n*, **exegesis** *n* *Exegesis*, the more familiar word, means a detailed explanation of written or printed material, most often part of the Bible. *Eisegesis* has a similar meaning, but it emphasizes the interpreter's own beliefs and theories, not what the text actually says. *Eisegesis* comes from Greek words for "leading into." The interpreter tries to lead hearers or readers into accepting hiser interpretation.

Epiphany *n* The January 6 Christian festival in commemoration of Christ's appearance before the Magi. Uncapitalized, the word refers to a sudden insight (in real life or in literature) into the essential but personalized meaning of an important human truth. <This was his epiphany: Now he knew that his must be a life of service to others.>

fakir *n* Not to be confused with faker, although such confusion has led to use of *fakir* to mean a swindler. From an Arabic word for "he was poor," *fakir* in the Muslim and Hindu faiths refers to an apparently devout ascetic, sometimes a beggar and often a monk, who is believed to be capable of producing wonders. (No doubt some fakirs have been impostors.)

fertility cult *n* A religious group that employs ceremonial dances or other rituals to assure that its members, its livestock, and its fields will produce richly.

fideism *n* In their search for philosophical or religious truths, some people rely largely on faith rather than on reason. Latin *fides*, "faith," has given us our name for such a basis of belief—*fideism.*

inerrancy *n* "The Bible is the word of God, and God never lies. Therefore every statement in the Bible is true." That is the heart of belief in inerrancy, "freedom from error, infallibility." Opponents argue that the Bible was written by many human hands and that translations differ from one another and often convey more than a single meaning for a given passage. They add that "Even the devil quotes Scripture" and that the Bible sometimes seems to contradict itself.

irenics *n* In classical mythology Irene was the personification of peace. *Irenics* refers to attempts to secure or enhance peaceful relations among Christian churches, usually on the ground that their similarities are greater than their differences.

lordolatry *n* *Lordolatry* implies title worship, adulation of a lord or other noble because of rank rather than more positive qualities. <Even Americans, or maybe especially Americans, exhibit lordolatry.> Perhaps there should be a word *lordolatrous*, but dictionaries do not record it.

manitou *n* The Algonquian Indians believed that a Great Spirit, the manitou (also spelled *manito, manitu*) controlled nature, including human existence. In some versions, numerous spiritual powers were personified, and a Great Manitou (Kitchi-Manitou) headed them all. Manitowoc, Wisconsin, is named for the Great Manitou.

monogeny *n,* and related words. Monogeny, also **monogenism,** is the belief that all human races descended from the same pair—for example, Adam and Eve—or at least from a common ancestral type. One who holds this **monogenous** belief is of course a **monogenist.** In contrast, **polygeny** or **polygenism** is the belief that humans descended from two or more distinct ancestral types. **Polygenous** is the adjective for this belief, and one who holds it is a **polygenist.**

numen *n* (pl. numina) Numina are the spirits that animists believe inhabit trees, stones, or other natural objects and phenomena. <J. Ferguson, 1874: "a cathedral town where all unite . . . in . . . adoring the sacred and historical numen of the place">. By extension, numina may be creative forces, the indwelling geniuses that push some people on in their artistic or other endeavors.

panatheism *n* Panatheism goes a step beyond atheism, reasoning that if God does not exist, nothing is really sacred or holy—not the Bible, any utterance, any place, anything at all.

pantheism *n,* **pantheist** *n* Some pantheists, such as poet William Wordsworth, believe that God exists in brooks, stones, flowers—everything in nature. Other pantheists believe that God is not *in* everything but rather that all things together *constitute* God. Still others say that their pantheism is an acceptance of all gods and creeds; they point out that the original Greek words mean "all gods."

physicism *n* The belief that there is a physical or materialistic explanation for all things, including creation, is physicism.

plutolatry *n,* **plutomania** *n* The worship of Mammon, excessive devotion to wealth, is plutolatry. When carried still further it may become plutomania, a mental condition in which one is almost solely concerned with acquiring, retaining, or dreaming about wealth, or has delusions about wealth.

psilanthropy *n* The belief that Jesus was only a man and not of divine birth.

Sabbatarian *n, adj* Three basic meanings: (1) one who regards Saturday as the Sabbath, (2) one who advocates very strict rules for Sunday observance, and (3) (adj) pertaining to the Sabbath and its observance. <My father's Sabbatarian practices chiefly involved sleeping and eating, but my mother's were more orthodox.>

sanctimonious *adj* The pretense of being more religious than one really is; artificial piousness. <He's a crook. Don't be fooled by his sanctimonious language.>

schism *n,* **schismatic** *adj* A schism is a division, most often of a church, into two or more opposing groups. It may lead to a physical separation, also called a schism. A person who encourages a schism may be described as *schismatic.*

sin money *n* At least according to dictionary definitions, sin money is not that which is spent on sinful pursuits. Rather, it is that which is paid for expiation of sins: <He paid the church $350 in sin money that year.> The concept of such payment is very old; the term is translated from Latin *pro peccatis,* which itself was a translation of Hebrew *keseph hakippūrim.*

speaking in tongues *n* Sometimes schizophrenics or others speak a long string of incomprehensible "sentences," gibberish (technically called *glossolalia*). Such speaking in tongues occurs in some religious situations: A person who appears to be in a trance may continue the speaking for several minutes, and members of the congregation may believe that heshe is divinely inspired.

syncretism *n* In religion, syncretism may be the gradual changes of belief and practice that result at least in part from interaction with other religions. It may also be any reconciliation or combination of beliefs between two religions or sects, and by its opponents may be considered an illogical, senseless compromise. Thus the word may have either positive or negative connotations, depending on who is using it.

testimony meeting *n* A church service or other meeting in which people talk about benefits attained or observed in their religious experiences.

thearchy *n* (1) the rule of God. <One who does not believe in a thearchy is likely to be an atheist.> (2) The hierarchy of gods. <In ancient Greek religious beliefs, Zeus and Hera were at the top of the thearchy.>

theism *n* The scores of English words in which *the-* or *theo* means "god" come from Greek *theos* "god." Theism, in its simplest definition, is merely belief in a god or gods. However, it may also mean belief in a single God, or it may be a whole philosophic system based on belief in God or a number of gods.

theocentric *adj* A theocentric view of life puts God at the center: <Some churches battle internally—perhaps unaware of the battle—between theocentric and homocentric emphasis.>

theogony *n* Theogony traces the family trees of the gods; thus it is genealogy on a cosmic scale: <According to theogony, Aphrodite was the daughter of Zeus.>

theolatry *n* Theolatry is worship of a god—sometimes excessive worship: <Their theolatry extended to praying to golden calves.>

theological virtue *n*, **theoretic virtue** *n* The theological virtues are faith, hope, and charity, which are believed to reside in service to God and to lead humanity to the ideal life. The theoretic virtues, in contrast, are not religion-centered; they are understanding, science (in the old sense of "knowledge"), and wisdom.

theologism *n*, and related words. Theologism may be either discussion and speculation about theology, or the act of extending theology to cover other disciplines: <The young seminarians spent hours each evening in theologism.> <His theologism by now encompassed not only biology but also history.> A **theologist** is the same as a theologian, "one who studies religious theory intensively." Heshe may **theologize,** "theorize about religion," during much of hiser time. A student planning to enter the ministry or other religious service is sometimes called a **theologue.**

theomachy *n*, **theomachist** *n* In several mythologies there are stories about theomachy "battles or serious arguments among gods." One who resists gods or the will of God is a theomachist.

theomania *n* A mental condition in which one believes that heshe is God or that God is speaking through himer.

theomorphism *n* The book of Genesis tells us that God created humanity after His own image. Theomorphism is the acceptance of this belief.

theonomy *n* God's rule; the condition of being subject to the rule of God.

theophagy *n* An example of theophagy, "god-eating," is a communion service in which communicants are told, "This is my body; eat ye all of it." More frequently, though, the term is restricted to certain rites of more or less primitive tribes who believe that by eating a symbol of a god that they worship (say, a wolf), they can attain the favorable characteristics (for example, strength, valor, cunning) of that god.

theophany *n* A brief appearance of a deity to an individual. <The Old Testament has accounts of several theophanies, as when God appeared in the shape of a burning bush.>

theosophy *n* An intuitive, rather mystic religious philosophy supposedly vouchsafed in its entirety to only a few especially perceptive persons.

total depravity *n* Adam and Eve sinned, and according to Calvinist doctrine their sin has been inherited by all their descendants, making them sinful, too. Only complete and devout adherence to His teachings can overcome that innate and total depravity.

Mastery Test

Fill in the missing letters.

1. A person who believes in several or many gods is described as p__________c.
2. Belief in two gods is d______m.
3. One who worships or deals with the devil is a d_______t.
4. A brief appearance of the deity is a t_______y.
5. The belief that man was created in God's image is t__________m.
6. A God-centered life can be described as t_________c.
7. Faith, hope, and charity are the t_________l virtues.
8. Worship of money is p________y.
9. Spirits inhabiting trees, stones, streams, etc., are n____a.
10. Excessive regard for a church as an institution is e___________y.
11. One who believes that God created everything from nothing is a c_________t.
12. Reliance on faith as the source of religious truth is f_____m.
13. Worship of a clan's symbol, such as an animal, is t______m.
14. A spirit inhabiting a tree may be a h_______d.
15. The belief that God inhabits everything in nature is p_______m.
16. Something paid for expiation of misdeeds may be s__ m___y.
17. The belief that Jesus was not divine is p__________y.
18. Genealogy of the gods is t______y.
19. A person planning to enter the ministry may be called a t_______e.
20. Fire-worship is also known as p_______y.
21. A s____m is a split—for example, in a church.

22. Saturday is my day of worship. I am a S__________n.
23. Some Native Americans believed in a Great Spirit called a m______u or m_____o.
24. People who advocate i______s work for peaceful relations among church groups.
25. A b__ m______h welcomes a Jewish girl to the adult Jewish religious community.

15
THE WAY WE TALK

Adam and Eve and the serpent all began talking just about as soon as they were created, and Adam and Eve have been at it ever since. (The serpent seems to have retrogressed.) Just as workers often discuss their tools, so people in general occasionally talk about the most useful of human tools, language. In this chapter we'll take a look at some of the mainly unscientific words they use for this purpose, and in the next chapter we'll see some of the terms that a professional linguist is more likely to apply. Some terms could be treated in either chapter.

A living language never stays put. Words and forms of words keep developing or dying out. Every significant societal change is reflected in linguistic change; the packaging industry, for example, largely a twentieth-century phenomenon, has already inscribed several thousand terms on the language. A new word or usage is a **neologism** (accent the second syllable): <Because of their daily discoveries, scientists more than anyone else are responsible for neologisms.> **Neology** may be a synonym of **neologism,** but also can refer to the use of new expressions and not just to the expressions themselves: <Always a conservative, he detests neology.> (Outside linguistics, a neology can be a new doctrine or theological interpretation: <Most church splinter groups result from neologies.>) One who makes up a new word is a **neologizer** or a **word-coiner.**

Some words tend not to be used outside a given region. These are **regionalisms,** words characteristic of the region: <*Tonic* is a regionalism for "soft drink."> A **linguistic geographer** can prepare maps to show characteristic expressions, pronunciations, etc., and can draw in lines, called **isoglosses,** to show the approximate boundary between one characteristic and another: <the isogloss in central Illinois between *greasy* with an /s/ and with a /z/>.

Superstitious people, and many who would tell you that they are not superstitious, believe in **word magic.** Among belief indicators are knocking on wood to ensure that something bad will not supersede something good that has just been spoken of, or saying things like "Don't talk about your good fortune or you'll lose it." The old custom of putting a verbal curse on someone is another example (still reflected in "Damn you" and "Darn you"), as is the survival of incantations in some children's games or in words like *hocus pocus.* Pennsylvania Germans, given a plant, often say "I won't thank you for it or it won't grow." In short, word magic is any supposed magic involving belief in the supernatural power of words.

Some people particularly enjoy playing or working with words. A **phrasemaker** coins effective phrases such as may be borrowed by many other people: <In his day Teddy Roosevelt was regarded as quite a phrasemaker.> Less kindly, *phrasemaker* suggests someone who coins high-sounding but essentially empty and rhetorical expressions. A **phrasemonger** borrows and uses extensively such expressions: <Many politicians are phrasemongers who delight in talking about "this great nation," "the will of the people," "the glories of democracy.">

In general *monger* carries unfavorable connotations. A professional writer doesn't like being called a **wordmonger,** because of the implication that heshe uses words more for show than to convey meaning and emotion. Heshe wouldn't like to be known as a **wordcatcher,** either, a disparaging term for "lexicographer" or for someone who quibbles unnecessarily about words and other people's supposed misuse of them: <Some teachers of composition are mainly wordcatchers.> **Verbomania** is an obsession with words or an excessive use of them, and of course a **verbomaniac** is a person afflicted with such a mania. (We need another word for a person who loves words, loves them gently, lifts them up and caresses them, studies them. I suggest *verbophile,* with *verbophilia* as the name of hiser harmless preoccupation.)

Verbicide is literally "word-killer." That which kills may be a pun or any other intentional distortion of the meaning of a word: <Even in tragedy he could not resist verbicide. When his fat wife looked at the scale and then shot herself, he said, "That was the weigh to go."> <The White House use of *inoperative* to mean "false" was more than verbicide; it was a confession of misconduct, of deceiving the American people.> *Verbicide* may also mean a person who commits such slaughter: <Verbicides are less likely to be punsters than they are to be businesspeople and politicians who use the language to mislead rather than to inform.>

Smaller misuses of words have resulted in numerous additions to the vocabulary. There's a dialectal **glibbery,** "smooth, slippery, not trustworthy." Because of its resemblance to *glib,* it merits greater use, to apply to a speaker who is glib and of dubious honesty: <a glibbery used-car salesman>. Another dialectal word is **grex.** "Don't grex so much," a Pennsylvania German father may tell his grumbling child. The word comes from German *grechsen* "to grumble, complain, or groan," which is derived from an older *krachitzen* "to cry hoarsely." **Bloviate** is a humorous blend of *blow* and *orate* and means "to orate in a windy, verbose manner." A person who bloviates generally resorts to **windbaggery** "empty, boastful talk": <the windbaggery of the traveling patent-medicine salesman>.

The discourse of many young people today seems more filled with **embolalia,** or **hesitation forms,** than was true in the past: "Like, well, uh, you know, man, what's his name is waitin'." That sentence opens with several hesitation forms, which are sounds we make when we aren't quite sure of what we want to say or how we want to say it; collectively the use of such forms is embolalia. Almost all of us stammer around a bit and toss in fillers while we arrange our thoughts or find the words to express them. But it is unfortunate, you know, when like hesitation forms, you know, fill like a sizable part of each sentence, particularly when, like, they're repeated like forever, you know.

A **howler** is a ridiculous or hilarious blunder in speech or writing. Often the howler is a dangling modifier (generally involving a participle that doesn't clearly modify what it's supposed to), such as "Peering down into the river, her head swam." A **spoonerism** is another sort of howler. The British Rev. William Spooner (1844–1930) would be less well remembered if his tongue hadn't slipped as often as it reportedly did. Specifically, he had a gift for transposing initial sounds of words, with comic results: "Will you please *s*ew the lady to a *sh*eet," "It is *kiss*tomary to *cuss* the bride," "It is pleasant to ride a well-*b*oiled icicle." A spoonerism is any such transposition in which two legitimate words remain. Thus "fank and rile" (for *rank and file*) is not technically a spoonerism, but "head rat" (for *red hat*) is. To **spoonerize** is to make spoonerisms: <spoonerized names of poets, like "Sheats and Kelley">.

A priest whose Latin was deficient used to say "mumpsimus" instead of "sumpsimus" in the Mass. When criticized, he said that he wouldn't change to any of these newfangled ideas like "sumpsimus." In his dishonor **mumpsimus** has come to mean anyone who stubbornly persists in error; also, the error in which heshe persists: <this narrow-minded bigot, this recalcitrant ass, this mumpsimus> <the mumpsimus that the earth is flat and has four corners> <the mumpsimus that "between you and I" is "correct">. (The word **sumpsimus** is sometimes used to indicate employment of a correct form.)

To **engaud** is to make unrealistically resplendent. The verb is used especially to mean the application of high-flown names to ordinary things or people. Examples of such engauding are calling a slum a "depressed area," poor people "economically underprivileged," and someone who greases your car a "lubritician." Engauding is often one of the characteristics of **officialese,** also called **governmentese,** which is the jargon or gobbledegook frequently used in official statements and publications. It is easy to recognize because of its pompousness, wordiness, polysyllabism, obscurity, abstract and general nouns, and passive verbs.

A **bigmouth** is a loud, braggartly speaker. A **flannelmouth** is either (1) a person whose speech is slow or halting, or (2) one whose speech is glib but untrustworthy. **Mealymouthed** speech is usually insincere and hypocritical but also may be overdelicate, nice-nellyish. **Mushmouth** is slang for a person who sounds as if heshe is talking with a mouth full of mush.

More Words About Words

antonymous *adj* *Antonymous* is antonymous to *synonymous.* Two words that have approximately the same meaning are synonymous, but two words that have nearly opposite meanings are antonymous. <*Hot* and *cold* are antonymous.>

aposiopesis *n* (pl.*-peses*). Sometimes you start a sentence but break off and say or write something else: "Helen and David—but you aren't interested in Helen and David, are you?" The name for this failure to complete a thought is *aposiopesis,* from Greek *siōpē* "silence." <Writers of realistic conversation frequently illustrate aposiopesis.>

billingsgate *n* Men and women fish peddlers at the market at Billingsgate in London were long noted for their colorful, abusive, profane language—so vitriolically scornful that only a very accomplished swearer could equal it. In their memory any vigorously uttered condemnatory profanity may be called by the name of their habitat—*billingsgate.*

breviloquent *adj,* **breviloquence** *n* Breviloquent speakers speak briefly but (usually) well. Breviloquence is brief but effective speech.

carriwitchet *n* A word of unknown origin, for a pun, quibble, or riddling question. A slang dictionary of 1874 defined it as "a hoaxing, puzzling question: 'How far is it from the first of July to London Bridge?' "

confabulate *vi*, **confabulation** *n* Generally used with humorous or disparaging intent, to confabulate is to prattle, to hold an informal conference, to hold a powwow. The noun form, *confabulation*, is also used humorously or disparagingly.

debabelization *n* Removal of obstacles to communication, especially the lack of a common language. <It was once argued that the widespread use of English would result in the debabelization of India.>

demegoric *adj* Greek *dēmēgorikos* means popular orator, and the English adaptation *demegoric* means pertaining to public speaking: <Bryan's demegoric talent was immediately obvious.> *Demegoric* thus differs from *histrionic*, which means pertaining to acting or the theater, staged.

demotic *adj* Literally "popular, pertaining to the people," *demotic* refers particularly to language: <demotic rather than aristocratic speech>. Still more specifically, it may refer to a simplified form of writing such as existed among those ancient Egyptians who employed characters less complex than the hieroglyphs of scholars. In modern Greek, a simplified form of the language, characterized especially by few inflections, is called demotic.

diplolingo *n* Informal or slang for "language used by diplomats." Its words are carefully chosen, usually to avoid offense. It tends to be calm, unemotional, understated, and often intentionally ambiguous.

double entendre *n* A word, phrase, or sentence with two (usually intentional) meanings, one of which is risqué. A famous example is Mae West's "Come up and see me sometime," a generally innocent invitation that lost its innocence because of West's tone and facial or bodily expression.

doublespeak *n*, **newspeak** *n* George Orwell's *1984* introduced *newspeak*, a form of political language in which meanings were twisted to their opposites. Three of Big Brother's slogans (inscribed on the building of the "Ministry of Truth") were WAR IS PEACE, FREEDOM IS SLAV-

ERY, and IGNORANCE IS STRENGTH. The phrase "our new happy life" was used repetitively to describe what was actually an almost completely restricted life. Doublespeak is an Americanized version in which ambiguous or evasive language is common: "California roast" for "chuck roast," "downsizing" for "wholesale firing," "mobile maneuvering" for "retreat," and "accidental delivery of ordnance equipment" for "We bombed our own troops."

dysphemism *n* A euphemism is a mild word chosen so as not to shock or offend someone; its motive is kindness. A dysphemism, however, is a strong word chosen because it is intended to be disagreeable, unpleasant, disparaging —for example, *old lady* for "wife," *embezzled* for "borrowed."

educationese *n*, **pedagese** *n* Language used by some (usually stuffy) educators, especially in their writing, characterized by unnecessarily abstract nouns, polysyllabic words when short ones would serve as well, passive-voice verbs, occasional convoluted sentences, and overuse of whatever educational jargon is popular at the time.

equivoke *n* Any form of verbal double meaning is an equivoke (sometimes spelled *equivoque*). A pun is a simple example, as when Shakespeare plays with *awl* and *all*, or as when William Riley Parker called a school for recalcitrant children "P.S. de résistance." An equivoke may also be a double entendre, as in the apparently innocent question "How did you make out last night?" which to some people can be a question about sexual success. Or it may be the use of a word without distinguishing among its meanings; *socialism*, for example, is an equivoke unless one designates the brand of socialism one is talking about.

farrago *n* Not to be confused with **virago**, "a loud, domineering, masculine woman." *Farrago* comes from a Latin word for mixed food for livestock, but in English refers particularly to an unorderly mixture of ideas or words, often incorporating both fact and fantasy: <The testi-

mony in regard to Irangate was a wild farrago of truths, half-truths, untruths, exaggerations, and denials.>

instantiate *vi, vt* To give an instance, a concrete example: <Don't just generalize. Instantiate.> <Failure to instantiate broad statements is the greatest weakness in most amateur writing.>

litotes *n* (three syllables) Litotes is a particular kind of understatement—one in which an affirmative idea is expressed negatively: <Sandy Koufax wasn't a bad pitcher [meaning that he was excellent].>

magniloquent *adj* Literally, "big speech." Magniloquent talk is high-flown, noisy, bombastic, boastful. (See also *bigmouth.*)

mellifluous *adj* A term to describe a lovely, flowing manner of speaking. The word is based on Latin words for "honey" and "flow."

mussitation *n* From a Latin word meaning muttering, mussitation is the act of moving the lips as if in speech but making no sound. In the early days of talking pictures, some actors and actresses with unpleasant voices resorted to mussitation and someone else dubbed in the sounds. Some stage performers move their lips while an offstage recorded or live voice sings—another form of mussitation. Also called **lip-synch.**

natter, *n, vi,* **yatter** *n, vi* Empty chatter; to talk endlessly and uninformatively.

nefandous *adj* From a Latin negative and a verb meaning to speak, *nefandous* means not to be spoken of, and is used to describe anything so sacrilegious or horrible that it is considered unmentionable: <nefandous crimes committed by soldiers against the deserted children>.

nonce word *n* A nonce word is one coined for a particular occasion and perhaps never used again. Thus in "It's too straight for a rain*bow;* maybe it's a rain *arrow,*" *rain arrow* is a nonce word. (*Nonce* results from faulty division of *then anes,* an old form of *then once,* misdivided as "the nanes" or "the nonce.")

overpronounce *vt* To pronounce each word in an exaggeratedly careful way.

palaver *n, vi* *Palabra* is Spanish for "word" or "talk," and Portuguese *palavra* has the same meaning. An English *palaver* may be a conference, a long discussion, or mere empty chatter. As a verb, *palaver* may mean "to confer" but more often "to talk much while saying little." <The eight senators and the twelve representatives palavered for three hours but settled nothing.>

persiflage *n* Light, jocular, often flippant banter: <Some of her acquaintances mistook her persiflage for serious statements, but her friends smiled or laughed.>

phatic communication *n* "Good morning, Mrs. Jackson. Lovely day, isn't it?" Any such seemingly insignificant remarks, intended only to greet, suggest friendliness, and build goodwill, constitute phatic communication.

pilpul *n* Hairsplitting analysis or argument, such as that attributed to Jewish scholars discussing fine points of the Talmud.

pleonastic *adj* Redundant, repetitious, using more words than necessary, repetitive (like this definition). Other examples: "my mother she," "repeat that again."

preambulate *vi* To make a preamble: <He preambulated for twenty minutes before getting to the point.>

querulous *adj* Sometimes confused with *quarrelsome*. A querulous person, remark, or tone uses or typifies a complaint. <The child's querulous tone was almost a whine.>

roboanchor *n* A slang term for a TV anchorperson or news reader who apparently does not understand what heshe is reading. The delivery may include hesitations and mispronunciations, pauses at the wrong places, omissions, and occasional running together of sentences.

salacious *adj* Derived from Latin for "lustful" and an earlier Latin verb for "to spurt," *salacious* means "lustful, obscene" and may be applied to persons, remarks, writings, or pictures that the current prevailing moral climate may consider indecent or pornographic. Opinions of what is salacious may vary from group to group and from one time to another. <Some moderns consider Chaucer's fourteenth-century tales salacious, but others call them great literature.>

sententious *adj* In Latin a sententia is a maxim, a statement of belief. *Sententious* means like a maxim: brief, epigrammatic, aphoristic, perhaps too moralizing. Occasionally it may mean only brief, terse: <His advice was sententious: "Work.">

sesquipedalian *adj* Latin *sesquipedalis* means a foot and a half long, and figuratively that is the length of a sesquipedalian word, which is one consisting of several syllables. A writer or a speaker has a sesquipedalian style if heshe uses many long words.

stultiloquence *n* From Latin *stultus*, "foolish," and *loquens*, "speaking," *stultiloquence* refers to just what its derivation suggests: foolish talk, babble.

tautological *adj* In "this modern world of today" the use of *modern* and *today* is tautological: the words say the same thing twice in different ways. "Widow woman" is tautological because every widow is a woman. The noun form is **tautology.**

trope *n*, **tropology** *n* A trope most commonly is a figure of speech (simile, metaphor, irony, etc.) in which two unlike things are compared—for example, the simile in Sir John Suckling's "Her feet beneath her petticoat/ Like little mice, stole in and out." Tropology is the use of figurative language: <superb, evocative tropology>.

tub-thumping *adj*, *n* Ranting, impassioned speeches or writing, usually characterized more by emotion than by reason: <His tub-thumping lasted for over an hour.> As an adjective, *tub-thumping* means excessively emotional and partisan: <tub-thumping politicians>.

weasel word *n* When a weasel eats an egg, it sucks out the contents and leaves the shell—apparently whole, but actually empty. A person who uses weasel words leaves a good impression, too, but hiser words are really empty, equivocal, often seeming to promise much but firmly guaranteeing nothing. Weasel words are ambiguous and lacking in forthrightness.

word-hoard *n* Dating back to Old English, *word-hoard* is a colorful way to say "vocabulary." It suggests careful storing away for future use.

word-music *n* The musical quality of spoken language:

<Even her recitation of the Gettysburg address was word-music to his ears.>

wordplay *n* Puns or other witty plays on words.

word-sign *n* A character, such as a hieroglyph or a shorthand symbol, used as the equivalent of a word.

wordsmith *n* A careful builder with words, a word expert, or a professional writer.

Mastery Test

Match each word with the best clue or descriptor in its group. (The clues are not necessarily definitions.)

	Word		Clue
___	1. isogloss	a.	one obsessed with words
___	2. phrasemonger	b.	Well, like, you know.
___	3. verbomaniac	c.	We were interrupted.
___	4. grex	d.	Heshe freely borrows other people's colorful expressions.
___	5. embolalia	e.	You may never hear it again.
___	6. mumpsimus	f.	pertaining to public speaking
___	7. aposiopesis	g.	erroneous belief stubbornly held
___	8. demegoric	h.	soundless movement of the lips
___	9. mussitation	i.	You might find one on a map.
___	10. nonce word	j.	what some little Pennsylvania German boys may do
___	11. sesquipedalian	k.	polysyllabic
___	12. nefandous	l.	Heshe quibbles a lot.
___	13. stultiloquence	m.	The rejection dealt me a blushing crow.
___	14. neologizer	n.	foolish talk, babble

___	15. word-catcher	o.	lubritorium
___	16. glibbery	p.	It might be deleted from a transcript.
___	17. spoonerism	q.	too horrible to describe
___	18. engaud	r.	harsh word intended to disparage
___	19. billingsgate	s.	Heshe is an inventor, of a sort.
___	20. dysphemism	t.	slick-talking
___	21. pedagese	u.	"Ignorance is strength."
___	22. newspeak	v.	a spring day in May
___	23. double entendre	w.	complaining
___	24. querulous	x.	a sexual ambiguity
___	25. tautology	y.	educational jargon

16
LINGUISTS TALK ABOUT LANGUAGE

The study of language has been a growth industry during much of the twentieth century, especially the second half. Most colleges now offer courses in linguistics, and most large universities have linguistics departments, which in turn may be subdivided into divisions of Asian languages, African languages, sociolinguistics, psycholinguistics, and so on.

Like all specialists, linguists develop their own esoteric jargon. In this chapter we'll glance at some of their terms that may warrant wider circulation.

As a product of people and as something used every day, language is an intimate part of the people who produce it and receive it, and it enters constantly into their interrelationships. **Psycholinguistics** is the study of language and the individual; for example, how a child learns to speak, the effects of bilingualism, speech pathology, the relationships between thought and language, how the mind decodes spoken messages. **Sociolinguistics,** an even newer field, is concerned with language as an instrument in personal interaction; for example, study of the reactions shown by listeners or groups of listeners to words, statements, or speeches, or study of language used by females contrasted with that of males. **Metalinguistics** is a more inclusive term embracing both social and psychological phenomena with regard to language. Among the types of metalinguistics, according to H.A. Gleason, are "the social implications of phonological and grammatical differences . . . and the general problem of relationship between language and the rest of culture."

Differences in the ways people use language are of much interest to the linguist, whose intent is always to describe and classify, not criticize. The **dialectologist,** whose specialty is of course **dialectology,** tells us that everyone speaks some sort of dialect, so obviously a dialect is nothing to ridicule or be ashamed of. Heshe examines **geographical dialect** (that of a given area) and **social dialect** (that of a somewhat isolable social group). The dialect geographer sometimes finds a **relic area,** a locality or region that has retained certain speech forms that have been lost or considerably altered in most places: <Some secluded American communities are relic areas in which vocabulary and usages of three or four centuries ago may be heard.> A **focal area** is one whose characteristic speech tends to be imitated elsewhere: <The great focal area of English long was, of course, London.> A **graded area** or **transition area** is affected by the speech of two or more focal areas: <the graded area between New York and Boston>.

A **speech community** is a group of people who are largely alike in the language they use: <the speech community of the Mexican-Americans of the Southwest> <Every school is a speech community somewhat different from other schools.> A **localism** in speech or other behavior is a local peculiarity, such as *candy tree* for "sugar maple." (Outside linguistics, though, *localism* refers to concern or affection for the area where one lives, feelings sometimes so strong that one pays little attention to national or international matters. A **localist** is one who holds such concern or affection: <He's such a localist that he speaks of people from the next county as "outlanders.">)

If you and I both speak English (or another tongue) as our

native language, we are **colingual** persons, or **colinguals.** But we are not if for one of us the language in question is a second acquisition, not native. And, of course, if we speak more than one language, native or not, we are **bilinguals** or **multilinguals** or **polyglots.** A language that we have learned chiefly to enjoy the culture represented by that tongue (rather than for commercial or linguistic reasons) is for us a **culture language.**

When a linguist looks at a language, heshe may study it as it is (or was) at a given time—a **synchronic** study. Or heshe may study if from the point of view of its changes over a considerably longer period—a **diachronic** study. <His dissertation, a synchronic study, dealt with variant pronunciations of American English in the 1980s.> <A diachronic analysis of grammatical changes from Chaucer to Shakespeare occupies most of her time.> The corresponding nouns are **synchrony** and **diachrony.**

Since about 1950 an awareness has grown that much of our communication is nonverbal, and popular books (for example, Julius Fast's *Body Language*) have fed that awareness. The study of gesture is **pasimology.** Touching, for which the scientific name is **haptics,** has attracted much interest, some of it no doubt prurient. Strokes, slaps, pats, tickles, and other kinds of touch communicate emotions and suggest or reveal the quality of relationships between or among two or more people. A **haptic** person has a predilection for the sense of touch (rather than hearing, seeing, etc.); the old joke says that heshe learns anatomy by the Braille system. <The fatal flaw of the haptic Lenny, in *Of Mice and Men*, was his desire to stroke soft things.> **Proxemics** is the use or study of distance in communication; in some societies, for instance, as proxemics has shown, conversationalists are uncomfortable unless they are almost nose-to-nose, but Americans usually prefer a space of three feet or more. The terms **personal distance** and **personal space** are used in the same connection.

The suffix *-eme*, "a significantly different structural unit," is one that linguists find indispensable. It appears in these words:

glosseme the smallest unit in language that signals meaning; for example, the word *a*, the ending *-ed*, an intonation, the word order *he is* vs. *is he*, the choice of a plural verb, the prefix *un-*.

grapheme a letter of the alphabet: <We spell with graphemes.>

lexeme a word; a speech form that carries meaning as part of the vocabulary of a language.

morpheme a meaningful linguistic unit that cannot be further broken down into meaningful parts; for example, a prefix or a suffix, or a word (like *law*) that has no affix. The meaning of a morpheme is called its **sememe;** for example, *frogs* has the sememe *frog* and the sememe *-s* that means "this word is plural."

phoneme the smallest unit of spoken sound that meaningfully distinguishes one utterance from another; for example, the phonemes /p/ in *pan* and /b/ in *ban* distinguish the two words. Individuals do not pronounce /p/ or any other sound exactly alike; the same person may in fact use several variants. Differences so small as not to affect the meaning are ignored in identifying phonemes. The slightly varied forms are called **allophones.**

semanteme a word or a base that carries a definite meaning; thus both *chronology* and its constituent base words *chrono-* and *-log* are semantemes. *Semanteme* is obviously related to *semantics* and to *sememe.*

toneme In a language like Chinese that relies heavily on tones for meaning, a toneme is a particular tone, one that can distinguish one meaning from another. The term is sometimes used also of languages that make less use of tone. Thus when Lady Macbeth says "We fail," if the actress uses one set of tonemes, she seems to be saying matter-of-factly, "We'll fail and that's all there's to it," but different tonemes make her say, "We—fail! Why, failure is completely impossible!"

For many years linguists were much more interested in form than in meaning, but recently they have more clearly realized that one cannot really understand the intricacies of language unless the interrelationships of form and meaning are known. In consequence words like *sememe* and *semanteme* (above) are now in all linguists' repertoire. A **polysemant** is a word with more than one meaning: <*Run* is a polysemant.> **Polysemantic** and **polysemous** mean having more than one meaning: <*Re-* is a polysemantic (polysemous) prefix.> **Polysemy** is an abstract word signifying multiplicity of meaning: <Her words were filled not just with *double entendre* but with polysemy.> **Semiotics** is a theory of signs and symbols of any sort. It deals with syntactics, "sentence structure," semantics, "meaning," and pragmatics, "relationship between linguistic expressions and their users." <Semiotics delves much more deeply into language than did old-fashioned grammar, which was concerned with superficialities of structure.>

An **acrolect** is the language of the upper classes, the one closest to whatever is considered "standard." In contrast, a **basilect** is furthest from the standard. A **mesolect** is about halfway between an acrolect and a basilect. An **idiolect** is the speech patterns of an individual: <No two idiolects are exactly alike.>

More Words of Linguists

Anglo-Vernacular *adj* People who can use both English and their native tongue are sometimes said to be Anglo-Vernacular. During British rule, Anglo-Vernacular schools included those of Burma, Ceylon, and India.

assembly (or **assembler**) **language** *n* A computer language that uses symbolic equivalents of the machine language "understood" by a specific computer.

catachresis *n* From Greek *katachrēsis*, "misuse." Catachresis is the misuse of words or the use of a forced or unlikely figure of speech. Examples: the use of *affective* for *effective;* her eyes were *hard as diamonds.*

comparatist *n*, **comparative linguist** *n* The alternative names for a linguist whose specialty is the comparison of two or more languages, usually of the same family: <Her work as a comparatist dealt with the structural patterns of English and Russian, both of which are derived from Indo-European.> (*Comparatist* may also mean a scholar in comparative literature.)

context of situation *n* If you say "I hate Tom" (or anything else), the total meaning of your utterance goes far beyond those few words. It includes, for example, your previous relationships with Tom, his feelings toward you, recent incidents involving him, and the person to whom you are speaking. The total of all such considerations is the *context of the situation.*

counterword *n* We use a few words over and over again in a very general sense. Thus *nice* is a counterword showing general approval, *awful* a counterword of dislike, *line* ("What's his line?") a counterword covering many occupations, and *fix* a counterword vaguely having to do with repairing. <Almost all slang consists of words that become counterwords.>

dactylology *n* The art of communicating by manual signs, such as deaf people are often taught, is dactylology. A different sign for each letter of the alphabet is sometimes used, so dactylology may be a form of spelling. *Sign language* is a broader term that may include both dactylology and other manual gestures or other types of gestures. **Signing** is the use of sign language for communicating.

deep structure *n* Transformational-generative grammarians say that underlying the surface structure of an utterance—for example, "The letter was signed by Anthony Gray"—lie certain patterns or formulas of sound, syntactic structure, and semantic structure that enable countless similar sentences to be constructed. Those patterns or formulas represent the deep structure of the utterance. They are learned by children through hearing much speaking and can also be "taught" to a machine.

diglossia *n* In many languages, including modern English, two overlapping basic varieties of language exist.

In *The Appropriate Word* I classify the English varieties as FF (Family and Friends) and SWE (Standard Written English, also used in formal speech). In some languages, such as modern Greek Demotic and Katharevuan, the differences are considerably greater than in English. The existence of two such forms is called *diglossia.*

disambiguate *vt* To remove ambiguities: <Several sentences in Mr. Klemm's speech draft could have been misinterpreted, but his secretary disambiguated them.>

discourse analysis *n* A grammarian is interested in parts of words, in words, and in sentences. A specialist in discourse analysis is concerned with larger units, such as the relationships between and among sentences, and the structure of paragraphs or larger units.

distance language *n* A means of communicating at a distance longer than the speaking voice can carry, for example, by whistles, drums, or horns (but not telephone, radio, or telegraph): <A distance language in the form of twitters and tweets is used in Kuskoy, Turkey, to communicate from one mountain to another.>

dysarthria *n,* and related words. A number of words starting with *dys-* "abnormal" refer to problems with language:

dysarthria difficulty in articulating words because of a problem in the central nervous system
dyslalia difficulty in articulating because of a problem in the speech organs
dyslexia disruption of the ability to read
dyslogia problems in speaking caused by problems in reasoning ability
dysphasia defective use or understanding of language caused by brain damage
dysphrasia defective speech caused by impairment of the intellect

error analysis *n* Not all foreigners learning a language have the same problems, partly because of differences in their native languages. Some researchers and teachers conduct error analysis to determine which kinds of items in the target language need to be given most attention by each learner or homogeneous group.

etymon *n* *Etymology* comes from the same source and gives a clue to the meaning of *etymon,* "literal meaning of a word according to its origin." In English, *etymon* preserves this Greek meaning but also may refer to the earliest-known form of a word either in the same language or in an ancestral one, or to a "parent word" from which other words in the same language are derived: <The etymons of *recalcitrant* are Latin *re-* and *calcitrare,* literally "to kick back."> <*Value* is the etymon of *valuation, devalue, valuable,* and other words.>

folk etymology *n* Sometimes people hear a word and decide that the speaker really meant to say something else. For example, French *crevice* came into Middle English as *crevis;* this creature lived in water, so people thought that *-vis* was meant to be *fish;* as a result of this misunderstanding, we today say "crayfish" or "crawfish." Some folks say "spare grass" or "sparrow grass" for *asparagus,* and "cold slaw" for *cole slaw. Belfry* arose from misunderstanding *berfrey,* probably because the structure usually contained a bell; *saltcellar,* in Middle English *saltsaler,* has nothing to do with a cellar. Any such alteration of words to make them sound like something familiar is called *folk etymology.*

homograph *n,* **homophone** *n* Homographs are two or more words that are spelled alike but are different in meaning, pronunciation, or derivation. For example, *plant* "to sow" and *plant* "factory," or *bass* "fish" and *bass* "low singing voice," or the verb *mean* from Old English and the noun *mean* from Old French—all are homographs. Homophones are words pronounced the same but different in spelling, meaning, and derivation, as *night* and *knight.* The more familiar term *homonym* is often used when *homophone* would be more precise, and the latter word is preferable if the sameness of sound is to be emphasized. Sometimes homonyms are both spelled and pronounced alike but differ in meaning or derivation, as *prune* "to trim" and *prune* "dried plum." (In that example, *prune* and *prune* are also homographs.)

hypercorrection *n,* **hyperurbanism** *n* Some speakers use nonstandard expressions such as "for he and I" or nonstandard pronunciations such as "tyoo" (for *too*) because they have been misled into believing that these are "correct" or "the way educated city people talk." Their mistakes are sometimes called *hyperforms* and are caused by *hypercorrection* and may be *hyperurbanisms.*

ideogram *n* Any one of the elaborate symbols used in Chinese and much other Oriental writing is not a letter but an ideogram (also called *ideograph*). An ideogram represents an entire object or idea, not a sound. In European languages and many others, a series of letters, each standing for a sound, are assembled (spelled) in a prescribed order and make the equivalent of a single ideogram.

lallation *n,* **lambdacism** *n* One meaning of *lallation* is "a child's or childlike pronunciation." (The word comes from Latin *lallare,* "to sing a lullaby.") *Lallation* may also refer, as does *lambdacism,* to troubles in saying the sound of /l/: substituting another sound for /l/, substituting /l/ for another sound, or articulating /l/ defectively. Thus difficulties of some Asians in pronouncing /l/ and /r/ illustrate lallation or lambdacism.

linguistic stock *n* A long-defunct language called Indo-European was the parent of most European and some Asian and Middle Eastern languages. Indo-European and all its descendant languages make up one linguistic stock, a central core belonging to all. More narrowly, the term may refer to the languages of one branch of the tree, such as Latin and its "children": French, Spanish, Italian, Portuguese, Provençal, Catalan, Rhaeto-Romanic, Sardinian, and Ladino.

logogriph *n,* and related words. Greek *logos* means "word, reason, or speech," but most often "word." Its progeny are numerous. Here are a few that you may not know:

logogriph a word puzzle, such as an anagram

logomachy an argument about words; also, a game of making words, like Scrabble

logomania, logorrhea excessive talkativeness, "verbal diarrhea"
logopedics study and treatment of speech defects
logophile a word-lover

manualist *n* A manualist may be anyone who works with hiser hands, but most often it is one who uses, teaches, or advocates the manual alphabet in teaching and otherwise communicating with the deaf.

merism *n* In rhetoric a merism is a pair of conflicting terms, such as *here and there, near and far, hot and cold, through thick and thin.*

minor sentence *n* Some of our expressions are equivalent to sentences in meaning, intonation, and punctuation but do not follow the grammatical structures of sentences—for example, "Yes." "On the contrary." "Wow!" These are known as minor sentences.

Mischsprache *n* (pl. *Mischsprachen*) This German word has been borrowed to indicate a language said to have come from the mixing of two or more languages: <She considered Middle English a Mischsprache because of the considerable amount of Norman French that became mixed with English.>

morphology *n* The study of how words are formed. It includes (1) derivation—for example, *television* is derived from a Greek word for "far" and a Latin verb for "see"; (2) inflection—for example, the final *-s* in most plurals, or the final *-ed* in the past tense of most verbs; and (3) compounding—for example, *barnyard.*

paralanguage *n* When we speak, we use different tones and talk more or less loudly and emphatically and more or less rapidly. Those are all characteristic of what is called our *paralanguage* (*para* from a Greek word for "beside"). Gestures and facial expressions are also sometimes named as ingredients.

pejoration *n* A process of changing for the worse. *Pejoration* and its opposite, *elevation* or *amelioration,* are often used to name what may happen to the connotation of a word. Thus *knave* once meant boy, but then declined to rascally boy and then to rascal—an example of pejoration. *Marshal,* in contrast, rose from meaning one who holds horses to meaning a high official—an example of elevation.

phoniatric *adj* A doctor or other person specializing in speech defects is doing phoniatric work.

phonology *n* Phonology is the science of speech sounds, involving description of the sounds used in a given language or languages, and perhaps involving also a history of sound changes: <Many histories of languages devote more attention to phonology than to morphology, syntax, and semantics.>

pooh-pooh theory *n,* and related words. Various theories of the origin of language have been ridiculed, unfairly perhaps, by attaching pejorative labels to them. The pooh-pooh theory holds that the earliest language consisted of interjections, the **bowwow theory** that it consisted of imitations of sounds in nature, and the **dingdong theory** that there is a natural relationship between observable things and the vocal sounds that early man used to represent them. Since no tape recorders were available in prehistoric times, we may never find out how language really originated, but there seems little justification for ridiculing any theories seriously put forth and possessing even minimal theoretic supportability.

rhotic *n* In your dialect do you say *farm* and *lover* or *fahm* and *lovuh?* If you customarily pronounce *r* before a consonant *(farm)* and at the end of a syllable *(lover),* your dialect is called *rhotic.* If you do not (*fahm* and *lovuh*), it is not. (Some speakers are inconsistent.)

semasiology *n* The word is sometimes used as a synonym of *semantics* but more often refers to the study of semantic change—how words change in meaning.

sonograph *n* A machine for translating sounds into phonetic symbols.

spelling pronunciation *n* People who pronounce the *b* in *subtle* or use ĕ as the main vowel of *pretty* are influenced by the spellings to disregard the customary pronunciations. These mispronunciations are examples of spelling pronunciations, which give letters of a given word their usual sounds even though most speakers of the language say something else.

stylogram *n* Computers can be programmed to analyze a printed passage to show the percentage of words that are used as nouns, verbs, or other parts of speech, or that refer to selected topics such as economics or agriculture. The results may be shown in a profile called a *stylogram.*

syllabary *n* An alphabet uses a symbol (a letter, a grapheme) to represent one or more sounds. A syllabary, in contrast, uses a symbol to represent a syllable; for example, *represent* would be written with three symbols: <The syllabary developed by Sequoyah for his Cherokee people made use of eighty-six characters and was employed in teaching and in the publication of newspapers and books.>

synesis *n* In grammar, synesis is a construction in which the sense of a passage rather than grammatical rule determines the form an individual chooses. Thus after "Macbeth, as well as other generals, . . ." the rules stipulate a singular verb since the subject is *Macbeth.* But many persons, feeling that the sentence is really about Macbeth and other generals, too, bow to synesis and use a plural verb.

syntacticon *n* One's personal lexicon consists of the words that heshe knows well enough to use or at least recognize. One's personal syntacticon consists of the syntactical constructions heshe knows well enough to use or at least recognize: <The nominative absolute is seldom in the syntacticon of young children.> The syntacticon may also refer to the entire body of syntactical constructions available to the users of a given language: <the syntacticon of English>.

time depth *n* The length of time during which a language, or sometimes a culture, has been developing: <Indo-European languages have a time depth of several thousand years.>

transliterate *vt* Not the same as *translate.* In transliteration you simply change characters (letters or other symbols) of one language into those used in another. <For Chinese or Russians to get their names into Amer-

ican telephone books, the names must be transliterated from Chinese ideographs or the Cyrillic alphabet into the Roman alphabet that we use.>

triglot *n* The polyglot knows several or many languages, the triglot only three.

two-word verb *n* "In the last race, Ella *got ahead* at first, but Sue *caught up with* her and *nosed out* her opponent at the tape." The italicized words are among the two thousand or three thousand two-word verbs widely used in English. A synonym is *merged verb.* The basic verb in each is supplemented by a preposition or adverb that changes the basic verb's meaning. Occasionally the "two-word verb" actually has three words: *put up with.*

usageaster *n* A person who claims to be—perhaps is—an authority on language usage.

word family *n* A group of words within the same language and of the same derivation: <*Slay, slayer, slaughter,* and *slaughterous* are members of a word family.>

Mastery Test

For each definition, find the word being defined.

___ 1. disruption of the ability to read
- a. dysarthria
- b. dyslogia
- c. dyslexia
- d. dysphrasia

___ 2. literal meaning of a word according to its origin
- a. etymon
- b. synesis
- c. catachresis
- d. sememe

___ 3. a letter of the alphabet
- a. semanteme
- b. toneme
- c. morpheme
- d. grapheme

___ 4. study of language and the individual
a. dialectology
b. psycholinguistics
c. sociolinguistics
d. dactylology

___ 5. communication by touching
a. proxemics
b. pasimology
c. semiotics
d. haptics

___ 6. word used with vague meaning
a. counterword
b. lallation
c. syntacticon
d. localism

___ 7. people who speak the same native language
a. speech community
b. synchrony
c. colinguals
d. Mischsprachen

___ 8. word with more than one meaning
a. polysemy
b. polysemant
c. polysemous
d. semanteme

___ 9. art of communicating by manual signs
a. distance language
b. culture language
c. folk etymology
d. dactylology

___ 10. words pronounced alike but different in spelling, meaning, and derivation
a. homophones
b. homographs
c. logomachies
d. logogriphs

___ 11. science of speech sounds
a. phonology
b. assembly language
c. basilect
d. ideograms

___ 12. change from one alphabet or set of ideograms to another
a. translate
b. logophile
c. transliterate
d. disambiguate

17
JOURNALISM AND LITERATURE

Anyone who wants definitions and examples of a large number of literary terms should consult such a book as the well-known *Handbook to Literature* by Thrall and Hibbard or the more recent *Modern English: A Glossary of Literature and Language* by Lazarus, MacLeish, and Smith. The few words I'll discuss here are for the most part not treated in those books and include also a handful of journalistic terms.

The urge to write is an old one, still sometimes referred to by its Latin name, **cacoëthes scribendi,** "mania for writing." English used to have the useful adjective **scripturient,** now obsolete, that meant having a strong desire or compulsion to write or to be an author (the two are not necessarily the same): <R. Ward, 1710: "He labour'd under the Scripturient Disease.">

Victims of this disease almost always start out with abundant hope and towering expectations—if not to write the Great American Novel, at least to get rich with a best-seller. What some of them, especially the idealistic reformers, have in mind is the writing of a **thesis novel,** which dramatizes a point of view: <*The Grapes of Wrath*, a thesis novel, is devoted in large part to portraying the evils of big business and the inherent virtues of poor people.> Other writers are content to experiment with the short story, including the **short-short,** which usually occupies only a page in a magazine and generally has a surprise ending. The **storiette** is similar but often lacks the surprise ending and the dense, taut narration that characterizes the short-short. The storiette is frequently just a pleasant, sometimes moralistic little story such as may be published in a Sunday school weekly.

Quite often the would-be serious novelist finds that no one will publish what heshe has written, so heshe lowers hiser sights and tries **fictioneering,** producing low-quality fiction that may be salable because of its sensationalism or its adherence to a currently popular formula. <Pearl Buck produced several fine books, but also did much fictioneering under several pseudonyms.>

Some writers still try their pens at poetry, even though at any given time in the United States no more than a handful of writers can make their livings at it. **Concrete poetry** attracts some attention; it is poetry in various physical shapes—owls, typewriters, or what have you—that are related to the themes of the unorthodox verse. Concrete poetry should not be confused with **physical poetry.** In early-twentieth-century America a school of poets called Imagists attempted to gain their effects primarily through the use of picture-generating words. They were exponents of physical poetry. Part of an Imagist Manifesto said that their major purpose should be "to present an image. We are not a school of painting, but we believe that poetry should render particulars exactly, and not deal in vague generalities, however magnificent and sonorous."

Miscellaneous types of writing attract many of the scripturient. **Reportage,** for example, which may be day-to-day newspaper reporting, may also be more thoughtful and analytical than quick deadlines permit; some weekly or monthly articles in the *New Yorker* or the *Atlantic* represent the type. **Ecography,** as the name suggests, is ecological description or any writing about ecology: <Rachel Carson was an early popularizer of ecography.> Writing may even be as specialized as that of **enigmatography,** the composing or stating of enigmas, which are riddles but also may be apparently inexplicable happenings or circumstances. So the person who writes a book of riddles for children is an enigmatographer, but so is the philosopher who poses any of the serious puzzles of human life.

Other Literary and Journalistic Words

biblioclast *n.* and related words. Most people know *bibliography* and *bibliophile* and a few other words from the Greek *biblion,* "book," but some relatively unknown words from the same source may be only a little less valuable:

biblioclast a destroyer or mutilator of books
bibliofilm microfilm used particularly for photographing pages of books
biblioklept one who steals books
bibliolatry excessive liking for books; **bibliolater, bibliolatrous**
bibliopegy the art or craft of binding books
bibliophage a bookworm or anything else that eats books

Your unabridged dictionary may introduce you to several other useful words starting with *biblio-*. Note that in all *biblio-* words the emphasis is on the physical book itself, not the contents.

black comedy *n* Comedy that is devoted largely to unpleasant or absurd subjects such as suicide, drug addiction, or talking amoebas is called *black comedy* or *black humor.*

breakover *n* When a newspaper or magazine story must be continued on a later page, the continued part is a breakover.

chosism *n* A French word based on *chose* "thing," *chosisme* (anglicized by dropping the *e*) is a writing practice like that of French author Alain Robbe-Grillet, who sometimes devotes long passages to minute descriptions of a single thing or scene, as detailed as a clear photograph, and deemphasizes characterization and plot.

collective biography or **prosopography** *n* A book or other compilation consisting of biographies of a number of people is a collective biography, also called a prosopography: <*Who's Who in America* is a prosopography.>

concinnity *n,* and related words. Latin *cinnus* means a kind of mixed drink. The Romans must have been skilled mixologists, for from this word have come several English words referring to skill or stylishness in putting things together—though usually not liquid refreshments. *Concinnity* means studied elegance of design: <the concinnity of the well-made play>. To **concinnate** (accent the first syllable) is to place parts together harmoniously. The adjectives **concinnate** (accent the second syllable) and **concinnous** both mean characterized by concinnity; elegant; well designed: <the concinnate personal essays of E. B. White>.

criticaster *n* The *-aster* in this word is from a Latin suffix meaning somewhat similar to, and often used to signify inferiority, pettiness, imitativeness, or worthlessness; it appears also in *poetaster.* A criticaster is an inferior critic, especially one who picks on insignificant details. Although the word is most often used with reference to literature and other arts, it can also be applied in other contexts: <the criticasters of this administration>.

croquis *n* (pl. *croquis*) In French *croquer* means to know a person slightly; to sketch. In English a croquis is a sketch in words or drawing, such as a brief character sketch or a drawing preparatory to something more elaborate.

cutline *n* The caption accompanying a printed photograph.

deconstruction *n* A movement chiefly in vogue in literary criticism but influential, too, in art and architecture. Essentially negative, a deconstructionist argues that words cannot depict reality and that therefore readers must make their own interpretations, which may vary greatly.

desktop publishing *n* The advent of computers has made it possible to prepare and print newsletters, pamphlets, specialized trade journals, and the like at home or in a small office without recourse to outside printers or publishers. Such desktop publishing is feasible for short pieces or works intended for limited circulation, not ordinarily for large books or print runs of thousands of copies.

deus ex machina *n* In Greek drama a problem was sometimes resolved by using a machine offstage to carry down from above a "god" (Latin *deus*) who would use hiser powers to set things right. A similar device is often used in modern novels and in movies—as when the U.S. cavalry, not previously involved in the action, arrives in the nick of time to rescue the hero.

dialogic *adj,* **dialogism** *n* *Dialogic* means pertaining to dialog or consisting of dialog: <the dialogic form of Plato's works>. *Dialogism*, an archaic word, refers to an author's use of dialog to present hiser ideas: <His dialogism degenerates into questions from a straight man and answers from himself as an "expert.">

docudrama *n* In television a docudrama is a fictionalized play based (often very loosely) on actual occurrences such as a Civil War battle or the invention of the atomic bomb.

donnée *n* Not to be confused with **donee,** "one who is given something, such as a blood transfusion." A donnée is a basic fact or assumption, in literature or in life, that shapes later developments: <The author's donnée is that mothers and daughters are inevitably in conflict.>

dramaturgy *n* *Playwriting* refers to the actual composing of plays, but *dramaturgy* is more theoretical—the study of the principles, the art, the technique of writing plays: <Professor Clayton's course in modern drama stresses the dramaturgy rather than the human relationships that the authors delineate.>

DWEMs *n* The acronym, heard on college campuses, refers to the authors of much of the literature studied. It stands for "Dead White European Males."

electronic journalism *n* Reporting of news by television.

epigone *n,* and related words. Seven Greek leaders lost a battle at Thebes. Their seven sons, a few years later, imitatively marched on Thebes, which they captured and burned. They were called the Epigoni, or "Descendants," from the Greek *epigonos*, "born after." In modern times an epigone is any imitator born in a later generation: <T. S. Eliot and his thousands of epigones>. Intellectual, artistic, or literary imitation (especially of dead people) is **epigonism.** The adjectival form of *epigone* is **epigonic:** <the epigonic followers of Milton>.

eye dialect *n* To suggest dialect some writers misspell common words that are not really pronounced differently by the speakers than by others. *Sez* and *duz* are examples: the misspellings hint something about the speaker even though heshe probably pronounces these words as most other people do. The spelling *wuns* for *once*, or *wunz* for *ones*, would be other examples of eye dialect. *Oncet*, however, or *wunst*, does not represent eye dialect, since the speaker is shown to be using a nonstandard pronunciation.

hard news *n* Journalists refer to news stories of wide interest (politics, international relations, etc.) as hard news—constrasted with feature stories and news chiefly local in impact and interest.

historicism *n*, **historicity** *n* *Historicism* has several meanings. One is veneration, sometimes excessive, of the past. Another is the belief that processes outside the power of man to change have altered history; a third is the writing of history from this point of view. And finally, historicism is the belief that in writing history one must not impose the value judgments of one's own time and culture but accept each era in its own terms. *Historicity* is much simpler, meaning only historical accuracy, authenticity: <The historicity of Parkman's account has been questioned.>

historiographer *n* A writer of history, especially a person appointed or employed to keep an official record of the history of a country, an organization, etc.

informance *n* In a few stage and many TV presentations of plays, ballets, or music, an author, artist, or commentator may spend a few minutes telling the audience about the origin, structure, or meaning of the piece. The event may be called an *informance.*

infomercial *n,* **infotainment** *n* At present at least one TV channel offers pictures and interesting commentary on places to which one may want to travel—combining information with commercials, often sponsored by an airline or tourist bureau. Any such combination of information and commercials (not necessarily about travel) may be called by the blend name *infomercial,* sometimes *informercial. Infotainment* is a similar blend of information and entertainment.

interactive fiction *n* Most poetry and fiction demand some cooperation from the reader. However, in interactive fiction (including some video games) the reader or player may choose among several possible endings for an adventure story: <A long-running Chicago comic mystery, *Shear Madness,* is interactive fiction: The audience votes on who the murderer is, and the cast plays the last act in accordance with the majority vote.>

magazinist *n* One who edits or customarily writes for a magazine.

narratage *n* In Thornton Wilder's *Our Town,* the stage manager inserts bits of explanation or narrative to tie the story together. In many other plays and films someone, a "narrator," supplies a beginning and an ending, creating the illusion that the central part is a dramatization of what heshe is saying. The author's technique of using this storytelling device is called narratage: <Martin's use of narratage is skillful and well justified by the story.>

nemo *n* Broadcasters sometimes use *nemo* to mean a radio or television broadcast originating outside the studio—for example, an athletic contest or a parade. The origin of the term is uncertain, but it may be an alternative form of *remote.*

photojournalism *n* The magazines *Life* and *Look* in their glory days served as examples of photojournalism, which stresses pictures more than words: <Some London tabloids, with their sensationalizing pictures, represent photojournalism at its worst.>

pilcrow *n* The unfamiliar name for the familiar symbol of a paragraph: ¶.

prolepsis *n* Greek *prolēpsis* means anticipation. English *prolepsis* means, among other things, a preliminary summary that will later be expanded and detailed, like a lawyer's statement, "We intend to prove such and such." Prolepsis may also be speaking figuratively of an expected event that has not yet occurred, as Hamlet does when he says, "Horatio, I am dead."

prosaist *n*, **prosify** *vi, vt* A prosaist is a writer of prose. To prosify is to write in prose, or to make something prosaic: <He is so dull that he prosifies even the miracle of spring.>

prosopopoeia *n* Sometimes a writer impersonates an absent, dead, or imaginary speaker, or an abstraction. Thus Plato used prosopopoeia to record the dialogs of Socrates and his friends, Shakespeare used it constantly in his historical plays, and old-fashioned poets used it when Liberty or Winter or Everyman said anything.

pseudostatement *n* To a literary critic, a pseudostatement is one, such as in a poem, that cannot be verified: <"Beauty is truth, truth beauty" is a pseudostatement.> To a grammarian, a pseudostatement is one that is syntactically "correct" but that does not make sense, as "The rabid stone shuddered limpidly."

purple passage or **purple patch** *n*, **empurpled** *adj* If a writer (or possibly a composer) writes a piece that is mainly uncolorful and commonplace but inserts something that in comparison seems extraordinarily brilliant, the insertion is a purple passage or purple patch. Because of the unevenness that results from such an insertion, the term is most often employed disparagingly. *Empurpled* means characterized by purple patches: <in this empurpled novel>.

rhapsode *n* One who rhapsodizes, "speaks with great enthusiasm": <"Dylan Thomas sang other poets' poems as well as his own, read beautifully, and traveled not only as the Poet himself but as the Voice of Poetry, rhapsode and reciter."—Donald Hall, in *The American Scholar*>

Scheherazadian *adj* In *The Arabian Nights*, Scheherazade is the bright, imaginative woman who saves her life by keeping the sultan amused by telling him a series of interwoven, weirdly wonderful tales. A Scheherazadian incident or story is fanciful, incredible, but interest-holding.

scribblative *adj* Writing that is hasty, wordy, and poorly organized may be described as *scribblative.*

stock character *n* In fiction, especially drama, a character who represents a "type." Heshe may be, for example, a confidant or confidante and occasional helper, such as Sherlock Holmes's Dr. Watson, the Lone Ranger's Tonto, or Cleopatra's maid in Shakespeare's *Antony and Cleopatra.*

stylebook or **style sheet** *n* Many large newspapers and other publishers have their own stylebooks or style sheets, which give the rules to be followed by their own copy editors and printers. They generally indicate which spellings, punctuation marks, principles of syllabication, etc., are to be chosen in cases where usage is not universal, and may also give information about headlines, typefaces, etc.

stylistics *n* Stylistics involves study of aspects of literary style such as word choice, sentence length, and use of figurative language.

tetralogy *n,* **pentalogy** *n* On the ancient Greek stage four more or less related plays were often presented in sequence—a tetralogy, or *tetralogia* as the Greeks called it. All four plays might be tragedies, or one might be a comic satire. Today any series of four connected works—plays, novels, operas—may constitute a tetralogy. (In medicine, when a disease has four characteristic symptoms, they, too, are known as a tetralogy.) A pentalogy is a series of five books.

think piece *n* In journalism a think piece gives background and depth to an important news story and often includes opinions and theories of its author or of supposed authorities on the subject.

time copy *n* Printer's copy, usually preset, that can be used in a newspaper whenever there happens to be a place for it.

Mastery Test

Match each word with the best definition in its group of ten.

___ 1. thesis novel	a.	verse that uses picture-painting words
___ 2. concrete poetry	b.	device used in *Our Town*
___ 3. physical poetry	c.	writing about conservation of natural resources
___ 4. ecography	d.	narrative containing impersonations of dead or abstract speakers
___ 5. fictioneering	e.	writing inconsequential narrative
___ 6. croquis	f.	long fiction intended to make a point
___ 7. black comedy	g.	a sketch
___ 8. narratage	h.	factual but often analytical account
___ 9. prosopopoeia	i.	verse in a special shape
___ 10. reportage	j.	a funny play about an unpleasant subject

___ 11. bibliolatrous	k.	a collection of short biographies
___ 12. prosopography	l.	imitative, but considerably later
___ 13. concinnity	m.	usually too ornamental bit of writing
___ 14. dialogic	n.	unbelievably fanciful
___ 15. epigonic	o.	in the form of conversation
___ 16. prolepsis	p.	hurried, not well designed
___ 17. purple passage	q.	preliminary summary
___ 18. DWEMs	r.	book-loving

___ 19. Scheherazadian	s.	certain dead Caucasian authors
___ 20. scribblative	t.	careful planning; excellence of design
___ 21. scripturient	u.	continued part
___ 22. bibliophage	v.	a “given,” something basic in a story
___ 23. pilcrow	w.	the theory of play construction
___ 24. breakover	x.	eager to be an author
___ 25. criticaster	y.	a writer, but not of poetry
___ 26. donnée	z.	symbol representing a paragraph
___ 27. dramaturgy	aa.	unverifiable assertion
___ 28. prosaist	bb.	sometimes a kind of worm
___ 29. pseudostatement	cc.	inferior reviewer
___ 30. concinnous	dd.	well designed

18
FOR THE PAINTERLY AND THE DITHYRAMBIC

People much concerned with arrangement, style, or extrinsic social forms are adherents of **formalism,** or **formalists.** Thus in traditional courts formalism may consist of scores of taboos and required niceties. Many of the practices prescribed in etiquette books are formalisms. And in artistic work of any kind, stronger attention to form than to content is also formalism.

Perhaps the least likable of the formalists in music is a **beckmesser.** What a pedant is to literature, a beckmesser is to music. Heshe pettily criticizes all music that does not follow "correct" principles, or, if a teacher, heshe insists that each pupil adhere rigidly to a prescribed technique. The name comes from Richard Wagner, who ridiculed Herr Sextus Beckmesser in *Die Meistersinger von Nürnberg.*

One example of what the beckmesser detests could be drawn from the ancient Greeks, who called a wild, pulsating musical chant or poem in praise of Dionysus a *dithyrambos.* Today the object of praise of a **dithyramb** need not be Dionysus, but **dithyrambic** music, language, style, etc., is still celebratory, wild, pulsating, and unpredictable.

Herr Beckmesser wouldn't like **ceiling climbing** either. During jazz improvising, the playing of high notes to show off one's ability is slangily called by that name. A **ceiling note** is one of remarkably high pitch, especially when played by a jazz trumpeter. By extension, the two terms can be used with reference to other music, and by further extension, with reference to any endeavor in which the performer surpasses normal boundaries in a display of hiser virtuosity.

It is dubious that a beckmesser really likes music very much; heshe seems more interested in what heshe considers purity. In abrupt contrast, a **melomaniac,** one who has **melomania,** has an excessive or abnormal liking for music and is often quite eclectic in hiser musical tastes. **Melomane,** the adjective, means exhibiting melomania: <melomane Russian and German noblemen of the eighteenth and nineteenth centuries>.

People whose major interest is painting rather than music have always been numerous, and the variety in what they could look at has been considerable. Fads have abounded, although many art forms have been too long-lasting to be thought faddish. There was, for instance, the **iconographic** art of early Christianity, with its highly formalized figures in which each gesture, each facial expression, and even the angle of an arm or a foot carried its own symbolic meaning. The **symbolic images** of medieval and Renaissance painting are well known to art students: for example, the owl for heresy, the toad as the devil, the egg representing sex.

The mediums of painters have been and are quite varied. **Tempera,** used for many centuries, traditionally is pigment mixed with egg yolk, although exact ingredients and proportions differ from time to time or from painter to painter. **Buon fresco,** used for murals, involves rough-cut plaster to which specially prepared pigments are applied. **Sgraffito** (related to the familiar *graffito*), for exterior walls, requires a series of thin plaster layers under a two-inch top surface. **Encaustic** painting involves application of a heated iron to a finished painting. **Casein** uses curds of cheese with pigment. Today an **acrylic resin emulsion,** a plastic paint, is popular with many painters. And some modern painters have abandoned the brush for the spray gun, the roller, or the electric light bulb. **Conceptual art** may be no more than a verbal description of the artwork that for some reason the artist cannot execute in tangible materials.

The following small assortment of words can give laypersons only a hint of the tremendous number of things that may show up in the vocabulary of professionals.

More Words from Music and Other Arts

appassionato (-ta) *adj* A musical term for "impassioned": <Beethoven's "Appassionata" sonata is one of his best known.>

automatism *n* In surrealistic art, automatism is a method of producing art by letting the artist's hands and choices of color be guided only by impulse or instinct, not by conscious design.

backbeat *n* The relentless, repetitious underlying rhythm, often supplied by a drummer, in much rock music.

baritenor *n* The conventional classifications of singing voices are oversimplifications, as the baritenor exemplifies. He has a baritone voice but almost the range of the tenor. *Baritenor* may refer to either the person or the voice.

barococo *n, adj* The word is a combination of *baroque* and *rococo* and refers to an extravagant, overly fussy, curvilinear, and even grotesquely ornate form of art.

bondieuserie *n* From the French words for "dear Lord," *bondieuserie* refers to cheap, shoddy religious art produced primarily to make a profit: <Imagine paying sixty dollars for such a piece of bondieuserie!>

bravura *n,* but often used as a modifier. *Bravura* goes back to an Italian word meaning to show off. In music, either a brilliant and unusual composition or exceptionally vivid playing may be described as bravura. Similarly in other fields, a daring performance or an unusually confident air may be called bravura.

broken consort *n,* **broken music** *n* Music played together by different families of instruments (for example, woodwinds and brass) is broken music, and the musical instruments so mixed constitute a broken consort.

burla *n* A humorous, playful musical composition or movement, or a short comic episode in a commedia dell'arte, is a burla, originally Italian for joke. The plural is *burle* or *burlas*. *Burlesque* comes from the same source.

calando *adj, adv* A musical term for diminishing in loudness and/or rapidity; dying away. Applied elsewhere by extension: <The engineer reduced the power, and the machinery proceeded calando.>

cellocut *n* A woodcut is a print made from a design cut in wood. A cellocut is similar, except that the design is made in plastic.

cembalist *n* If you play any keyboard instrument in an orchestra (though most often a harpsichord) you are a cembalist. The word comes from Italian *cembalo*, "clavichord."

character piece *n* A translation of German *Charakterstück*, *character piece* refers to a short musical composition that conveys only one specific impression or mood.

chiaroscuro *n* The contrast of light and shadow is the chief characteristic of the type of art known as *chiaroscuro*, from Italian words for "light" and "dark."

chinoiserie *n* From time to time, especially in the eighteenth century, European nations have been influenced by Oriental decorative arts. Thus much eighteenth-century furniture, clothing, and architecture showed Chinese influence in their rococo qualities. This style is called *chinoiserie*, from the French word for Chinese: <the chinoiserie of the Tivoli amusement park in Copenhagen>.

chordophone *n* *Chordophone* is the comprehensive name for these stringed instruments: harps, lutes, lyres, zithers, and their close kin.

choreologist *n* A person who studies or records dance steps (usually ballet). A twenty-sided figure (an *icosahedron*) was invented by choreologist Rudolf Laban to represent the twenty major directions of movement by a dancer.

citybilly *n* A slang word for a "country" music singer from New York or some other city; coined, of course, by analogy with *hillbilly.*

clave *n* Ever wonder about the name of those little sticks that percussion players sometimes strike together as, for instance, in the rumba? Well, they're called *claves,* from the Latin *clavis,* "key," which is also the source of *clef* and of *clavicle,* "the collarbone."

colorfield *n* Pertaining to a style of painting in which large areas of color predominate over field, texture, or anything even remotely representational.

contrasty *adj* Showing great contrasts in visual qualities, such as highlights and shadows: <Steichen's contrasty photographs>. The word could also be profitably used to indicate marked contrasts of other kinds: <contrasty life-styles of the four members of the family>.

crop mark *n* Photographers and workers in printing shops often need to cut off parts of pictures to make them more attractive or to make them fit a space. A crop mark is a line showing where the picture is to be cut, or cropped.

deaccession *n, vt* Sometimes to raise money, perhaps for buying other works of art, a museum may deaccession, or sell, something in its present collection.

deadee *n* A slangy and irreverent term for a portrait from a photograph of a dead person.

decoupage *n, vt* Decoration with cutouts of paper, linoleum, etc., with varnish or lacquer over it: <She decoupaged the bathroom with pastoral scenes.>

diapason *n* Although *diapason* has several technical meanings in music, to the layperson it signifies especially a full, deep, and generally pleasant outpouring of sound: <The bullfrog began his evening diapason.>

drybrush *n* A work of art in drybrush is one painted or watercolored with most of the pigment being squeezed from the brush.

eglomise *adj* M. Glomy, an eighteenth-century French

decorator, has his name concealed in *eglomise.* Glomy, it seems, used to take an attractive piece of glass and paint a picture or a design on its back. Other Frenchmen liked what he did and began to imitate it, coining the verb *églomiser* for the process; *eglomise,* which we have borrowed, is the past participle of that verb. Today most eglomise work is performed mechanically rather than by hand, but we see it occasionally in our houses on cupboard doors, clocks, and other conspicuous items with glass fronts.

eisteddfod *n* This is one of the few words that the English language has borrowed from Welsh, in which it means session, specifically a competitive session in which Welsh singers vie with one another. The word is occasionally used in the United States for almost any artistic competition, especially of singers or poets, with the competitive element sometimes played down.

esquisse *n* Italian *schizzo,* "sketch," gave birth to Dutch *schets,* from which our *sketch* comes, and to French *esquisse.* We use the word for the very first rough drawing of anything, such as a painting or a building: <Don't worry about details; this is only an esquisse.>

gamut *n* A twelfth-century Benedictine monk named Guido d'Arezzo developed a musical scale, a hexachord in which *gamma,* the third letter of the Greek alphabet, and *ut,* the lowest note of Guido's scale, were combined as *gamma ut,* later shortened to *gamut,* a word now used to designate an entire range not only in music but in other activities as well. "The whole gamut from A to Z" is a familiar phrase, although an unkind drama critic once described the portrayal of emotions by an actress as running "the gamut from *A* to *B.*"

grisaille *n* An art work, such as a painting or a cameo, done in a single color (usually shades of gray) is a grisaille. By extension, a grisaille may be anything else very similar throughout, yet not unpleasantly monotonous: <Wordsworth's years at Lake Grasmere were a grisaille; little happened, but he and Dorothy were generally happy.>

kinetic art *n* The combining form *-kinesis* is from Greek for "movement." Kinetic art involves movement. Its parts may be moved by hand, motor, wind, or other means, and shifting light may accentuate the movements. Even a simple homemade mobile may be called kinetic art.

longueur *n* A long, boring passage in a musical composition or a literary work: <At the concert she fell asleep during the first longueur.>

marinorama *n* Recent decades have seen a proliferation of *-rama* as in *panorama: Cinerama, autorama, futurama,* etc. The usual suggestion is of some sort of overview. A marinorama gives a wide view of the sea.

melodist *n* A melodist may be a singer, but is also one who composes melodies: <M. Kelly, 1826: "I compare a good melodist to a fine racer, and counterpointists to hack post horses."> The melodist's medium may also be word-music: <Swinburne, an unexcelled melodist>.

minimal art *n* An impersonal, unemotional, simple form of painting, sculpture, architecture, or music that developed in America in the 1960s. Minimalism in music, for instance, uses only simple sound patterns and rhythms.

painterly *adj* Artistic; like a painter; seeing or portraying something as a painter might do: free in form and shading rather than linear: <Developing his photographs, he succeeded in giving them a painterly appearance.>

pianism *n* The art of playing the piano: <Murray Perahia's Mozart recordings display a probing, thoughtful pianism.> Writing or adapting music, especially for piano, is also pianism.

pianologue *n* A comic monologue with a piano accompaniment.

pyrography *n,* and related words. Designs, lettering, or pictures made by burning: <The leather belt bore a superb example of the **pyrographer's** art.> <an impressive **pyrographic** portrayal of an elk hunt>.

refacimento or **rifacimento** *n* Literally "making over." A bit of Tchaichovsky, for example, is reworked and emerges as a popular song, or a novel is rewritten as a stage play or a movie. Any such reworking of a piece of music or literature, especially when it is adapted to a different form or medium, is a refacimento.

representational art *n* In contrast to abstract art, representational art attempts to portray its subject realistically, although some degree of interpretation is inevitable and also desirable.

reverse perspective *n* To the human eye, distant things appear small and those nearby appear large. Modern perspective in art, not invented until the Renaissance, imitates what the eye sees. Reverse perspective, however, was used earlier, as in Byzantine painting and medieval illumination. In it, distant objects look large, nearby ones small.

skirl *n, vi* The *chanter* of a bagpipe is a reed pipe on which the melody is played by covering and uncovering finger holes. A skirl is the high, even shrill sound made by the chanter. (The pipes that make the fixed, continuous tones of the instrument are called *drones*.) As a verb, to skirl is to make the high-pitched sound of the bagpipe, and nonmusically means to swirl: <Dust skirled in the street.>

socialist realism *n* China (and the Soviet Union before *glasnost*) insisted that art and literature portray the economic and social state of the nation as ideal, and the workers as industrious and living in a paradise, singing happily as they dragged loads of manure up steep hills. The prescribed artistic style was called *socialist realism.*

storiation *n* Some public or collegiate buildings are decorated with bas-relief or other ornamentation depicting or suggesting historical events. Such decoration is storiation, from medieval Latin *historiatus.*

townscape, cityscape *n* A picture of a scene in a town or a city; an urban or town scene that can be observed from one vantage point; in architecture, a group of urban buildings planned to offer a unitary impression.

verism *n* An operatic composer or a painter who uses modern everyday material—for example, a labor union dispute or a Salvation Army Santa Claus instead of a court intrigue or Lady Hoy de Toy—is illustrating verism in hiser artistic creation. The word is obviously related to *verity* and *verisimilitude.*

Mastery Test

There are no rights or wrongs this time. Just answer each question subjectively on the basis of your understanding of the italicized words, which are not necessarily in the same categories.

Would you rather

___ 1. be (a) a *beckmesser* or (b) a *ceiling climber?*
___ 2. (a) be a *choreologist* or (b) a *citybilly?*
___ 3. be (a) a *baritenor* or (b) a *cembalist?*
___ 4. play (a) a *burla* or (b) a *character piece?*
___ 5. create (a) a *chiaroscuro* or (b) a *cellocut?*
___ 6. create (a) an *eglomise* or (b) a *grisaille?*
___ 7. (a) create a *marinorama* or (b) do *pyrographic* work?
___ 8. in painting or music illustrate (a) *formalism* or (b) *verism?*
___ 9. (a) do a *pianologue* or (b) create a *refacimento* based on Debussy?
___ 10. have your artistic work praised as (a) *painterly* or (b) *contrasty?*
___ 11. (a) be a *melodist* or (b) play a *chordophone?*
___ 12. look at a display of (a) *chinoiserie* or (b) *bondieuserie?*
___ 13. (a) sit through a *longueur* or (b) be a *deadee?*
___ 14. look at (a) *kinetic art* or (b) *barococo?*
___ 15. see displays of (a) *minimal art* or (b) *social realism?*

19
SOMEWHAT LEGAL

"Why don't you sue him?" a friend suggests, even though the offense may be minor. "I think you may have a case," says an ambulance-chasing lawyer after your car has been bumped by another. Such stirring up of needless lawsuits is called **barratry** by lawyers; the word obviously is related to *bar* and *barrister.* A person who does the stirring up is a **barrator** (also spelled *barrater* and *barretor*). Loosely, anyone who foments any quarrels (and not just lawsuits) may be called a barrator and be said to engage in barratry.

If an act or a statement really does offer ground for legal action, it may be called **actionable.** The noun is **actionability. Litigable** and **triable** are approximate synonyms of *actionable;* all three words mean capable of being contested at law.

Many acts other than the obvious ones like theft, rape, and murder are actionable. We'll look at a few examples. If a driver does not slow down when driving through a parking lot, and if as a result heshe strikes a car backing out, heshe may be charged with failure to exercise **ordinary care,** also called **ordinary diligence** or **ordinary prudence.** Each of these terms refers to the degree of carefulness that can sensibly be expected of a reasonable, mature person and that when not exercised can cause legally actionable damage.

Respectable though the noun *deacon* is, the verb **deacon** suggests deceptiveness that comes close to breaking the law and sometimes may indeed crack it. For example, one deacons if heshe packs a box of apples with the choicest ones on top, customarily packages meat with the best side exposed, adds water to wine or vinegar, or moves a boundary marker of hiser land a foot or so.

Subreption, which is related to *surreptitious,* means unfair, unlawful, or otherwise unethical presentation of information, including willful concealment of facts: <Even his own lawyers could not deny that the defendant was guilty of subreption, since charred bits of key documents had been found in his fireplace.>

A **public nuisance** causes annoyance or harm to members of the public who happen to be in the area: <The unauthorized flashing light beside the highway was judged a public nuisance.> A **private nuisance** affects only a particular person or persons: <His vines spreading across his neighbor's property were a private nuisance.> A **mixed nuisance** is a public nuisance that also affects a particular person or persons: <The illegally parked trucks were a mixed nuisance, for they obscured drivers' vision and also blocked Helen Turk's driveway.>

If two moving ships run together, it's a *collision,* but if a stationary ship is struck by a moving one, it's an **allision.** Why not use the latter word also when someone's car strikes a parked car, a telephone pole, or some other unmoving object? or when any moving thing strikes a stationary thing? Years ago, this use of *allision* was recognized, but it is now called obsolete; yet it seems worth reviving. And while we're at it, let's also revive the obsolete verb **allide,** "to strike something stationary," not the same as *collide,* which implies reciprocity of motion.

A **street offense** is any one of a set of misdemeanors that may be committed on or beside a street—for example, removing or altering public signs, loitering, soliciting, posting bills illegally, making unnecessary noise.

Some street offenses, as well as others, may be the acts of a **stubborn child** or a **wayward child.** A stubborn child is not just a perverse, unyielding child, but in the law of some states is a minor who persistently and harmfully disobeys hiser parent or guardian and is subject to placement in a correctional institution. A wayward child may also be disobedient, but more specifically heshe steadily associates with known criminals or other immoral persons and prefers an environment conducive to crime rather than one more socially approved.

Contempt of court isn't, in the eyes of the law, always the same thing, although a layman may not think the differences significant. **Direct contempt** occurs directly in the presence of a court in session, or at least close enough to be disruptive; alternatively, it may involve obstruction of the activities of a legislature. **Criminal contempt** is a form of direct contempt but involves a show of disrespect to the court and more or less open obstruction of justice. **Constructive contempt** may be similar to either of the others but occurs away from a court in session or a judge acting in hiser judicial capacity —for example conduct that disobeys a court order might be construed as constructive contempt.

In some legal systems, when an offender has been convicted of a certain number of serious crimes, the law requires that heshe be sentenced to life imprisonment (or at least for a specified number of years) as a habitual criminal. The felony immediately preceding and resulting in this sentence is in some places called a **technical felony.**

Some sort of judgment ordinarily results from a court case. The law, like the Lord, both giveth and taketh away. **Adjudge** is a relatively familiar word. One of its meanings, to deem or pronounce to be, is illustrated in <His claim to the estate was adjudged valid.> **Abjudge,** however, means to *take away* by decision of a court or other judge, as when a nineteenth-century theologian wrote: <"Even if one of the three [pastoral epistles of St. Paul] were abjudged it would still keep its place in argument as a good imitation of the apostolic manner.">

Other Legal Words

abalienate *vt,* and related words. If you legally deed over a piece of property to another person, you are *abalienating* it—a word that goes back to a term in Roman law. The noun form is **abalienation.** Figuratively, the act of removing or transferring feeling may also be abalienation: <I soon discovered my affection being abalienated from Jane to Joan.> **Alienation of affection** is not quite the same thing, since it refers to the act of luring one person's affection from someone else: <In the 1920s many actors and actresses, as well as other people, brought suits for alienation of affection.>

allograph *n* Your own signature on a letter or other document is your *autograph.* But if your secretary or someone else signs for you, the signature is called an *allograph,* from Greek *allo-,* "other," and *graphein,* "to write." <There may be an argument about whether his allograph is legally binding.>

blockbusting *n* Unscrupulous real-estate dealers sometimes use racial prejudice to induce homeowners to sell to them at a low price, claiming that people of another race or ethnic heritage are infiltrating the neighborhood and that property prices will plummet as a result. Then they make a big profit by reselling at an inflated price or by charging high rent. The tactic is known as *blockbusting.*

chirograph *n,* and related words. From the Greek words for "hand" and "writing," a chirograph is a formally signed legal document such as a bond or a note. One who studies handwriting is a **chirographer. Chirography** is a synonym for handwriting, penmanship, and calligraphy. **Chirographic** means pertaining to or in handwriting.

cohabitation law *n* The increasing number of couples living together without marriage has caused a boom in practice of cohabitation law, which concerns property rights of each individual during and especially after cohabitation.

consensual *adj* The noun *consensus* is familiar, but its adjectival form is comparatively rare. *Consensual* means made by mutual consent, without formal action: <a consensual obligation not to go on strike>.

coyote *n* In slang a coyote can be either (1) a person who smuggles aliens into the United States or (2) a fire fighter poised to rush to any forest fire.

demandant *n* In law, a plaintiff is sometimes called a *demandant;* so is a person who makes a legal demand or claim: <The demandant insisted that the defendant's livestock must be fenced in.>

deponent *n* One who testifies, especially in writing.

discovery rule *n* Statutes of limitation say that after a specified time a person cannot be legally tried for an alleged crime. Discovery rules in some states, however, provide that the time of application does not begin until the wrongful act is discovered: <Although the embezzlement was committed in 1985, the loss was not discovered until 1990, and the discovery rule says that the statute of limitations time limit starts with the latter date.>

dishome *vt,* **dishouse** *vt* A person is dishomed or dishoused if hiser home/house is taken away: <Several thousand persons were dishoused by floods along the Missouri River.>

dolose *adj* In Roman, civil, and Scots law, an act of criminal intent is described as *dolose:* <His injury of the child is regrettable, but it was not dolose.>

Draconian *adj* Draco, a statesman of ancient Athens, drew up a code of extremely severe laws. Modern Draconian (or *Draconic*) laws—especially punishments—are unusually severe, even cruel.

earwitness *n* Someone who hears but does not see an event.

easement *n* You own a piece of land. Neighbors need to cross it to get to their property. You may give or sell them a legal easement to provide access for them, but you still own the land.

eminent domain *n* You own a piece of land, but the state wants to get it for its own purposes, such as to build part of a highway. Under the law of eminent domain, the state may take your property but must pay you a fair price for it.

Enoch Arden law *n* Alfred Lord Tennyson wrote in 1864 a poem called "Enoch Arden" (once required reading in many literature classes) concerning a sailor whose shipwreck kept him from his wife and children for ten years; on his return, he found that his wife, presuming him dead, had married his best friend. Many states and nations now have what speakers of English call *Enoch Arden laws,* which provide presumption of death and permission for a spouse's remarriage after one has been inexplicably absent for a set period of years, usually seven.

exlex *n* In Latin, *exlex* means "bound by no law, outside the law." In English, the usual meaning is "with no legal authority or jurisdiction": <an exlex action by a jury member>.

filiate *vt* From Latin *filius,* "son." To determine through judicial proceedings who is the father of a child, usually one born out of wedlock: <The court filiated John Smith as the father.>

flotsam *n,* **jetsam** *n,* **lagan** *n* The law recognizes essential differences in these three kinds of floating materials. Flotsam is the wreckage of a ship or parts of a wrecked ship's cargo found afloat in the sea. Jetsam, however, consists of ship parts or cargo intentionally thrown overboard (jettisoned) to lighten a distressed ship. Lagan (also spelled *lagend, lagon, ligan, ligen,* and *logan*) is like jetsam, but a buoy is fastened to it for future location and recovery.

gravamen *n* The most serious and substantial of several charges made against a defendant: <Clearly the gravamen in this case is the accusation of accepting a bribe.>

handhabend or **handhaving** *adj* A person who is in possession of stolen goods (especially if heshe is caught with them in hiser possession) is described by the Old English *handhabend,* "having in hand," or the newer *handhaving:* <There is a strong presumption but not a certainty that a handhabend person is guilty of crime.>

holograph *n* A document written entirely in one's own hand is a holograph: <His will, a holograph, was not contested even though it had not been witnessed.>

infract *vt* To infract is to break, violate, infringe upon. Like its familiar noun form, *infraction,* the verb is generally used of abstract rather than concrete things. Thus one probably doesn't infract a vase but may infract, or violate, a law.

kangaroo court *n* A kangaroo court is one not following established legal principles and procedures. Some groups of prisoners, for example, try their fellows and occasionally enforce arbitrary, cruel, and/or perverted punishments. In the West a comic show may be made of a kangaroo court, with "dudes" or others being tried for trivial or imaginary offenses. An authorized court may be called a kangaroo court if its procedures are high-handed, irresponsible, and of doubtful legality: <Lynchings were often preceded by trials in kangaroo courts.>

mandatory injunction *n,* **prohibitory injunction** *n* A legal or quasi-legal injunction is mandatory if it compels the defendant to do something or to stop doing something. A prohibitory injunction, in contrast, restrains himer from carrying out some desired, proposed, or threatened act: <Because of a prohibitory injunction he could not go to his wife's new residence.>

metalaw *n* It is heartening to know that human beings, in thinking about creatures from other worlds we may someday visit or be visited by, have evoked the concept of metalaw—a variation of the Golden Rule, saying that we shall have to treat intelligent space creatures in the way they want to be treated—at least up to certain limits. (In case these folks from another world turn out to be perpetually hungry for human flesh, metalaw may be in trouble.)

no bill *n,* **true bill** *n* Grand juries decide whether enough evidence exists to justify an indictment and probably a trial. If the evidence is too slight, the result is *no bill*, but if it is strong enough, the grand jury will endorse a *true bill*.

parapherna *n* Through a prenuptial agreement a woman may legally set aside some of her property as only her own, completely outside the control of her husband. Such unshared property is her parapherna. The word comes from Greek for "alongside the dowry," as does *paraphernalia*, a word that has greatly extended its meaning.

probatum *n* A probatum is something that has been proved. Although primarily a legal term, *probatum* may also be useful in family or saloon arguments: <You'll admit that his being a convicted robber is a probatum.>

replevin *n* If Johnson has a car or other possession belonging to Brown and refuses to return it, Brown may obtain a writ of replevin to force Johnson to give it up. The verb is *replevy*.

saving clause *n* In a legal document or any statement representing a promise or an intention, a saving clause is an expressed condition, exception, or exemption. Thus in "All my cousins named in paragraph 2, except Jane Snyder, shall divide equally the residue of my estate," *except Jane Snyder* is a saving clause. Insurance policies may contain saving clauses exempting the company from payment under certain conditions such as suicide, arson, etc.

secondary evidence *n* In law, primary evidence is direct, firsthand evidence, as from an eyewitness or in the form of an original document. Secondary evidence is less direct and may be secondhand—for example, evidence that indicates that the accused was in the neighborhood of a crime, or a copy of a document rather than the original: <The president's tapes as used in the Watergate trials were regarded as primary evidence, but transcripts of the tapes were secondary evidence.>

subauditur *n* Latin for "it is understood." A subauditur is anything that is implied or understood in connection with what is said openly—a hidden meaning: <Somewhere in his words, I was sure, was a subauditur that I was failing to grasp.>

suborn *vt* If you suborn someone, you persuade himer by secret or unethical means to perform an undesirable or illegal action, such as perjury: <The father suborned his children into supporting his alibi.>

succussion *n* The act of shaking vigorously or the state of being shaken vigorously: <The succussion was so violent that Radford was arrested for assault and battery.>

testate *adj* A person who dies without leaving a will dies intestate. Obviously, then, a testate person has left a will. Also, anything given away by the terms of a will is testate property.

title by occupancy *n* When parts of the world were still legally unclaimed, a nation might gain title by occupancy—that is, by merely settling there. Similarly, in American Colonial days, a person might settle on unoccupied land and thus lay claim to it.

tort *n* Many legal cases involve torts and are tried in criminal courts. Torts are willful or negligent acts that cause loss or injury to someone else. Breaches of contract or trust are not included here but are handled under civil laws.

usufruct *n* The legal right to use something, as the income of an estate: <The will granted him the usufruct of 260 acres of land during his lifetime, with certain restrictions.>

Mastery Test

Choose the best completion for each sentence.

________________ 1. If you encourage litigation that may not be necessary, you may be a *(deacon, wayward child, barrator, demandant)*.

________________ 2. Your signature if signed by someone else is a(n) *(allograph, holograph, chirograph, autograph)*.

________________ 3. Loitering is likely to be classified as *(a private nuisance, criminal contempt, a technical felony, a street offense).*

________________ 4. To take something away by legal decision is to *(adjudge, abjudge, abalienate, dolose).*

________________ 5. Something that has been proved is a *(metalaw, subauditur, parapherna, probatum).*

________________ 6. A person who leaves a will may be described as *(intestate, testate, usufruct, consensual).*

________________ 7. To run into a stationary object is to *(deacon, infract, allide, collide).*

________________ 8. Material that is thrown overboard to lighten a ship and that is not marked by a buoy is *(flotsam, jetsam, lagan, exlex).*

________________ 9. An action requiring a person to do something or to stop doing something is a *(mandatory injunction, prohibitory injunction, saving clause, private nuisance).*

________________ 10. Willful concealment of facts is one example of *(allision, subreption, constructive contempt, an Enoch Arden law).*

________________ 11. A finding issued by a grand jury may be a *(filiate, retainer, true bill, deponent).*

________________ 12. An extremely severe law or punishment is *(Draconian, a gravamen, a tort, a cohabitation law).*

20
WHEN PEOPLE TRY TO GOVERN

Greek *arkhos,* "ruler," is familiar to us in words like *anarchy, monarch,* and *matriarchy.* Slightly less familiar is **oligarchy,** from Greek *oligos,* "few," a form of government in which the power rests in the hands of a few: <A democracy can almost imperceptibly become an oligarchy.> In places where landed gentry exert considerable political influence, that group may be called a **squirearchy** (or *squirarchy*): <The speaker declared that early America, especially the South, was governed by a squirearchy.>

A government conducted by three persons is a **triarchy,** or alternatively a **triumvirate** or (in a Russian term) a **troika,** which refers basically to a carriage pulled by three horses harnessed abreast. A **tetrarchy** is joint rule by four persons, a **pentarchy** by five. If women can do a better job of running affairs than men have so far done, perhaps each nation should be a **gynarchy,** "government by women," rather than an **androcracy,** "government by men." (*Gynecocracy,* an awkward word, is sometimes used as a synonym of *gynarchy.*) A **gerontocracy** is a government led by elderly people, perhaps in the form of a council.

Greek *kratos,* "strength, power," is a root of words like *androcracy* and *democracy.* Theories as to who should or does hold the governing power have been numerous and are reflected in our vocabulary. To Aristotle, Greek *timokratia* (our **timocracy**) referred to a stage of political development in which the wealthy held most of the political positions and received most honor. Plato, however, had used the same Greek word for a stage in which honor and glory, rather than wealth, was the ruling principle. One form of timocracy in the United States was a **slavocracy** (also *slaveocracy*). Before the Civil War there was a faction of slave owners and slavery advocates in the South who were influential enough to control effectively the reins of government; they were known collectively as a slavocracy, and each individually was a **slavocrat.**

Mobocracy, as the name suggests, is government by a mob, or a mob as a ruling group. <Mme. D'Arblay, 1788: "Mr. Wilkes . . . quarreled with a gentleman for saying the French government was become a democracy, and asserted it was rather a mobocracy."> <Gangsters, forming a mobocracy, ruled the city.> Greek *pornē* means harlot, and **pornocracy** is therefore government by harlots—perhaps with reference to the influence of loose women during some periods of the Roman Empire and in other times and places. A **stratocracy,** from Greek *stratos,* "army," is a military government or one dependent on the army to stay in control: <In Latin American countries, stratocracies were more numerous than elsewhere.> **Thalassocracy** means command of the seas: <England's thalassocracy was chiefly responsible for her once-huge empire.>

An **ideocracy** is a government founded on theory or abstract ideas. Both democracy and communism are at base ideocracies, but necessarily and properly the theories of both have had to be translated into concrete terms that sometimes bear little resemblance to the underlying philosophies. One form of ideocracy, much discussed in the depression of the 1930s, is a **technocracy,** which is a government by technical experts who follow principles laid down by technicians. The technicians, as well as anyone else favoring technocracy, are called **technocrats,** and they follow **technocratic** policies. No nation has yet been governed as a technocracy, and the concept has been criticized as excessively materialistic and inadequately attuned to social, psychological, and artistic considerations.

There have been many **kleptocracies,** "government led by thieves," but the word has no legal status and has not become familiar. If drug dealers ever obtain complete control of a government (as seems possible), the country will be a **narcokleptocracy.** Quite different would be a **meritocracy,** managed by people chosen for their ability and talent.

In ancient Greek elections, at a time when nearly all voters were illiterate, each voter would drop into a box a pebble, called a *psēphos.* (Italians later used a *ballota,* "little ball or pebble," to vote; our *ballot* comes from the Italian.) The color of the pebble the Greek chose indicated hiser preference. The custom survives after a fashion in **psephology,** "the scientific study of voting or elections." One who conducts such a study is a **psephologist;** hiser studies are described as **psephological. Psephomancy,** however, is hardly scientific; it means divination by pebbles, and hence is about as trustworthy as **phyllomancy,** which is divination by reading tea leaves or other leaves.

It has been alleged that in some elections ballots have been cast in the names of people who have died or moved away. These illegal ballots collectively are called the **graveyard vote.** Use of such a vote may be a mark of a **malversation,** "corruption in administration." A malversation may include any of a number of misdeeds, whether criminal or merely unethical: bribery, mishandling of funds, embezzlement, extortion, misappropriation, subversion of the Constitution, treason, corruption, dishonesty, crimes against persons, breaking and entering, concealment of felonies or misdemeanors, cheating in elections, and so on; the possibilities are quite rich.

Sometimes a government is not crooked (at least not *very* crooked) but just doesn't accomplish much. The French have a word, *immobilisme,* for governmental policy that involves little positive action and much discussion, with frequent compromise resulting in scanty changes. Similar **immobilism** exists in other countries, and the term is also sometimes applied to a business, a family, or other group that talks much but does little. (Creative writers and other artists are often victims of immobilism.)

Civicism is praiseworthy, unlike the political abuses we have been noticing. It is devotion to civic causes: <Her regular attendance at meetings of the town and school boards confirmed her civicism.> To create or infuse such civicism is to **civicize:** <She had been civicized by her mother's example.> **Civism** is much like civicism but refers particularly to the good qualities themselves: <G. C. Warr, 1800: "Roman 'civism,' the tradition of self-sacrifice for the public good">.

Other Words About Government

capitation *n* A tax or a payment of dues that is the same for each person—for example, a poll tax or the amount of dues per head that a local union pays to the parent union. In Latin, *capitatio* means poll tax; it came from *caput*, "head."

centrist *n* A moderate in politics, neither left- nor right-wing. Heshe stands for **centrism.**

citizenly *adj* Pertaining to a citizen: <Her only citizenly activity was the drafting of countless petitions, on any subject that she felt strongly about.>

clawback *n* (1) Governmental retrieval, through tax maneuvering, of a benefit granted earlier. The term is British, but the tactic is known in the United States, too: <Many recipients of Social Security payments were hit by a clawback, with one half of each payment made subject to income tax.> (2) An agreement by a country to pay higher interest on a loan in return for sizable orders of one of its products: <The secretary of commerce remarked to the ambassador, "Perhaps for more uranium, we can arrange a clawback.">

closed society *n* A society in which people are not allowed to emigrate or to speak and write freely.

Crown corporation *n* A Canadian term for a commercial company owned and managed by the government.

dawk *n* A slang term for a person who is neither a hawk nor a dove (neither for nor against a very strong military stance).

death-qualify *vt* To be rejected for jury duty because of one's attitude toward the death penalty. The prosecution may want to death-qualify those who oppose it, and the defense may try to death-qualify those who favor it. The term is informal and not yet in dictionaries.

deep six *n, vt* Perhaps most Americans had not heard the slang phrase *deep six*, "throw overboard, get rid of," until the Senate Watergate hearings of 1973, when a White House official reported that some possibly embarrassing or incriminating papers had been "deep sixed" or "given the deep six." Presumably the expression refers to putting something under six fathoms of water.

defalcation *n* Misappropriation of funds held by a government official. Comparable to embezzlement in business.

dollar diplomacy *n* (1) Use of American economic strength to achieve victories in diplomatic decisions. (2) Governmental assistance to citizens or companies engaging in business in or with other countries, to strengthen relations. (Other countries may engage, of course, in ruble, mark, or yen diplomacy.)

dynast *n* A strong ruler, especially one who has inherited the position. A sequence of hereditary rulers constitutes a *dynasty*, although that word is also used in private life for a family that over the years has been extraordinarily wealthy and powerful.

Gleichschaltung *n* Dictatorial governments discourage independence and variety and work for uniformity of belief, cultural forms, habits, methods of work, and almost everything else. The policy and process of encouraging such extreme sameness and conformity (well illustrated in Germany, the Soviet Union, China, and elsewhere during parts of our century) is known by the German word *Gleichschaltung*, literally meaning "similar direction."

heteronomy *n*, **heteronomous** *adj* *Autonomy* means self-rule, but *heteronomy* means rule by someone else. A person subject to anything other than hiser own rule is heteronomous: <Small children are necessarily heteronomous to a considerable degree.>

juridical *adj* Often confused with *judicial*, but actually different in meaning. *Judicial* refers especially to judges and the act of judging: <the judicial process> <a judicial decision>. *Juridical*, in contrast, refers in general to courts of justice, to their structure and proceedings, and to the whole body of laws, legal principles, and legal precedents: <juridical precedents> <juridical constraints>.

laborism *n*, **laboristic** *adj* In England, *Labourism* refers to the beliefs of the Labour Party. More broadly, laborism is an economic and political philosophy and system that favors the cause of labor as opposed to that of management: <Laborism made few substantial advances until the twentieth century.> *Laboristic* means pertaining to policies favoring labor: <Laboristic abuses are often as deplorable as those of the plutocrats.>

liberticide *n* Destruction of liberty, or a person who destroys liberty: <A democracy is constantly in danger of liberticide, but most greatly so when freedom of the press is threatened.>

nativism *n* (1) Any governmental policy that favors native inhabitants over immigrants. (2) Policies to encourage, preserve, or revive native culture: <Greater attention to nativism was needed, the speaker said, to redress earlier wrongful treatment.>

party question *n* A party question is one about which political parties disagree, even though the question may otherwise be of minor importance: <"Who spends more —Republicans or Democrats?" is really only a party question, since both parties have consistently run the country into debt.>

patrial *adj* Anything that is patrial relates to one's fatherland: <the patrial mountains that she longed for in this flat country>. The name for an inhabitant of a country is a patrial name—for example, *Frenchman* for a person from France.

revanche *n* This French word for revenge is usually limited in English to meaning governmental policy aimed at recovering lost territory: <For centuries revanche was a chief motive of central European states.>

revisionist *n* To a Marxist, a revisionist is one who attempts to revise Marxian socialism gradually to make it conform to actuality or to present conditions. More generally, a revisionist tries to make gradual changes in any widespread attitude or doctrine.

sansculotte *n* Members of the most radical and perhaps the most violent party in France in the French Revolution were nicknamed *sans-culottes* "without breeches," because they wore pantaloons or other attire not in general use. Today's English uses the term with no reference to clothing but to indicate extremists in politics, especially those who use violent tactics: <sansculottes in some Middle Eastern countries>.

snopes *n* The unscrupulous Snopes family, prominent in novels of William Faulkner (particularly *Sartoris* and *The Hamlet*), is remembered in this little-used name for a businessman or small-town politician of low morality but perhaps a little crude charm: <a real snopes—lying, cheating, staying one jump ahead of the law>. Plural *snopeses.*

spinnish *n* To influence public perceptions, spokespersons for presidents or other high officials often put a "spin" on announcements of decisions, official statements, or events, usually to make them appear better than they really were, or to make them appear worse if the opposition is responsible. The informal name for such use of interpretations or misinterpretations is *spinnish* or occasionally *spinnage.* Neither term is yet in dictionaries. <The press secretary used spinnish to reduce taxpayers' probable hostility to the president's statement.>

statism or **stateism** *n,* **statolatry** *n* Statism is highly centralized government, with the economy directly under the control of a few persons: <So-called communistic governments of large countries have illustrated statism in almost pure form.> Statolatry, literally "worship of the state," is strong advocacy of centralized government.

syndicalism *n* A radical political movement that flourished in Europe in the first quarter of the twentieth century and that was embraced in part by the American Industrial Workers of the World. Syndicalists wanted to replace the capitalistic system with one run by labor unions and other workers' cooperatives. Their chief weapon was the general strike.

World Federalist *n* A supporter of a movement, officially begun in 1947, toward a world government charged especially with promoting peace.

Mastery Test

Fill in the missing letters.

1. t_______y	government by four persons
2. i_______y	government based on theory
3. t_________y	government by technical experts
4. p________y	scientific study of elections
5. i________m	much talk, little action
6. c______m	devotion to civic causes
7. d_____r	co-ruler
8. h__________s	subject to rule by someone else
9. j_______l	pertaining to the act of judging
10. p_____l	pertaining to the fatherland
11. s_________m	belief that labor unions should govern
12. s_____m	highly centralized government
13. s_________e	French revolutionary
14. g______y	government by women
15. a________y	government by men

16. o_______y	government by the few
17. s_________y	military rule
18. g________ ___e	illegal ballots
19. c________n	same tax on each person
20. l______m	political policy favoring labor
21. s______h	distorted emphasis in public statements
22. d_________n	misappropriation of public funds
23. g__________y	government by the elderly
24. n______________y	government by drug dealers
25. c______t	neither right- nor left-wing

21
IN THE LEXICON OF BUSINESS

Probably the proportion of dishonesty among businesspeople is about the same as that in the population at large, but since most of us buy things every day, we have opportunity to learn directly about the petty cheating of some shopkeepers and indirectly about the machinations of big business. The fact that dishonesty is not new is attested by the word **venal.** Its ancestor, Latin *venum*, simply means sale, and *venal* used to mean salable. Now, though, it has come to mean corrupt, unscrupulous, open to bribery. A venal businessperson is ruled by greed; a venal politician may sell hiser vote to the highest bidder. The word should not be confused with **venial** "easily forgiven"; a venial sin is considered much less serious in the Roman Catholic Church than is a mortal sin.

President Eisenhower warned about the potential evils of **agribusiness** (as well as the **military-industrial complex**). *Agribusiness* covers everything from the plowing of a field to your purchase of a box of cornflakes or other farm-based commodity. It designates the roles of the farmer, the processor or manufacturer, the transporters, and the distributors, as well as various related workers such as seed and fertilizer salespersons and rural elevator operators.

Simple cunning or shrewdness in selling, etc., perhaps even when slightly deceptive, is a **dolus bonus,** literally "good deceit." A **dolus malus,** "bad deceit," however, is a fraudulent act and is punishable by law. Perhaps an example of dolus bonus, at least of shrewdness, is a charge known as **corkage.** This involves charging a customer (usually in a restaurant or a place of entertainment) for allowing himer to drink an alcoholic beverage that heshe has brought along. The word also means a restaurant surcharge for each bottle of liquor or each drink served. Ways of extracting money from customers are endless.

Businesspeople, like everyone else, must often take chances. In Latin, *alea* is a dice game, *aleator* is a dice player or other gambler, and *aleatorius* means pertaining to a gambler. English **aleatory** similarly refers to chance-taking, though not necessarily with dice. Lawyers and businesspeople may include aleatory provisions in contracts, requiring larger or smaller payments in case of good or bad luck, as with weather. (*Aleatory* is also a useful word to mean pertaining to luck: <the aleatory effects of being born in a palace or a hovel>.)

Instances of possible bad luck include **droppage** and **spillage.** In an orchard, part of the fruit, the droppage, falls off before harvest, and losses result from unusually high droppage. In various kinds of work, such as painting and spraying, part of the material may be dropped and therefore become unusable: this, too, is droppage, or if a liquid, spillage.

Dockage, too, may involve loss for someone. It may be (1) money charged for the use of a dock, (2) the act of docking a ship, and (3) facilities for docking a ship, but also (4) an amount withdrawn (as from a salary or a price) because of some failure or flaw, or (5) weed seeds and other material that should not be in grain. Meanings 1–3 derive from Middle Dutch *docke,* "a dock for a ship," and the others from Middle English *docken,* "to cut off the end of a tail or other appendage."

A renter loses when heshe has to pay what for centuries

has been called **rack rent,** which is excessively high rent, sometimes almost as much as the value of land. The term goes back to the torture instrument called the *rack,* which stretched a person's body unbearably. In 1800 Maria Edgeworth wrote *Castle Rackrent,* a novel about the Rackrent family's vicious oppression of their Irish tenants. The tenants, like many other people, lived in **illth,** a word formed by analogy with *wealth* and almost its opposite in meaning. Illth is poverty and misery, or that which causes them: <Most illth, like most wealth, is created by human greed.>

Advertisers have special techniques. One of these is the **advertorial.** This word, a blend of *advertisement* and *editorial,* refers to a paid statement, often by a corporation, setting forth its reasons for holding a particular view of a current matter. For instance, when oil shortages began developing in the 1970s, oil companies paid for many full-page (tax-deductible) advertorials to explain why the most recent price increases were justified at a time when company profits were already at record levels.

Despite criticisms that may be leveled against many businesses, some businesspeople become increasingly aware of the **human equation.** Regardless of how complex our machinery or how sophisticated our computers or how advanced our economic and political planning, the human equation remains. This is the group of human characteristics that affects the results of all activities in which people and their machines and institutions are involved.

In consideration of the human equation, some industrialists talk in terms of **human engineering.** This may be, for instance, the planning of machinery and its placement so as to be most comfortable for its operators and easy for them to use efficiently. Or it may be industrial management of human beings so as to gain maximum productivity and yet keep workers contented. In large factories or assembly lines, for example, many tasks have been mechanized or made so routine that little skill is demanded of the worker; the tasks have been **deskilled,** and as a result some jobs have become dreadfully monotonous. In the early days of this century, as Upton Sinclair's *The Jungle* dramatized, employers paid no attention to workers' complaints about monotony or anything else, but now, in an era of human engineering, at least some attempts are made to make work safe and less boring, as well as much more rewarding monetarily.

Other Businesslike Words

agiotage *n* Have you ever bought and sold stocks speculatively? If so, you were engaging in agiotage. <W. S. Landor, 1829: "Vanity and agiotage are to a Parisian the oxygen and hydrogen of life.">

anticipointment *n* (Note the spelling.) If you have eagerly anticipated a touted new TV program or a new cereal, dress, etc., and then been disappointed when you got it, you have suffered anticipointment. The term was apparently coined by a CBS vice president of advertising, Mike Mischler.

aquiculture or **aquaculture** *n,* and related words. If you raise fish or other edible water creatures in enclosed ponds, you are engaged in aquiculture, which is an **aquicultural** activity, and you are an **aquiculturist. Hydroponics** is not the same, since it involves growing plants in a nutrient solution. *Pisciculture,* discussed elsewhere, refers to growing only fish.

barcode reader *n* You can't read the group of lines that you see on a can of beans or thousands of other products. You can't, but an electronic device, a barcode reader, can and does.

bracket creep *n* You get some salary increases that move you into a higher income tax bracket. Because both prices and your tax payments increase, your real income may be diminished. This unhappy phenomenon is called *bracket creep.*

catazine *n* Some catalogs include as fillers and attention grabbers some little informative or amusing paragraphs, short human-interest stories, and the like, thereby serving as both a catalog and a magazine—a *catazine.*

coasters *n,* **flyover country** *n* Businesspeople (sometimes actors, too) whose work is done only on the coasts—say, New York and Los Angeles—are coasters. They ignore—may even speak contemptuously of—the flyover country and its residents, the *flyover people.*

consequential loss *n* If your house burns, you will lose not only your property but also probably time from work, cost of temporary housing, expenses for finding new housing, and so on. Any loss that is a consequence of some other loss is a consequential loss and is covered by some insurance policies.

continentalize *vt* To continentalize is to broaden something until it becomes continental in scope: <After trial runs in the Midwest, the advertising campaign was soon continentalized.> Sometimes the verb refers specifically to the continent of Europe, in which case it may be the equivalent of *Europeanize* and is often written with a capital: <He hoped to Continentalize America's musical taste.>

cost-push (and **wage-push** and **demand-pull**) **inflation** *n* Inflation has three main causes. If manufacturing costs, such as those of materials, rise, a company's prices also rise: cost-push inflation. <Raw materials now cost us more, and such cost-push inflation makes us raise our prices.> If wages go up, so do the company's prices: wage-push inflation. <Wages went up 3 percent that year, resulting in wage-push inflation.> If demand increases but supplies do not, the demand pulls the prices higher: demand-pull inflation. <Sales of the dolls were so brisk that the factory could not keep up with the demand, so our higher prices were caused by that demand-pull inflation.>

cross-train *vt* To make workers more versatile and also to increase a company's ability to adapt to changing circumstances while keeping the same personnel, a worker may be cross-trained: taught several usually related jobs.

cybernation *n*, **cybernetics** *n*, **datamation** *n* *Cybernation*, also called *datamation*, means the use of computers in automatic processes. *Cybernetics* is the study of the use of computers in performing actions traditionally done by human beings.

debit card *n* If you have a debit card, you may use it to pay for purchases as you would a credit card. However, the debit card automatically debits the amount from your bank checking account without going through a credit card company.

dehire *vt,* **deselect** *vt,* **riff** *n, vt* *Dehire* and *deselect* are euphemisms for *fire* or *discharge. Riff,* which is short for "reduction in force," has the same meaning but may also be a noun: <The company riffed two hundred of us. The riff will probably be permanent.>

demand-side *adj, n,* **supply-side** *adj, n* Demand-side economists believe that consumer demand is and should be the major determining force in the economy. Supply-siders believe that reducing taxes for corporations and the well-to-do will have a trickle-down effect and eventually benefit the less affluent: <Supply-side theories characterized Reagan's economic policy.>

dittograph *n* In writing or typing, perhaps you have unintentionally repeated a letter or a a word (as I have just done). The repeated element is a dittograph.

dollar averaging *n* You invest a fixed sum (such as a hundred dollars) in the same stock or other security at regular intervals (such as once a month), even as the price per share fluctuates. The number of shares you buy each time thus changes, but over a period of time you end up paying approximately the average price of that stock. That process is called *dollar averaging.*

double-bill *vt, vi* Double-billing is cheating, especially on expense accounts, by billing the same costs to two different companies or two accounts in the same company.

dreck *n* Although Yiddish *drek* apparently first meant rubbish or filth, the English derivative now often means a piece of clothing made of poor material or with flawed workmanship: <This dress is dreck! Just look at the stitching!> (It's an indelicate word, like *crap.*)

fractionation *n* Selling item by item instead of as a package. Example: The price of a meal in most restaurants used to be all-inclusive. Then the cost of a beverage was listed separately, and then the cost of an appetizer and a dessert. Now the total bill for a full meal is higher because of this fractionation.

golden parachute *n* A larger-than-usual severance payment to induce a key executive to leave quietly. In a merger or sale, the new directors, not wanting to keep the executive, use the "parachute" to let himer down gently. On some occasions the executive may find it advantageous to suggest that heshe is open to such a deal if it is "golden" enough.

hyperinflation *n* An extraordinarily high inflation rate, as in Germany after World War I or, more recently, in Israel, Brazil, and Argentina.

indirect labor *n* When a product is being manufactured, many workers in the plant (for example, office personnel, janitors, repair people) do not work directly on the product, yet their wages or salaries are chargeable at least in part to the product. Such labor is indirect labor, contrasted with direct labor, that of the workers who actually handle the product.

instantize *n* To make foods—possibly other products, too—usable in a very short time: <Rice and other cereals were among the first foods to be instantized.>

kanban *n* A Chinese word borrowed by the Japanese and then by the Americans. Kanban involves keeping inventories low and thus reducing storage costs by having most supplies delivered just before a factory needs them.

key bargain *n* When several companies bargain with union representatives for a new contract, the terms of one agreement tend to influence or determine others. Such an agreement is a key bargain.

live load *n*, **dead load** *n* Basically a live load is the weight of cargo or passengers that a vehicle carries, and a dead load is the constant weight of the vehicle itself, including its permanent attachments.

lowball *vt* An unethical but not necessarily illegal manufacturing or building tactic: underestimating costs at the time of submitting a bid and then later collecting much larger amounts because of cost overruns. <The government spends untold billions each year because of lowballing by many of its largest suppliers.>

miscorrect *vt* To make a new mistake in trying to make

a correction: <The typesetter miscorrected the spelling from *physcology* to *psycology.*>

monopsony *n,* and related words. In a monopoly there is one seller with many buyers, but in a monopsony the reverse is true: many sellers with only one buyer. The words **duopsony** (two buyers) and **oligopsony** (a few buyers each strong enough to influence the market) also exist but have limited usefulness except among marketing specialists.

moratory *adj* Pertaining to delay in paying a debt or other obligation: <His moratory tactics alienated his friends.> <a moratory statute authorizing delay in payment of the highway bonds>.

notehead *n* A letterhead is a letter-sized sheet of paper with a printed or engraved heading. A notehead is the same, but a smaller sheet.

obligee *n,* **obligor** *n,* **mortgagee** *n,* **mortgagor** *n* An *obligee* is one to whom another owes an obligation (usually legal). An *obligor* is the person who owes the obligation: Heshe is expected to pay. Similarly, a *mortgagee* receives the payments and the *mortgagor* must make them because heshe has placed the mortgage on the property.

oligopoly *n* Like a monopoly, but in an oligopoly a few suppliers, possibly through mutual agreement, control the market, usually forcing out small competitors.

original cost *n* In real-estate parlance *original cost* ordinarily does not really mean *original* cost, that is, the cost of construction. Rather, it is the cost to the present owner. Thus if the first owner paid fifty thousand dollars but the present owner paid eighty thousand dollars, the original cost is eighty thousand dollars.

outage *n* Most commonly today *outage* refers to an interruption of electrical power or gas line failure: <The outage lasted more than two days.> Less frequently it refers to the amount of something lost in transport or storage: <an outage of several thousand barrels of oil>.

owelty *n* Commonly referred to as "boot," as in "gave him ten dollars to boot," owelty is an extra payment made by one trader to another to equalize the values of the items being traded: <gave him ten dollars as owelty>.

PERT *n* *P*rogram *E*valuation and *R*eview *T*echnique. Continuous computer reporting and analysis of costs, income, labor status, profits, and anything else of importance to a business.

planned (or **built-in**) **obsolescence** *n* Example: One brand of submersible pump has an electric switch made to specifications that will make it stop working after ten or twelve years. Then workers must spend hours replacing it, the company makes a fresh profit, the installers benefit, but the customer pays unnecessarily.

psychotechnology *n* Some problems in industry or business can best be solved by application of psychological principles. Such application is psychotechnology.

replacement cost *n* The cost of replacing a tangible asset with something equally good: <The old house is worth twenty thousand dollars at most, but its replacement cost would be at least a hundred thousand.>

repressed inflation *n* The condition of having wage and price controls without elimination of the basic causes of inflation.

spendthrift trust *n* If you are wealthy but fear that an heir to your estate is likely to squander what you leave himer, you and your lawyer may establish a spendthrift trust, which will provide the heir with regular income but prevent himer from spending part or all of the principal (perhaps just until heshe reaches a specified age).

stagflation *n* An economic situation in which prices continue to rise (inflation) even though business activity and employment rates are both lower (stagnation): <considerable stagflation in the late 1960s and the 1970s>.

stope *vi, vt* A North Carolina man received a ticket for parking beside a sign that said "No Stoping." In court he produced a dictionary that proved his innocence, for stoping is mining ore by means of a series of steplike excavations.

sug *vi* A telephone caller says, "I am calling for the XYZ Market Research Institute. We are gathering information about consumer satisfaction. Are you satisfied with the quality of your (dishwasher, windows, or whatever)?" Later, heshe tries to sell you something. The caller is probably *sugging*. *Sug* is a British acronym for "*s*elling *u*nder the *g*uise of market research."

sweetheart agreement or **sweetheart contract** *n* Some labor union officials have been accused of negotiating sweetheart agreements or contracts which are beneficial to the employer and in which union members have little or no voice. The implication, of course, is that the union officials received money or other favors in return.

telemarketing *n* Selling by telephone. Also, in recent years, selling by television, especially on channels used solely for that purpose.

tree-hugger *n* A slang term for a person who, usually for reasons of financial security, spends most of hiser life working for the same company.

walk-in-walk-out *adj* This term, used especially in Australia, is used to describe a real-estate sale in which the purchaser buys a house, store, etc., just as it is, for immediate possession, and with the contents to be left intact. The adjective is presumably a short form of "When you (the buyer) walk in, I (the seller) will walk out." <a walk-in-walk-out agreement>.

Mastery Test

Mark each statement *true* (T) or *false* (F).

____ 1. The actions of a *venal* merchant are easily forgiven.

____ 2. *Aleatory* results are those attributable to good or bad luck.

____ 3. *Rack rent* is rent paid for display racks at conventions.

____ 4. *Agiotage* is speculative buying and selling of stocks.

___ 5. A *spendthrift trust* protects an estate against foolish spending.

___ 6. To *stope* is to mine ore by a particular method.

___ 7. A *sweetheart agreement* is a premarital agreement concerning financial matters.

___ 8. *Coasters* do most of their work on the East and West coasts.

___ 9. In some business agreements, a seller must allow *dockage* if heshe does not completely satisfy the terms of the contract.

___ 10. Manufacturers sometimes *deskill* jobs.

___ 11. *Hydroponics* is the use of tanks of water for growing anything.

___ 12. A *consequential loss*, as in a fire, consists of whatever the major loss is.

___ 13. A *dittograph* is a copy of a document or a picture.

___ 14. *Indirect labor* is that not involved directly in manufacture of a product.

___ 15. *Dreck* may be clothing of poor quality or workmanship.

___ 16. *Moratory* tactics involve delay.

___ 17. A *live load* on a vehicle consists of hogs, cattle, sheep, chickens, or other animate creatures.

___ 18. A *golden parachute* is reserved for top Air Force officers.

___ 19. In making a trade, one party may sometimes pay an extra amount called *owelty*.

___ 20. *Repressed inflation* is that which has been replaced by deflation.

___ 21. In a *kanban*, prompt delivery of supplies is essential.

___ 22. *Oligopolies* are a result of *telemarketing.*

___ 23. *Double-billing* is one way to prevent *dollar averaging.*

___ 24. A *catazine* is a catalog with some features of a magazine.

___ 25. *Cross-training* may sometimes reduce *dehiring.*

22
ON BUILDINGS AND BUILDING

Architecture is the art or science of designing buildings, and **tectonics** is the art or science of constructing them. Since both the architect and the builder are likely to be especially concerned with roofs and windows—which give most houses and some other buildings much of their individuality—I'll devote this section to them and then move on to a miscellany of building terms.

Roofs are basically either flat or pitched. The **flat roof** is almost never completely flat, because some slope is needed to prevent water from standing. A carpenter measures slope in terms of the number of inches of vertical rise in each foot. Thus one-in-twelve would be a reasonable slope for an almost flat roof, and four-in-twelve for many pitched roofs. A **shed roof** has a single, gradual slant, perhaps like that on Grandpa's chicken house.

The most common pitched roof, shaped like an inverted V, is a **gable roof.** If the roof has a single slant at each side and also each end, it is a **hip roof.** A **curb roof** has a center ridge and a double slope on each of two sides. A **gambrel roof** is a type of curb roof in which the lower slope is considerably steeper than the upper one. A **mansard** roof has two slopes on all sides (not just on two); again, the lower is steeper.

Oddities among roofs include the **rainbow roof,** which has slightly convex slopes; the **skirt roof,** used mainly for decoration, consisting of a band of roofing material (usually shingles) that stretches around the entire structure or considerable parts of it; and the **sawtooth roof,** found almost exclusively in factories and consisting of several sections that resemble the teeth of a saw. In the sawtooth roof usually one slope is steeper than the others and may contain one or more windows, since with this design a considerable amount of natural light may be admitted to different parts of the factory.

Some roofs, especially on choice houses, are built with an **overhang,** the underside of which is called a **soffit.** The overhang extends beyond the edge of the house for several inches or perhaps two feet or more, and in addition to its function as a protection against bad weather or the hot sun, it has considerable effect on the appearance of the building.

The roof line may be broken by **dormers,** which are gables built out from the roof and which contain windows. There may also be a **shed dormer,** which has a roof that slants in the same direction as the main roof.

Fenestration is a term used by architects for the choice and arrangement of windows as contributors to the appearance and other qualities of a building. There are several types of windows. The most common one, capable of being raised and lowered from bottom and top, is the **double-hung window;** it often has only a single large pane of glass in each of the two sashes but may instead have a number of small panes. **Casement windows** have hinges and open like doors; they, too, may have single or multiple panes. **Sliding** or **traverse windows** open by sliding along top and bottom tracks. **Awning** or **projected windows,** often one above another, are hinged at the top and are opened by a crank or a bar; **hopper windows** are similar but are hinged at the bottom. **Louvered** or **jalousie windows** consist of narrow strips of glass installed horizontally in a frame; they are opened usually by a crank or a lever. **Strip windows,** generally installed high in bedroom walls for privacy, are narrow awning or hopper windows placed side by side. Sometimes casement and hopper windows are combined in a single frame, and sometimes a fixed pane is used in combination with louvered or awning or hopper windows. A **Palladian window** is rectangular except for a semicircular top; a smaller rectangular window is at each side. An **eyebrow** is a dormer projecting from a slanted roof; its roofed part is shaped like a human eyebrow.

A **bay window** is usually three windows forming an alcove, projecting from the wall of a building and often having its own foundation. Such a window affords a good place to display flowers or to sit and look out in any of three directions. A variety of bay window is the **oriel,** which is semihexagonal or semisquare and is usually cantilevered from a wall. A **lunette** is a window in the shape of a crescent or a semicircle—usually the upper half. An **oeil-de-boeuf** is a small round or oval window that is so called because it somewhat resembles the eye of an ox. Especially in some large modern office buildings, lines of windows stretch horizontally around most or all of the structure, making the building look like a series of ribbons one above another; hence the windows are called **ribbon windows.**

Assorted Words Pertaining to Buildings

abatjour *n*, **abatvent** *n*, **abatvoix** *n* French *abattre* means to throw down. Literally, these three devices respectively throw down the day (light), the wind, and the voice. The abatjour deflects light downward; if, for instance, you wanted to admit daylight to your room but keep it from shining into your eyes, you could devise an abatjour for your window. Sometimes a skylight is also called an abatjour. An abatvent keeps wind from blowing directly on you; its most familiar form is that of a slanting piece of glass, wood, or plastic inside a window. An abatvoix is a sounding board or similar acoustical device to send vocal or other sounds out into a room.

aquatel *n*, **boatel** *n* An aquatel is a marina, at which boats are moored, or occasionally a motel partly or entirely over the water. A boatel is a hotel or motel at a marina.

architrave *n,* **cornice** *n,* **entablature** *n,* **frieze** *n,* **pediment** *n* An *entablature* is at the top of a classical column, just below the eaves. It usually consists of a support called an *architrave,* which is topped by a decorative *frieze* and a projecting (sometimes decorated) *cornice.* Above the cornice may be a *pediment,* a low gable that can be either triangular or rounded.

ashlar *n* Carefully squared building stones that make possible the use of unusually thin layers of mortar.

brutalism *n* A style of architecture that pays more attention to strength and functionalism than to beauty—for example, large, unbroken expanses of concrete walls.

cenotaph *n* From Greek words meaning empty tomb. Sometimes a monument is built to a person buried elsewhere, and sometimes a body is moved to another tomb, leaving the first one vacant. Such a monument or empty tomb is a cenotaph.

cinerarium *n,* and related words. After Mrs. Smith's husband's body had been cremated in a **cinerator,** which is also called a **crematorium** or **crematory,** Mrs. Smith bought a **cinerary** urn to hold his ashes. She kept the urn in her living (!) room, and irreverent or uninformed visitors flicked their cigaret ashes into it. "Oh," said a friend one day, "I see that your husband has been gaining weight." Mrs. Smith might have been saved that embarrassment had she purchased space for her departed in a cinerarium, which is usually a commercially operated place for deposit of cremated remains. And whenever Mrs. Smith saw something **cinereous,** "resembling ashes," she would still have had a reminder of her loved one.

clerestory *n* (Also *clearstory*) Used mainly but not exclusively in a church, a clerestory is a windowed wall looking out over a lower roof and admitting light to a high-ceilinged interior such as a nave.

corbel *n* A bracket, usually of wood, stone, or brick, that protrudes from the face of a wall and helps to support an arch or a cornice.

demountable *adj* Capable of being taken apart for later reassembly: <Farmers built demountable livestock sheds that could be moved to where water was most plentiful.>

effloresce *vi* Although *effloresce* in the sense of "to start to blossom" is fairly familiar, it is less well known that owners of brick houses are saddened when the bricks begin to effloresce: to develop a white coating of hard-to-remove soluble salts.

ekistics *n* The study or science of human settlements, including, in part, community planning and design.

gazebo or **gazeebo** or **gazabo** *n*, **belvedere** *n* Squires and higher gentry of eighteenth-century England used to build gazebos or belvederes in especially attractive parts of their estates. They are small, open outdoor structures. *Gazebo* is supposedly derived from *gaze* plus a Latin future-tense ending, and so means "I shall gaze." *Belvedere* comes through Italian from Latin *bellus* and *videre*, "beautiful view."

geodesic dome *n*, **tetrahedron** *n* A geodesic dome is a light but very sturdy domelike structure developed by R. Buckminster Fuller. From the outside the dome looks like many adjoining triangles. The dome combines the properties of a sphere and a tetrahedron (a triangular pyramid).

half story *n* Usable space beneath a sloping roof, generally with one or more dormer windows for light.

half-timber or **half-timbered** *adj* Tudor and Elizabethan builders often put plaster or other masonry between the timbers used for framing a house or other building, leaving the timbers visible. Such construction, sometimes imitated today, is called *half-timber* or *half-timbered.*

lightening hole *n* Some plates or structural parts of a ship are made with holes, which reduce weight, eliminate waste of material, and cost less, but are no less strong than a solid piece. Such holes, which may be seen also in bridges and other structures, are lightening holes.

loggia *n* A roofed gallery, open on one side, especially when it is one or more stories above ground level: <Many motels are now built with loggias on which one can circumambulate the entire building.>

ogee *n* A frequently used shape of molding that combines a partly concave and partly convex curve.

pilaster *n* A shallow columnlike projection from a wall, adding strength and often an attractive appearance.

possum-trot plan *n* The plan for a house consisting of two parts with a breezeway between.

riser *n* *Riser* has several meanings, one of which is the upright part of a stair, between two treads.

shacktown *n* Unlike many ghettos, a shacktown has no large buildings such as apartment houses but has a large number of small shacks used as dwellings: <the shacktowns of Hong Kong and Singapore>. **Shantytown** is a synonym.

smoke door *n*, **smoke pocket** *n* In the roof over the stage in a theater may be a door that can be opened in case of fire, so that smoke and flames will tend to go out there instead of into the auditorium. There may also be a smoke pocket, a metal angle at the end of the asbestos curtain, for the same purpose.

voussoir *n*, and related words. An arch made of stones or bricks consists of these basic parts: a *keystone* at the top; a number of wedge-shaped pieces called *voussoirs*, set side by side to form a gradual curve; and, at each end of the base, a differently shaped voussoir called a **springer.** (The arch may rest on a **pier,** the top part of which is called an **impost.**)

wellhole *n* Besides the obvious "hole or shaft of a well," a wellhole is the space in one or more floors that is occupied (or to be occupied) by a stairway, or the open space that serves as a center for a circular staircase.

Mastery Test

Fill in the missing letters.

1. A c______t window is one that swings open like a door.

2. A j______e window is made of several narrow strips of glass.
3. S____windows are placed side by side high on a wall.
4. A device placed inside a window to deflect air currents is an a______t.
5. A place to keep the ashes of a deceased person is a c_________m.
6. Something that can be taken apart and reassembled is described as d_________e.
7. A small structure where one may sit and enjoy a view is a g____o.
8. The open space in the center of a circular stairway is a w______e.
9. A g_____l roof has two slopes per side, the lower being steeper.
10. A s___ roof is a single roof slanting only slightly.
11. A roof shaped like an inverted V is a g____ roof.
12. The art or science of building is t_______s.
13. An empty tomb, a memorial to a person buried somewhere else, is a c______h.
14. If bricks develop a white coating of salts, they are said to e________e.
15. The upright part of a stairstep is called a r____.
16. A house consisting of two parts with a breezeway between is said to follow a p_____ t___ plan.
17. A l____a is a roofed galley open on one side.
18. Openings made to reduce weight in structural parts are called l_________ h___s.
19. One type of bay window is an o____.
20. Only the upper part of a P_______n window is rounded.
21. An e_________e is at the top of a classical column.
22. An o__e is a double-curved molding.
23. A windowed wall, most likely found in a church, is a c________y.
24. A c____l is one kind of bracket.
25. A s___t roof is used mainly for decoration.

23
IN AND OUT OF THE LABORATORY

If one were to attempt to classify on a semantic basis all the words in an unabridged dictionary, beyond question heshe would find more entries for the physical and biological sciences than for any other classification. There are, for instance, thousands of names of chemicals, thousands of names of plants, thousands of names of birds and animals. In this chapter I shall attempt to list only a few dozen scientific terms of fairly wide potential use by laypeople. Some other chapters include additional words from one science or another—for example, astronomy.

Physical Sciences

Every branch or subbranch of science develops its own vocabulary. Take, for example, **anemology,** "the study of wind," from Greek *anemos,* "wind." An **anemometer,** an instrument with revolving lightweight cups, measures wind speed; the process or act of such measurement is **anemo-**

metry. An **anemograph** records what the anemometer shows. The written record made by the anemograph is an **anemogram.** A more sophisticated instrument is the **anemetrograph,** which records wind speed, pressure, and direction.

For another example, consider **seismology,** "the study of earthquakes," from Greek *seismos,* "shock, earthquake." A **bradyseism** is a slow upward or downward movement of the earth's crust: <Bradyseisms are constant, the **seismologists** tell us.> A **seismograph** records and measures earth's tremors; so does the very sensitive **tromometer. Temblor** (also **tremblor, trembler**), from Spanish *temblar,* is a name used especially in the Southwest for an earth tremor or earthquake. In 1896 (ten years before the San Francisco earthquake) a California publication bragged. "One freshet of an Ohio river a dozen years ago took more lives than all the temblores [*sic*] in California in a century and a half have taken."

Other words from *seismos* include the adjectives **seismal, seismetic,** and **seismic,** all meaning pertaining to earthquakes; **seismisity,** the relative tendency of an area to have earthquakes; **seismological,** pertaining to the study of earthquakes; and **teleseism,** which is a faraway earth tremor recorded locally. Besides earthquakes there are **waterquakes,** vigorous shaking of the water as the result of an underwater earthquake: <The submarine was slightly jarred by what the captain said was a waterquake.> And when a large mass of ice suddenly breaks, a loud concussion accompanying a shaking of nearby ice or even land is often observed; this phenomenon is known as an **icequake.**

In the twentieth century, scientists are more clearly aware than before that no one of the sciences exists independently but that all are interrelated. Names have been invented for various combined fields, in some of which the century's major research is being done. Consider these combinations involving the study of electricity:

electrobiology biology dealing with the electricity of living things

electrochemistry study of the relationships between electricity and chemical change

electrodynamics physics concerned with the interaction of electrical currents and other physical phenomena

electrokinetics physics concerned with the motion of electricity

electromagnetism physics concerned with physical relations between electricity and magnetism

electrometallurgy metallurgy concerned with use of electricity in creation of heat or electrolytic deposition in metals

electrophysiology physiology dealing with electrical phenomena in human and other animate bodies

Other Words from Physical Sciences

catastrophism *n,* **uniformitarianism** *n,* and related words. Some geologists, called catastrophists, believe that major changes in the earth's crust have been brought about by sudden cataclysmic events that are not now occurring. Their belief is called *catastrophism.* Opposed to it is *uniformitarianism,* whose proponents hold that the geological forces are constant and can account for earth-crust changes without any supposition of cataclysms. Similarly in philosophy and religion, some persons believe that major changes in human events and outlooks have resulted from cataclysms, but others are **uniformitarians.**

critical mass *n* In atomic physics, the amount of fissionable material needed to sustain a constant chain reaction. The term has been broadened in popular use to mean the amount of anything needed to effect a given result: <Letters flooding in to Congress created what one senator called a critical mass of opposition to the bill.>

cryopedology *n,* **cryopedologic** *adj,* **pedology** *n* *Pedology* means the study or science of soil. Cryopedology is literally the study or science of cold soil, and is especially the study of soil frozen hard and the results of severe frost action. *Cryopedologic* means pertaining to permanently frozen soil (as in the Far North): <Cryopedologic studies have uncovered bacteria still alive after being frozen perhaps a million years.>

deliquesce *vi* In physics, to become liquid by absorption of moisture from the air, as some salts do. In botany, to divide into many branches.

dosimeter *n* Unlike a Geiger counter, which measures radioactivity in a given place or thing, a dosimeter measures the amount of X rays or radioactivity to which a person has been exposed.

geochronology *n,* and related words. History is interpreted mainly as the story of human activities. Geochronology, however, is the story of the earth, the chronology of past events, as revealed by geological study. It is also called **geochrony,** which refers especially to the system of geological time divisions—Archeozoic, Proterozoic, Paleozoic, Mesozoic, and Cenozoic. A specialist in geochronology is a **geochronologist,** whose studies are in **geochronological** or **geochronic** areas and who may specialize in **geochronometry,** "measurement of past time by use of the tools of geochronology," which are **geochronometric** tools. The **geochemist,** whose field is **geochemistry,** is interested in the composition of the earth's crust and the geological explanations of how it got that way. The **geophysicist,** a specialist in **geophysics,** is concerned with hydrology, magnetism, meteorology, oceanography, petrology, radioactivity, seismology, and volcanology. Public officials sometimes need to think about **geoeconomic** factors, which relate economics to geography.

geodetic surveying *n* When surveyors mark the boundaries of a little 70-foot by 150-foot suburban lot, they need not be concerned with the curvature of the earth. But to a surveyor of a large part of the earth's surface, the fact that the earth is a ball rather than a flat expanse is of great significance, since failure to account for curvature could lead to considerable error. Geodetic surveying, also called *geodetic engineering*, takes curvature into account.

geotechnics *n* This developing science has as its aim making the earth more habitable. Its practitioners concern themselves especially with the discovery, conservation, and wise use of the earth's resources of oil, coal, minerals, water, etc.

Grundriss *n* (pl. *Grundrisse*) This German word means literally "a drawing of the foundation." A Grundriss is a carefully prepared explanation or overview of the basic concerns of a science: <This freshman-level textbook in physics is the best available Grundriss for this complex subject.>

hydration *n* We seem to talk more of dehydration, "removing water from something," than of its opposite, hydration. But the addition of water in physical and chemical processes is often essential for success in manufacturing and even in the sustenance of life itself.

hydrology *n*, **hydrogeology** *n* The combining forms *hydr-* and *hydro-*, from Greek and Latin for water, are used in several hundred English words. Among them is *hydrology*, which is the study of water particularly as it exists on and in the earth and in the atmosphere, and of water movements as in precipitation and evaporation. Hydrogeology is the geological science dealing especially with the storage of water in the earth and the long-term effects of water on the surface structure of the earth—for example, as in water erosion and the movements of glaciers.

hydrosphere *n* There are two basic meanings for this word. One is the water in the form of vapor that permeates the atmosphere. The other is more inclusive: the vapor in the atmosphere plus the water in all the bodies of water on the earth's surface, plus all the water beneath the surface.

igneous *adj* From Latin *ignis*, "fire," *igneous* means pertaining to fire. Thus *igneous fusion* is fusion caused by heat, and *igneous rock* means rock like that from a volcano, formed in the cooling of molten lava.

luminiferous *adj* Anything that directly produces or

transmits light may be described as *luminiferous*—for example, fireflies, certain eels, certain chemicals: <Parnell, 1842: “The principal luminiferous constituents of coal-gas . . .”>.

macrochemistry *n*, **microchemistry** *n*, and related words. Macrochemistry is chemical study or application unaided by microscope or microanalysis; in contrast, microchemistry deals with substances or properties not ascertainable by the naked eye. Similarly, *macro-* and *micro-* team up with names of other sciences or objects of scientific interest: *economics, linguistics, physics, biotics, climate, cosmos, fauna, flora, pores, seisms,* and others.

mesosphere *n*, and related words. The portion of the atmosphere nearest the earth’s surface and extending up to about seventeen kilometers at the equator or six to eight kilometers at the poles is the **troposphere.** Above that, up to about fifty kilometers, is the **stratosphere.** Then comes what is called the *mesosphere*, “middle region,” the highest part of the “lower atmosphere.” The upper atmosphere consists of the hot **thermosphere** (up to about two hundred kilometers), and the **exosphere,** which may extend to several hundred kilometers. The three lowest levels are sometimes referred to collectively as the **homosphere,** and the ones above these three as the **heterosphere.** Atmospheric scientists also refer to an **ionosphere,** a vast area from about fifty-five kilometers up for several thousand kilometers, in which many of the atoms and molecules have become electrically charged.

micrograph *n*, and related words. *Ripley’s Believe It or Not!* sometimes featured extremely tiny writing or engraving, such as engraving the Lord’s Prayer on the head of a pin. An instrument for writing so minutely is a micrograph. The term is used also for a graphic copy of something seen through a microscope. The verb *to micrograph* also exists. One who micrographs is a **micrographer. Micrography** is study with a microscope, or the process of making micrographs. **Micrographic** means pertaining to micrographs or micrography.

Moho *n* Short for *Mohorovicic discontinuity*, after Yugoslav geologist Andrija Mohorovicic. Drill down a few miles and you'll find materials considerably different from those on the earth's crust. The Moho is the level (say, from five kilometers under deep oceans to seventy kilometers under the Andes) at which the change becomes apparent. (*Mohole* has been suggested as the name for a hole drilled to the proper depth.)

particulate *n* Tiny separate particles: <Countless radioactive particulates drifted over the countryside.>

persistence of vision *n* The phenomenon that makes it possible for pictures to "move." Actually, a motion picture is a set of still photographs, but when a series of these is shown rapidly, one image remains briefly on the retina so that the next overlaps it, and the images appear to move. This brief retention of an image is persistence of vision.

phonautograph *n* Sounds can be mechanically changed to visible form, generally as wavy lines. A machine for making such a translation is a phonautograph.

photophone *n* A device for transmitting a voice or other sound by modulation of a beam of visible or infrared light. A photoelectric cell receives the light signal, which is retranslated into sound by a receiver.

plate tectonics *n* To the geologist, tectonics is concerned with folds and faults in the earth's crust. Plate tectonics is the name of the concept that the earth's surface is divided into a number of huge "plates" whose movements are responsible for earthquakes, orogenesis (mountain making), and other changes in the earth's crust.

radon *n* A radioactive gaseous element produced by decaying radium. It is a health hazard, especially when it is emitted from rocky soil into tightly enclosed areas nearby.

receding color *n* Some colors, especially greens, blues, and violets, are called *receding colors* because they appear to be farther from the eye than others equally distant.

residual phenomena *n* When a scientist conducts an experiment, heshe can usually explain whatever happens. But sometimes one or more of the observed phenomena have no explanation known to himer. These are residual phenomena, which heshe may merely note or, if a purist, do further work to explain.

Saint Elmo's fire *n* Saint Elmo is a patron saint of sailors. The "fire" is actually a reddish (positive) or bluish (negative) electrical discharge sometimes seen on mastheads or yardarms of ships in stormy weather, and also on the wingtips of airplanes, tops of steeples or tall trees, or other prominent exposed points.

service ceiling *n* The height above which a particular airplane or type of airplane cannot climb easily and efficiently. In England and the United States the service ceiling is said to have been reached when the possible rate of climb falls below one hundred feet a minute.

shard or **sherd** *n* A piece of earthenware or other brittle material: <From sherds found at various levels, archaeologists can draw a number of conclusions about a series of civilizations inhabiting a place.> (The determination of such a sequence is called *stratigraphy* by the archaeologists, from Latin *stratum*, "layer.")

speleologist *n*, and related words. A speleologist is one who studies and explores caves. If heshe is an amateur or a hobbyist cave explorer, heshe is usually called a **spelunker.** The scientific study of caves is **speleology,** which has **speleological,** "pertaining to speleology," as its adjectival form. Two other adjectives are **spelaean** or **spelean,** "living or occurring in caves," and **speluncar,** "pertaining to caves." All these words go back to Latin *speleum* or Greek *spēlaion*, "cave."

TBS *abbr* or *n* An abbreviation of "*t*alk *b*etween *s*hips," TBS is a system of radio communication between ships or other things and persons not far apart.

Biological Sciences

As is true of the physical sciences, each branch of biological science—each twig, even—develops its own vocabulary. Greek *ichthys*, "fish," gave us **ichthyology,** "the study of fish." One who specializes in that science is, of course, an **ichthyologist,** and anyone who likes to eat fish is an **ichthyophagist** and is **ichthyophagous** (*adj*) or, if you prefer, **piscivorous** (from Latin *piscis*, "fish"). **Piscatory** or **piscatorial** means pertaining to fishing. And **pisciculture** means the raising of fish, a growing industry especially in the South, there more commonly called fish-farming.

Or note a few of the words related to **conchology,** "the study of seashells":

conchiferous producing or characterized by shells
conchiform shaped like half of a bivalve shell
conchitic made of shells; having numerous shells
conchological pertaining to conchology
conchologist a specialist in conchology
conchologize to collect and study shells, especially as an amateur

Like physical scientists, more and more biological scientists study the relationships between or among fields. The **psychobiologist,** who specializes in **psychobiology,** is interested in psychological phenomena in relation to biology in general: <As a psychobiologist he chose as a field of study the physical effects of long-sustained fear or other emotions. Alternatively he could have studied the psychological effects of sustained illness or other biological problems.> Combinations of *biology* (from Greek *bios*, "life") are reflected in these self-defining words, which may exist in nounal, adjectival, or adverbial forms:

biochemical	**biogenetic**	**biophysics**
bioclimatic	**biogeographic (-al)**	**biosociological**
bio-ecology	**biomathematics**	**biostatistics**
bio-engineering	**biometeorological**	**biotechnical**

Other Words from Biological Sciences

apian *adj*, and related words. The debt owed by people to bees for food and pollination and as symbols of industry is considerable. Here are some of the words with *api-* (Latin *apis*, "bee") that acknowledge the debt:

apian pertaining to bees
apiarian pertaining to beekeeping or bees
apiary a place for keeping bees, especially a number of hives
apiculture beekeeping, especially when scientific and large scale. **apicultural** (*adj*)
apiology scientific study of honeybees
apivorous bee-eating: <Some birds are apivorous.>

autogenous *adj* Something that occurs or is produced without outside help can be described as autogenous, "self-generating": <the autogenous healing of a wound to which no medication is applied> <an autogenous change in a plant>.

aviary *n,* and related words. *Avis* is Latin for bird and has several well-known English offspring, such as *aviation.* A little less well known are *aviary,* "a place where many birds are kept," **avicide,** "the killing of birds," and **aviculture,** "the raising of wild birds in captivity," which has the adjectival form **avicultural.** <This zoo has an aviary with eight hundred birds.> <The senseless slaughter of the passenger pigeon is the best-known example of avicide.> <His avicultural activities consist of raising thousands of pheasant and quail.>

cryonics *n* Deep-freezing human or other bodies to be held for possible revival at a later date, perhaps for cure of an illness not now treatable.

cytology *n,* and related words. Cytology is the scientific study of cells. A person specializing in such study is a **cytologist.** The adjective may be either **cytological** or **cytologic.**

emersal *adj,* **demersal** *adj* If you hold a piece of lightweight wood under water and then release it, it becomes emersal, "rising to the top." It is also emersal in a different sense when it floats on the surface. <Emersal insect eggs float on water; demersal eggs, in contrast, stay on the bottom.>

herpetology *n* The study of reptiles and amphibians. The word goes back to a Greek verb for to creep.

heterosis *n* Also called hybrid vigor. <Harry L. Shapiro,

1974: "We know from many animal and plant experiments that when . . . inbred strains are crossed, they often produce hybrids taller and more vigorous than either parent. This is known as hybrid vigor, or heterosis.">

idioadaptation *n* *Idio-*, from Greek, means personal, one's own. In the course of evolution, each type of organism makes its own adaptations to its environment and at the same time loses characteristics it no longer needs. This slow process is idioadaptation, as exemplified in the breathing process of mammals, which differs from that of fish. By extension, the word may be used of shorter processes: <Harriet's idioadaptation to prison life reduced her former reticence and shyness.>

macerate *vi, vt* A body denied food and liquid for a considerable time withers, or macerates. Somewhat differently, a grain soaked in water macerates—that is, "softens." Maceration is also a process in perfume making: it involves extraction of fragrant oils by soaking fresh flowers in hot oil.

malacology *n* The branch of zoology concerned with mollusks—snails, mussels, oysters, etc. It is distinguished from conchology, which deals with shells rather than with their inhabitants.

mulm *n* If you have an aquarium, you note that organic sediment gradually accumulates at the bottom. This is mulm.

ophidian *adj,* and related words. Greek *ophis* means snake. *Ophidian* meaks snakelike: <ophidian eyes>. **Ophiolatry** or **ophism** is worship of snakes, and **ophiology** is the study of snakes. **Ophiophagous** means snake-eating.

pheromone *n* A chemical substance that is released by an animal and is usually attractive to the opposite sex. The word is based on a Greek word for "bring" and the last part of *hormone:* <Ms. Kline is experimenting with synthetic pheromones to lure mosquitoes into traps.>

spongiology or **spongology** *n* The scientific study of sponges.

subfossil *n* A subfossil isn't old enough to be a fossil, yet it is not recent. It has lost fat, protein, and the like but has not yet replaced these with minerals.

teratology *n,* **teras** *n* The creation of stories centered on monsters, or a collection of such stories, is teratology: <*King Kong* is one of the most famous cinematic examples of teratology.> Scientists use the word to refer to the study of greatly abnormal growth or malformation in an organism: <Dr. Rudolf specializes in elephantiasis and other varieties of teratology.> Organisms, including fetuses, that are grossly malformed are called *terata* (singular *teras*).

trichotomy *n,* **polychotomy** *n* *Dichotomy,* "a dividing into two parts," is a well-known word. *Trichotomy,* obviously, means dividing into three parts, and *polychotomy* into several or many parts (especially into divisions, subdivisions, subsubdivisions).

tropism *n,* and related words. *Tropism* is the name given to either an involuntary affinity for a stimulus or a dislike of it: <*Tropism* often refers to being attracted to or being repelled by something.> *Thermo,* referring to heat, combines with *tropism* in **thermotropism:** <Plants that like warm places and those that prefer cold ones both illustrate thermotropism.> **Neurotropism** ordinarily refers only to an affinity for nerve tissue: <Some viruses illustrate neurotropism, seeking out nerve fibers on which to settle.> (*Heliotropism* and *phototropism* are discussed on page 316.)

venter *n* A blunt and sometimes legalistic word for mother: <He fathered a girl by one venter, a boy by another, and twin girls by a third.>

Mastery Test

Choose the best completion for each sentence.

________________ 1. The study of tornadoes would most likely be included under (catastrophism, cryopedology, anemology, geotechnics).

______________ 2. The vapor that permeates the atmosphere is the (mesosphere, exosphere, ionosphere, hydrosphere).

______________ 3. A device for transmitting sound as light is a (photophone, micrograph, halation, venter).

______________ 4. Probably the best guide to a cave would be a(n) (conchologist, ichthyologist, speleologist, herpetologist).

______________ 5. The best place to keep bees is in a(n) (apiary, aviary, mulm, Grundriss).

______________ 6. If you make your living by raising pheasants, your work is in (cytology, malacology, apiology, aviculture).

______________ 7. A plant that shrinks away from heat illustrates (thermotropism, igneous fusion, hydration, Saint Elmo's fire).

______________ 8. Something made of shells can be described as (spelean, apian, demersal, conchitic).

______________ 9. The tendency for hybrids to be more vigorous than inbred strains is known as (idioadaptation, teratology, macroscian, heterosis).

______________ 10. If you wanted to measure the lifting power of a butterfly's wings, you would hunt up an expert in (biophysics, electrokinetics, apiology, microchemistry).

______________ 11. A good example of a receding color is (red, yellow, brown, green).

______________ 12. If you wanted to study the

Moho, your major tool would have to be (a hammer, pliers, a drill, an extra-long wrench).

__________ 13. Good evidence of persistence of vision is provided by (motion pictures, halos, moonlight, television commercials).

__________ 14. If you are keenly interested in shards, you are probably a(n) (housewife, archaeologist, gardener, astronomer).

__________ 15. If something is emersal, it is (leaping from the water, staying at the bottom of water, rising to the top of water, likely to drown).

__________ 16. If a body macerates, it (becomes thin, is badly cut, grows, freezes).

__________ 17. A subfossil (can never become a fossil, is inferior to a fossil, is found under a fossil, is probably going to become a fossil).

__________ 18. A pheromone is (a growth hormone, an attractor of the opposite sex, useful in cryonics).

__________ 19. With an anemometer you could measure (anemones, a Moho, the speed of light, wind velocity).

__________ 20. Geodetic surveying takes into account (the geology of the area, the curvature of the earth, geography, solid geometry).

24
SHAPED LIKE A HAND, SHAPED LIKE A HEART

Geometers have scores of words to designate various regular shapes. An icosahedron, for example, is a solid figure with twenty faces, but I always have trouble remembering the difference between two other geometers' words, *rhombus* and *rhomboid.* Botanists, to indicate the approximate shapes of plant parts, use perhaps as many different shape-words as geometers do. In this chapter, though, I'll be dealing with a variety of shapes, most of them less precise than those of the geometer and less technical than those of the botanist.

For instance, consider the shapes that people come in. Some anatomists say that there are three basic types of human beings as classified by bodily structure: the **ectomorph,** who is of slender build, lightly muscled, and sometimes described as **asthenic;** the **endomorph,** who is short, broad, and powerful and is sometimes labeled **pyknik;** and the **mesomorph,** who has a large chest, rather heavy body, and sturdy muscles, and is commonly called *athletic.* A look at people walking along the street or on the beach will show that many persons do not fit neatly into any of the categories, but enough do to make the classification fairly useful. <I was an ectomorph when I was a boy, then I became something like a mesomorph, but now I bulge enough in the middle that I don't know what I am.>

Habitus, also known as **constitutional type,** comes from Latin for appearance, condition, or character. In English it refers to bodily build in connection with a predisposition to physical disorders. Thus a very thin person may have a tubercular habitus, a very fat one a habitus for cardiac problems.

A human being is **bifurcate. Furcate** means forked, fork-shaped, branching out like a fork. If there are two prongs (for example, a person's legs or the prongs of a tuning fork), the object is bifurcate. **Bifurcal** is a rarer form. *Bifurcate* may also be used as a verb meaning to divide (a physical thing) into two branches: <The stream bifurcates here.> <To bifurcate such a hard metal rod will be difficult.> The noun **bifurcation** has several related meanings: separation into two branches, the point of such separation, or either one of the two prongs or branches in something bifurcate. There's also an adjective **trifurcate,** "three-pronged."

Topiary refers not to the shape of people but to something that some people do: training, trimming, or forming shrubbery or small trees into various shapes such as animals, birds, or abstract geometrical designs. The word may be used as an adjective or a noun: <Topiary art delights many Britishers.> <Would you like to see our topiaries?>

Other Shapely Words

arcuate *adj* Bent or curved in the form of a bow: <an arcuate shape> <The brace, the printer's mark { }, is arcuate.>

biform *adj* The mythological centaur was biform: He had the body and legs of a horse and the trunk, arms, and head of a man. Greek and Roman gods were also biform (or multiform) in another sense: Each could appear as someone besides himerself, as Zeus carried off the beauteous Europa while disguised as a bull. More mundanely, certain crystals and chemicals are biform, as are creatures that share characteristics of both plant and animal life, and also some intangible things such as arguments or cowardice.

claviform *adj* Latin *clava* means club, and *claviform* means club-shaped: <The upper section of an exclamation mark is claviform.>

cordate or **cordiform** *adj* Latin *cor*, "heart," which gives us *cordial, accord, courage*, and other words that pertain literally or figuratively to the heart, is also the source of *cordate* and *cordiform*, both of which mean heart-shaped: <Valentines are traditionally cordate.>

cruciform *adj* Shaped like a cross.

cuneiform *adj* Wedge-shaped. Some of the bones in the human foot are cuneiform. Linguists use the term chiefly to describe an ancient system of writing in which each character was in the shape of several connected wedges, which could easily be marked in soft clay by the use of a stylus.

decussate *adj, vi, vt* The first part of this word is from Latin *decem*, "ten," which as a numeral was written X. To decussate something (accent on the first syllable for the verb) is to cut or divide it in the shape of an X. Lines that cross each other so as to make an X are also said to decussate. The adjective *decussate* (accent on the second syllable) means X-shaped, although in botany it describes an arrangement of leaves on a stalk on which each pair of leaves is at right angles to the pair above or below.

deltoid *n, adj* The large triangular muscle that enables you to raise your arm from your side. The word is based on the shape of the Greek letter Δ (delta). The adjective *deltoid* or *deltoidal* means "delta-shaped": <Some leaves are approximately deltoidal.>

dolioform *adj* In Latin a *dolium* was a large jar, cask, or barrel. In English something (or someone) shaped like a barrel may be described as *dolioform*.

enfilade *n* In French *enfilade* refers to a row of something (from a verb meaning to thread). The English word is used primarily to refer to a straight line of troops whose position makes them subject to being raked lengthwise by gunfire; it is also the fire so directed. Additionally, though, *enfilade* may refer to other things arranged in a straight line, like rooms along a hotel corridor.

fictile *adj* From a Latin verb meaning to shape, *fictile* means shaped from clay or other soft material, or capable of being shaped. By extension, anything capable of being molded, such as public opinion, may be described as fictile: <The justification of a political campaign is the belief that people are fictile.>

full orbed *adj* Completely round, or having the appearance of complete roundness: <a full-orbed beet weighing three pounds> <the moon not yet full-orbed>.

-gon A combining form, Greek for "angled." It most often appears in *pentagon*, "a figure with five angles," *hexagon* (six), *heptagon* (seven), *octagon* (eight), *nonagon* (nine), *decagon* (ten), *hendecagon* (eleven), and *duodecagon* (twelve).

hexagram *n* Draw a regular hexagon. Then using each of the six sides in turn as a base, draw six equilateral triangles outside the hexagon. The result will be a symmetrical six-pointed star, called a *hexagram*. It will also be two interlocking larger equilateral triangles—the shape of the Star of David.

incurvate *vt*, **excurvate** *vt* To incurvate is to cause to curve inward, and to excurvate is to cause to curve outward. Generally used as a past participle: <an incurvated (or excurvated) line>.

napiform *adj* *Napiform* comes from Latin *napus*, "turnip," and means turnip-shaped.

obrotund or obround *adj* If you take a soft ball or other spherical object and press down on it so that the top and bottom are somewhat flattened, the resulting shape is obrotund or obround.

ostreiform *adj*, **ostreophagous** *adj* *Ostreiform* means shaped like an oyster: <The ostreiform mushrooms used in soup>. (Latin *ostre-*, "oyster," the source of this word, is also the source of *ostreophagous*, "oyster-eating": <ostreophagous jellyfish>.)

palmate *adj* Shaped like the human hand with fingers spread: <palmate leaves of this maple tree>.

patulous *adj* Something is patulous if it is spread wide from a center: <the patulous branches of the ancient oak>.

quincunx *n* A quincunx may be an arrangement of five objects, one at each of four corners and one in the middle, or an arrangement of any number of objects in squares or rectangles with one in the middle of each.

whorl *n* A circular, "spinning" shape, like that of certain leaves and shells. One of the turns of a spiral shell (ammonite, chambered nautilus, or others) may also be called a whorl.

Mastery Test

Supply the missing letters.

1. a shape like that of the five-side on a die — q______x
2. shaped like a turnip — n______m
3. a slender, unmuscular person — e_______h
4. having three prongs — t________e
5. shaped like a club — c_______m
6. to cut or divide in the shape of an X — d_______e
7. the shape of the Star of David — h______m
8. shaped like an oyster — o________m
9. shaped like a heart — c_____e
10. shaped like a sphere flattened at top and bottom — o_______d
11. shaped like the human hand with fingers stretched out — p_____e
12. short and powerful in appearance — p____k
13. to split into two branches — b_______e
14. one with an athletic body — m_______h
15. pertaining to shaping of bushes — t_____y
16. curved like a bow — a_____e

17. able to appear in two shapes b____m
18. shaped like a wedge c_______m
19. shaped like a barrel d_______m
20. to make (something) curve outward e_______e
21. shaped like a triangle d_____d
22. a twelve-sided figure d________n
23. shaped like a cross c_______m
24. a nine-sided figure n_____n
25. a circular, “spinning” shape w___l

25
ON THE MOVE

A high-school class once thought of over four hundred substitutes for *go.* Another class found over five hundred substitutes for *say.* These numbers may seem less surprising if we recall that moving and talking are occupations almost everyone engages in during nearly every waking hour.

If we were to try, like the first class, to find substitutes for *go,* we would probably come up quickly with a hundred or so like *walk, saunter, meander, stampede,* and so on, and with greater effort (or a thesaurus) arrive at *peragrate, nomadize, debouch,* and others. In this chapter, however, I'll be talking about some fifty or sixty verbs, nouns, adjectives, and adverbs that I like and that refer in one way or another to motion (or its lack) but that do not simply mean go. So few of these are closely related that I'll start at once on an alphabetical list.

ablate *vi, vt,* **ablation** *n Ablate* means in its Latin ancestor "to carry from." It is used in the sense of to remove, especially by stealing, cutting, eroding, melting, or evaporating. *Ablation,* the noun, often refers to removing by surgery, but may mean other sorts of removal: <Hakluyt's *Voyages,* 1589: "Marchants have sustained sundry damages and ablations of their goods.">

adamantine *adj* If you ever need a word meaning unyielding or not movable, but more visual and forceful, try *adamantine,* which goes back to Greek for steel or diamond and thus suggests extreme hardness, solidity, impenetrability: <a man of adamantine resolve>.

astatic *adj,* and related words. One meaning of *static* is stable, stationary, unmoving. *Astatic* is its opposite, meaning not stable or steady: <as astatic as a drop of mercury being carried in a dish by a shivering child>. A corresponding verb, **astatize,** means to make astatic. A noun, **astasia,** is a word sometimes used by doctors to mean lack of muscular coordination while standing: <Astasia is often a symptom of intoxication.>

autocide *n* Suicide by crashing the vehicle one is driving.

bogue *vi* A dialect word with no precise counterpart in standard English (*putter* may come closest), *bogue* refers to slow, aimless movement: <Grandma loves to bogue around her garden even in winter.>

brawn drain *n* *Brain drain,* widely known, is the movement of well-educated people from a country. Less well known is *brawn drain,* the emigration of needed strong blue-collar workers.

career *vi, vt* Although the noun *career* is well known, the verb is less familiar. It is primarily a term in horsemanship, but is sometimes extended to the driving of automobiles or other vehicles. It may mean to make a short gallop, to turn from side to side while running, to go in a reckless manner, or to cause a horse to gallop recklessly. <The horse careered viciously.> <He careered the car around a sharp curve, skidding the rear end as he did so.>

circumambient *adj,* **circumfluent** *adj* Both words have the meaning of moving around (something), but purists like to draw a distinction on the basis of etymologies: *-ambient* deriving from Latin *ambire,* "to go around," and *-fluent* from *fluere,* "to flow." Therefore anything that can flow around like a fluid is described as *circumfluent,* but anything that is more solid is *circumambient:* <a piece of coal that was bathed in circumfluent acid> <fearful of the circumambient pack of wild dogs>.

fillip *n, vt* If you curl your forefinger against the ball of your thumb and release it vigorously, the resulting light blow is a fillip. By extension, any short, sharp blow is a fillip. A small, decorative addition is also called a fillip: <an extra fillip in the plans for the convention>. Such an addition may be slightly exciting, so *fillip* also means a small added element that tends to excite: <Her sensational costume provided a fillip to the envy of everyone at the costume ball.> The word may be used as a verb in senses approximating those of all these nounal definitions.

flat-hat *vi,* **flat-hatter** *n* To flat-hat is to fly recklessly low in an airplane; also called to *buzz.* The verb comes from an alleged incident in which a man's hat was smashed by a low-flying plane—while the man was wearing it. A flier who flat-hats is called, of course, a *flat-hatter.*

frenetic *adj* Pertaining to frantic, frenzied movements. The twin words (doublets) *frantic* and *frenetic* came to us from Greek through Latin, French, and Middle English and at one time meant "delirious" or "insane."

galumph *vi* Invented by Lewis Carroll (remember *Alice in Wonderland*) by blending *gallop* and *triumphant.* To galumph is to move or march clumsily and heavily.

gambol *vi, n* There's a considerable difference between *gamble* and *gambol.* The latter means to dance or frisk about in joyous fashion, or, as a noun, lively physical behavior.

glent *vi* *Glenten* was a Middle English verb meaning to move quickly in an oblique direction. As *glent,* it still exists with that meaning in some British dialects, and has added the meanings to strike obliquely and then bounce off (like a pebble thrown against a tree) and to look sideways. It is a little hard to understand why this valuable verb has largely died out; it deserves reviving.

Although *glance* has similar meanings, it can be ambiguous because of its more common meaning "to look at quickly."

gracile *adj,* **lissome** *adj,* and related words. A person who combines slenderness with grace of movement may be described as *gracile.* The noun form is **gracility,** "the gracefulness of a slender person." *Lissome* and **lissomeness** are similar in meaning to *gracile* and *gracility,* since only a slender person is so described, but refer more to limberness than to grace. It is, of course, possible to be both gracile and lissome.

highroad *n* The highroad is the easiest way, the best way—whether literal or figurative: <on the highroad to London> <the highroad to financial independence>. (In England, *High Street* is generally equivalent to American *Main Street.*)

hither-and-thither *vi* To move more or less at random, usually with quick movements: <Rabbit, in *Winnie-the-Pooh,* does a lot of hither-and-thithering.>

homeostasis *n,* **homeostatic** *adj* *Homeostasis* is literally "the same condition." In general, it refers to remaining essentially the same regardless of external circumstances. It is illustrated in the tendency of the human body to keep a temperature of close to 98.6 degrees Fahrenheit even when the outdoor thermometer registers 0 degrees or 100 degrees, in the psychological ability to stay "sane" even when one is wrenched by grief, or in the tendency for family units to stay together in times of stress. (Note that all these are tendencies, not constants.) *Homeostatic* means pertaining to or characterized by homeostasis: <Most lower animals are even more predictable than man, for they are ruled even more than he by their being homeostatic.>

hurrah's nest or **hoorah's nest** or **hooraw's nest** *n* An expressive term for hubbub, mess, disorder. To my mind it brings a picture of people milling around, shouting, and quarreling, utterly confused and disorganized.

hysteresis *n* Greek *hysterein* means to come late, to be behind. *Hysteresis* refers to the lag between cause and effect. Few things occur instantaneously after a triggering impulse; there is a well-known hysteresis, for example, between educational research and its classroom application. Less noticeable are such hystereses as the physical changes involved in expansion and contraction (which do not occur immediately after touching with heat or cold). <the unavoidable hysteresis between seeing a child on the road and applying the brake> <Hysteresis must always be a concern of physicists working within close tolerance.>

illocal *adj* Anything not restricted to a particular place may be described as illocal: <Cases of diphtheria had become illocal; some were reported from two counties away.>

ingravescence *n*, **ingravescent** *adj* When someone says that the plight of the economy, education, or something else keeps getting worse and worse, heshe is talking about ingravescence, "a worsening, an increase in severity." The adjective *ingravescent* means becoming more severe.

invection *n* The act of carrying in—bringing in something not normally present: <the invection of cold air through the broken window>.

jeepable *adj* Shortly after jeeps were introduced to the army in World War II, military maps began to appear with some roads or trails marked *jeepable,* to indicate that they could be traversed by jeeps but not by less sturdy vehicles or those without four-wheel drive.

labefaction *n* Latin *labare* means to totter, and *facere* to make. Labefaction is, then, causing to totter, weakening, undermining, or overthrowing, and is used especially with reference to the deterioration of moral principles or the downfall of an established order. Thus the growth of social permissiveness necessarily involves the labefaction of older values and beliefs. The verb to *labefy,* "to cause to totter," is labeled obsolete but seems useful enough to be resuscitated.

levant *vi,* **levanter** *n* Although *levant* (or *Levant*) has several meanings, a little-known one is to abscond after failing to pay a debt or a bet: <After falling in debt to his bookie, he levanted.> A levanter, obviously, is one who levants.

limberly *adv* For some reason *limberly* appears to be used much less often than its companion, the adjective *limber*, yet it should be equally useful: <Although he's in his fifties, he plays handball vigorously and limberly.>

live parking *n* If you ever see a sign "Live Parking Only," interpret it to mean that parking is permitted only if a driver remains within the vehicle.

logily *adv* In a logy manner, sluggishly, lazily, dully, listlessly.

lollop *vi* If you ever need a verb to describe a bounding, bobbing motion, try *lollop:* <A huge jackrabbit lolloped across the field.>

manback *adv, n* Burdens may be transported on horseback, muleback, elephantback, or camelback, but no doubt much earlier were carried on manback, as many still are. The human back, as a carrier of burdens, is manback. The word may also be used adverbially: <ore carried manback from deep in the mine>.

maunder *vi* To maunder is to move or speak slowly, uncertainly, erratically. Some elderly people maunder about their neighborhoods on foot; a person maunders if hiser speech is disconnected or if heshe does not organize what heshe says.

microlevel *vt* To bring an elevator to an almost exact level.

misguggle *vt* A Scottish expression based on *guggle* or *gruggle,* "to crumple, rumple." One misguggles if heshe handles something or someone awkwardly or roughly: <Don't misguggle the eggs, lad.>

noctambulous *adj,* and related words. A noctambulous person walks at night (either while awake or asleep; a *somnambulist* is a sleepwalker). Walking at night is **noctambulation** and is done by a noctambulist. **Noctivagant,** an adjective, means night-wandering; the noun form is **noctivagation,** for the act of wandering at night, or **noctivagator,** for one who performs such an act.

onychophagy *n* If you ever need a highfalutin name for nail-biting, try *onychophagy.*

paseo *n* From Spanish *pasear,* "to walk," a paseo is a leisurely walk or a short, unpressured excursion: <a paseo in the park with his two Irish setters>. It may also be a public boulevard or promenade: <a shady paseo>. (A *paseo de cuadrillas* is the formalized entrance march of bullfighters.)

passe-passe *n* A well-executed feat in juggling, such as keeping several plates passing one another in the air, is a passe-passe. By extension, any other skillfully handled activity involving motion of several objects may be a passe-passe: <the well-coordinated passe-passe of ships in the huge port>.

revenant *adj, n* Although Thomas Wolfe said "You can't go home again," a revenant is a person who does just that. Heshe returns, although perhaps in the form of a ghost, to a place heshe formerly knew. As an adjective, *revenant* means coming back: <a revenant spirit> <revenant impressions of childhood fear and hate>.

rusticate *vi, vt,* and related words. A rustic is one who lives in the country; the term is often used pejoratively to indicate a dull, cloddish person. To rusticate is to go temporarily or permanently to live in the country; it may also mean to compel someone to live in the country, or to suspend (a student) from school or college. **Rustication,** the noun-form of *rusticate,* perhaps most often means retirement to the country. A **rusticism,** like a ruralism, is an expression associated with country-dwellers, but *rusticism* carries uncomplimentary connotations not generally shared by *ruralism.* **Rusticity** is lack of grace or refinement in manners or speech. To **rusticize** is to give a rustic appearance to something or someone: <He mussed his hair and put on a torn blue jacket in a feeble attempt to rusticize himself.>

saltatory *adj* In general something is saltatory if it proceeds by leaps rather than by smooth progression: <Grasshoppers are saltatory insects.> <saltatory discussion> <ideas advanced in saltatory fashion in a brainstorming session>. *Saltatory* is also used to mean pertaining to dancing, especially dancing that involves leaping: <proficient in the saltatory art>.

sashay *vi* To *chassé* is to take a gliding dance step. *Sashay,* an anglicized form, may mean chassé, to walk (especially in a gliding manner), to move in a showy way, or to move diagonally or sideways.

squawk sheet *n* Airline or government pilots may be asked to write a brief report indicating things needing inspection or correction in a plane they have just finished flying. Such a report, which may be on a special form, is a squawk sheet. (All car rental agencies might well ask their customers to fill out squawk sheets to call attention to repairs that should be made for safety.)

switchback *n* In mountainous country, since most vehicles (or pedestrians) could not climb in a steep, straight line, roads and trails are built to zigzag upward. Such winding ascents are switchbacks.

traipse *vi, vt* Dictionaries still label this word "informal," but the late Rudolf Flesch argued that this four-hundred-year-old word should not be kept out of formal company just because it means "to meander in an unbusinesslike manner."

volitate *vi* To fly aimlessly here and there: <A tiger swallowtail volitated among the flowers.>

wester *vi* To move toward the west: <the westering pioneers>. To shift or veer toward the west: <The weather vane westered.> (*Webster 3* lists corresponding verbs *norther* and *souther* "used chiefly of the wind," but no *easter.*)

wimple *vi, vt* To wimple (something) is to cause to ripple, or to cover as with a veil: <A light breeze wimpled the wheat.> <some gauzy stuff wimpling her breasts>. Intransitively, to wimple is to lie in folds, or to ripple: <wimpled cloth> <the wimpling water of the pond>.

Mastery Test

Mark each statement *true* (T) or *false* (F).

___ 1. Butterflies apparently *volitate* more than honeybees do.

___ 2. Something that has been *ablated* is no longer in its original place.
___ 3. *Homeostatic* refers to static such as you may hear on your home radio.
___ 4. Both a *gracile* girl and a *lissome* girl are slender.
___ 5. A tropical bird called a *hurrah* lives in a *hurrah's nest.*
___ 6. *Hysteresis* is an especially severe attack of hysterics.
___ 7. To *lollop* is to move in a slow, lumbering fashion.
___ 8. To *maunder* is to move in a slow, uncertain fashion.
___ 9. In an old-fashioned vaudeville show you might have seen some *passe-passes.*
___ 10. A *noctambulous* animal sleeps all night.
___ 11. Long grass sometimes *wimples* on a windy day.
___ 12. A *galumph* is a light, graceful dance.
___ 13. A person who sways when heshe stands is exhibiting *astasia.*
___ 14. A reference to a *circumfluent* forest or even to *circumfluent* birds is etymologically inaccurate.
___ 15. A bullet striking a metal shield may *glent.*
___ 16. *Homeostasis* refers to unchanging conditions.
___ 17. It is sensible to wager with or lend money to a known *levanter.*
___ 18. *Labefaction* is the act of propping up something weak.
___ 19. *Microlevel* is a small level used in tight spots by carpenters.
___ 20. A ghost revisiting hiser former surroundings is a *revenant.*
___ 21. To *traipse* is to walk in an unbusinesslike manner.
___ 22. *Frenetic* is closely related to *frantic.*
___ 23. *Autocide* is a form of suicide.
___ 24. *Brawn drain* means weakening of a human body.
___ 25. Buying a lottery ticket is a form of *gamboling.*

26
HOW BIG? HOW FAR? HOW MUCH? HOW . . .

Human beings might still be cave dwellers if they had not learned to measure and quantify. A carpenter can't build a house if heshe has no ruler and square. Every machine except the least sophisticated, every manufactured product depends on measurement. Medical diagnosis and treatment could not exist without it. Schools (if there could be schools without measurement) could not determine a child's needs or the extent of hiser accomplishment.

Measurement devices range from the simple, like the cup or tablespoon used by the cook or the foot ruler used by the student, to the intricate hardware sent on space missions at a cost of millions of dollars. The words used vary from informal, subjective estimates to those representing scientifically accurate measurement—for example, from **drinky,** "partly intoxicated," <drinky but not drunk> to **intoximeter** (popularly known as *drunkometer* or *breathalyzer*), which lets a precise amount of breath pass through a solution of potassium dichromate and sulfuric acid and results in a color density change that shows just what proportion of alcohol is in the subject's breath. Some huge industries—IBM, for example—exist mainly to manufacture machines that can count and measure and then manipulate the basic counts and measurements.

Dictionary entries by the hundreds reflect the importance of measurement in our lives. There are few dictionary pages that do not have, for example, any words with ***-meter*** or ***-graph*** as a component. I had difficulty, when preparing this chapter, in selecting which of many possible words to include; I finally settled on a rather broadly representative list that necessarily omits many other words of no less interest.

A number of measuring devices are related to people's health and well-being. Sometimes before a child is born, a physician will measure its head to determine whether delivery will be difficult because of its size. Such measurement, accomplished with a **cephalometer,** is called **cephalometry,** a term used also for measuring heads for other purposes—for example, to compare head sizes of members of different races, sexes, etc.

In general a **manometer** is a device that measures pressure; a barometer is a familiar type. In your doctor's hands a manometer is a **sphygmomanometer,** the gadget that heshe wraps around your arm, inflates, and reads so that heshe can tell how high or low your blood pressure is. Hiser **sphygmometer** measures the strength of your pulse. (*Sphygmo-* means pulse.)

Hemometer is the inclusive name for a number of instruments individualized to identify and measure a constituent of blood such as hemoglobin. An **inspirometer,** used in checking lungs, measures the amount of air the patient can inhale. **Tactometer** sounds like something that measures tact, but actually it measures the sharpness of one's sense of touch.

If a hedonist wants to know how much pleasure heshe is receiving from something, a device called a **hedonometer** supposedly could be used. The word is a humorous one, though, since no such machine exists (although the rate of pulse and of breathing and the measurement of certain other physical indicators might provide clues to the amount of enjoyment of certain activities).

People often need to know distances, heights, and depths, and in consequence have originated a number of instruments to provide such information. A **waywiser** (from Dutch *wegwijzer*, "one that shows the way") is an odometer, pedometer, or other device that shows how far one has traveled. (Many people say *speedometer* when they mean **odometer.** The speedometer shows speed, but it is the odometer that shows how many miles or kilometers a vehicle has traveled.) A **chartometer** or an **opisometer** is a handy little gadget to enable you to estimate the mileage of a trip. It consists of a little wheel that can be pushed along the highway lines of a map to show the approximate mileage between two points.

An **elevation meter** may be attached to a vehicle and pulled along a hilly road, where it registers changes in elevation. A **hypsometer** is any instrument for determining heights or elevations; it may, for instance, be a triangulation device for ascertaining heights of trees, or it may be an apparatus for finding the height of a mountain by checking the boiling point of water.

If you ever wonder how steep a hill is or what is the degree of slope or inclination of anything else, you need a **clinometer** to tell you. It's any of a number of kinds of instruments that surveyors, firers of large guns, and many other people find indispensable. A **tachymeter** (not to be confused with *tachometer*, which measures speed of rotation) is an instrument used by surveyors and others who need to know how far away or how high a distant object is. A **telemeter** also measures the distance of something; a range-finder, for instance, is a telemeter. Additionally, a telemeter may be a rocket-based instrument that records various observations (for example, speed, or amount of radiation) and radios them to a station on Earth.

One way to measure the depth of the ocean is to use an **echograph,** an instrument that does its job by automatic recording of the time required for an echo to bounce back from the ocean floor. A **bathometer** doesn't usually measure the water in a bathtub, although theoretically it could, since like the echograph it is a device for measuring the depth of water. *Bathus* is Greek for deep; *bathos*, for depth. It appears in such other words as **bathos,** "low, commonplace writing," **bathymetry,** "the measurement of depths as with a bathometer," **bathygram,** "a record from sonic instruments," **bathythermograph,** "an instrument that measures temperature as well as depth," and **bathyscaphe,** "a submersible ship used for deep-sea exploration."

Consumers profit from tests given products before marketing. Some universities have materials-testing laboratories where anything from the tensile strength of cloth to the durability of a bridge girder can be tested. A **fadeometer** (from a trademarked name, Fade-Ometer) uses a carbon arc lamp that approximates the characteristics of sunlight and measures the amount of fading in cloth, upholstery, etc., in a given period of time. A **launderometer** may test color-fastness during laundering, or may compare the cleansing effectiveness of various soaps and detergents.

It is often useful to know how flexible a piece of metal, plastic, rubber, or cloth is, and how well the flexibility is retained. The instrument for making such a measurement is a **flexometer.** Somewhat similar is the **elastometer,** which measures the amount of elasticity. Research hospitals also use elastometers for measuring the elasticity of body tissues, which tends to decline because of age or limited use.

One frequently hears "The road is rough!" But how rough? An instrument called, rather obviously, a **roughometer** has been designed to measure roughness of a road surface; it is used by some highway departments to help determine priorities in road repair work.

Manufacturers and consumers alike are much interested in the colors of paints, cloth, plastic, etc. A branch of optics dealing with color, especially hue and saturation, is called **chromatics:** <Before the twentieth century, chromatics was more intuitive and individual than scientific.> The science of determining or measuring colors is **colorimetry.** Its instruments include **colorimeters** and **spectrophotometers.** A **weatherometer** measures how well paints or other finishes will withstand the ravages of weather.

Pluviometry means measurement of rainfall. (**Pluviometer** is a fancy name for rain gauge.) A **hyetograph** is a chart of average annual rainfall. A **hyetometrograph** is a rain gauge that automatically records the amount of rainfall. A **hythergraph** records both rainfall and temperature.

A **thermograph** is a thermometer that keeps a record of temperature over a given period: <The thermograph consisted of a cylinder covered with graph paper; as clockwork slowly turned the cylinder, a pen marked the temperature on the paper.> A **cryometer** measures coldness, especially extremely low temperatures like those near **absolute zero** (−273.15 degrees Centigrade or −459.67 degrees Fahrenheit).

Hygro- is a standard combining form in the International Scientific Vocabulary (ISV) and means humidity, moisture. It appears in various technical terms such as **hygroexpansivity,** "expansivity attributable to humidity," and the fairly familiar **hygrometer,** "any instrument that measures relative humidity." A **hygrograph** is an instrument that automatically keeps a record of atmospheric humidity, and is of value not only to the scientist but also to workers in factories where unvarying humidity is required.

Some Miscellaneous Measures

barodynamics *n,* and related words. Greek *baros,* "weight," is most familiar to us in *barometer,* an instrument that measures the weight or the pressure of the atmosphere at a given time; a self-registering barometer is a **barograph,** and the written record is a **barogram.** In a weather station sometime you may see a **barothermohygrograph,** an instrument that records automatically the pressure, temperature, and moisture of the atmosphere. *Barodynamics* refers to mechanical characteristics of large, heavy structures like bridges or dams that may collapse on account of their weight and the pressures put on them.

chronograph *n,* and related words. Although *chronograph* is sometimes used loosely as a synonym for *watch* or *clock,* experts in the measurement of time usually restrict it to more sophisticated instruments, such as a recording device for reporting precise times of occurrence of astronomical and other events or for measuring elapsed time in projectile flight. The record made by such a device is a **chronogram,** which adjectivally and adverbially is **chronogrammatic** and **chronogrammatically.** Graphic methods of measuring time are **chronography.** A **chronometer** is an unusually accurate timepiece.

cliometrics *n* In Greek mythology Clio was the Muse of history. The application of rigid principles of measurement, especially computer science, to the study of history is cliometrics: <*Time on the Cross*, by Fogel and Engerman, is a rather controversial book applying cliometrics to the economics of American slavery.>

column inch *n* Some free-lance writers and clipping services are paid on the basis of the amount they get published and the extensiveness of the clippings they supply. The usual measure is in terms of the column inch: printed matter one column wide and one inch deep.

computist *n* A computist is a mathematician who specializes in computing such things as times of high and low tides, eclipses, dates, business accounts, and the like, in which specific answers useful in practical applications are the goal.

conditional probability *n* Many college departments of mathematics or statistics offer courses in probability theory—ways of measuring how likely something is to happen. The study is devoted mainly to conditional probability, concerning the likelihood that the thing will happen if this or that condition exists.

cusec *n* In measuring the flow of water or other liquid, a cusec represents one cubic foot per second.

dollop *n* A dollop is a blob, dash, splash, or any small, unmeasured bit, usually of something liquid or semiliquid: <a dollop of brandy, Worcestershire sauce, mustard, ice cream, whipped cream>. The word is also sometimes used for intangibles: <a dollop of Sandburg influence in his poetry>.

equitime point *n*, **howgozit curve** *n* Known also as "the point of no return," the equitime point is the moment in a long airplane flight at which the risks of going back and the time required would be the same as those of going ahead. It is not necessarily the geographic midpoint of the journey, since wind and other factors must be considered. An officer on a plane may keep what heshe calls slangily a *howgozit curve*, a running graph that shows distance, fuel consumption, and time, and that assists in determining the equitime point. Information about weather ahead may also influence the determination.

extrachance *adj* Greater than the degree of probability that chance alone would provide: <The weighting of these coins on one side results in extrachance results; heads turn up 60 percent of the time.>

Geodimeter *n* A trademarked name for a surveying instrument that measures distance through the use of a light beam.

gravimeter *n* A gravimeter may be either a device for measuring specific gravity or one for measuring differences in the strength of gravity at various places on the earth or elsewhere.

infiltrometer *n* Sandy soil absorbs water faster than does clay. Dry soil absorbs water faster than does damp or wet soil. A device for measuring the rapidity of water absorption by soil is called an *infiltrometer.*

loadometer *n* A loadometer is a machine designed to measure the weight carried by a wheel of a vehicle that passes over it. The word came from a trademark, *Loadometer.*

lunker *n* A month—and three retellings—after I catch a fairly large fish, it has transformed into a lunker—a giant of its kind. The word applies most often to a bass, sometimes to other fish, and only rarely to other very large things.

metrology *n* The science of measurement. *Metro* is from Greek for "measure," found also in *meter* and scores of other words.

phonometer *n* An instrument that measures the intensity of sound or the frequency of vibration. In one form it is sometimes called a *decibel counter.*

psychometrics *n,* and related words. Psychometrics is

mental measurement, particularly various kinds of tests such as those that purport to measure intelligence or personality. A **psychometer** is a measuring instrument used in psychometrics, and a **psychometrist** or **psychometrician** is one who attempts to perform mental measurement.

salinometer or **salimeter** or **salinimeter** *n* A device such as a hygrometer for measuring the amount of salt in a solution.

skosh *n* From Japanese *sukoshi,* an informal word for "a small amount"—equivalent to the likewise informal *a tad bit:* <just a skosh of vermouth in my martini>.

sodar *n,* **sofar** *n,* **sonar** *n* Three acronyms for ways to make certain special observations:

sodar **so**und **d**etecting **a**nd **r**anging—an acoustical system for checking atmospheric conditions to forecast the weather.

sofar **so**und **f**ixing **a**nd **r**anging—a system for locating the area of an underwater explosion.

sonar sound **na**vigation **r**anging—a device that uses sonic and ultrasonic waves to detect underwater perils such as a submarine.

spherometer *n* An instrument that measures the curvature of a sphere, used, for instance, to determine the extent to which a ball-shaped object is not truly spherical.

tare *n* The weight of a container without its contents. Thus if a truck with household goods weighs 14,600 pounds and the household goods weigh 4,000 pounds, the tare is 10,600. Or if a container filled with a pound of brown sugar weighs 18 ounces, the tare is 2 ounces.

testmanship *n* Skill in taking and passing examinations: <He was convinced that testmanship added several points to each of his examination scores.>

ton-kilometer *n,* **ton-mile** *n* A measurement of cost for hauling: the amount charged for moving one ton one kilometer or one mile: <charged twenty cents per ton-kilometer for hauling the coal>.

tonometer *n* Tonometers may measure pitch (rate of vibration), vapor pressure, or tension on the eyeball.

ullage *n* The amount by which a container is short of being full: <A five-quart pitcher containing three quarts of liquid has an ullage of two quarts.> In a rocket an ullage is the space not used for the liquid propellant—space needed for thermal expansion and accumulation of gases.

Mastery Test

If you wanted to measure each of these, what could you use? Fill in the missing letters.

1. the size of a head — c_____ometer
2. pressure — m__ometer
3. blood pressure — sph_______ometer
4. a quality of the blood — h__ometer
5. lung capacity — in____ometer
6. sharpness of the sense of touch — t___ometer
7. the number of miles traveled by a vehicle — __ometer
8. the height of any tall object — h___ometer
9. the distance from here to, say, a mountain — t__emeter
10. the depth of an ocean — e___graph
11. the depth and temperature of water — b____th____graph
12. fade-resistance of cloth — f___ometer
13. color-fastness in washing — l______ometer
14. elasticity — e____ometer
15. color — c____imeter
16. relative humidity — h___ometer
17. precise time — c_____graph
18. specific gravity — g___imeter
19. ability of soil to absorb water — in_____ometer
20. intensity of sound — ph__ometer
21. saltiness — s____ometer
22. curvature of a sphere — s____ometer

23. pitch t__ometer
24. mileage (on a map) c____ometer
25. flexibility f___ometer
26. distance as revealed by a light beam G___imeter
27. a constituent of blood h__ometer
28. rate of water flow c___c
29. a small amount of something s___h
30. the steepness of a hill c___ometer

27
TO TELL OF TIME

In the **dayspring** of humankind (*dayspring* means an early stage of any promising development) our distant ancestors observed the passage of the sun across the sky, the regularity with which night follows day, the movements of the moon and stars. **Thenadays,** as today, season followed season: Flowers blossomed and faded, trees and animals shed their apparel and renewed it. Children were born, became adults, and eventually died. **Primordial** people (*primordial* means first, earliest, existing at the beginning) shared inevitably in time, the fourth dimension, not knowing what a dimension is, but noting and feeling and participating in the harmonious or discordant rhythms of the universe.

Modern man has become insistent on precision of measurement, of time as of almost everything else. We define the length of the year, not as just 365 and 1/4 days, but as a **solar year** (from vernal equinox to vernal equinox) of 365 days, 5 hours, 48 minutes, 45.5 seconds, or as a **sidereal year** (the time taken by the sun to return to the same place in relation to other stars) as 365 days, 6 hours, 9 minutes, 10 seconds. There are also an **anomalistic year** (the time from Earth's nearest approach to the sun until another nearest approach; these approaches are called **perihelions**) of 365 days, 6 hours, 13 minutes, 53 seconds and a **lunar year** (12 "moon months") totaling about 354 days. On a scale that dwarfs all these little years is the **cosmic year,** about 225 million of our years, the time the solar system needs to revolve once around the center of our galaxy. And some philosophers and adherents to some religions believe in *eternity*, "time without end," and in **eternality,** "deathlessness," or, with Nietzsche, they believe in **eternal recurrence,** "cyclical repetition forever of all things and events."

At the opposite end of the time scale are the measures of short duration. A second, conventionally defined as 1/60 of a minute or 1/86,400 of a mean solar day, was redefined by the International Committee on Weights and Measures in 1956 as 1/31,556,925.9747 of the length of the solar year 1900. Alternatively, the second is measured in terms of the time of radiation from certain atoms, most often cesium-133. (Cesium is element 55; it is extensively used in photoelectric cells and television cameras.) So defined, a second is 9,192,631,770 cycles of radiation of a cesium-133 atom. One might think that no finer measurements could be conceived of, but it happens that there are also a **centrisecond**—a thousandth of a second, a thousandth of any of the durations just given—and a **millisecond**—only a tenth as long as that.

Most of us need not be concerned with cosmic years or milliseconds, but there are other time-words, more closely related to our **diurnal,** "daily" or "daytime," activities or our nocturnal doings. **Diurnation** is anything that happens each day to something in the plant or animal kingdom: <The appearance of trout in that pool was a diurnation during the summer month>, or it may be the habit of sleeping during daylight hours: <A characteristic of bats is diurnation.> Something that happens three times a day, like our meals, may be described as **terdiurnal.** (For those who eat four times a day, maybe we should coin **tetradiurnal** and **tetradiurnally.**) That which occurs at midnight or every midnight is a **midnightly** event. Shouldn't we have a corresponding **noonly,** as in <the noonly whistle>? We do have **noonlight** "the light at noon; very bright daylight."

We have no common single word for "to become dark in the evening," although we can use sentences like "Twilight falls" or "The sun sets and darkness gradually covers the earth." Scottish people can say "It **gloams**" or "It is **gloaming,**" using a verb that may be familiar through Annie Harrison's song that our great-grandparents loved, "In the Gloaming." *Gloam,* incidentally, is related to *glow:* Twilight is characterized by a decreasing glow. Perhaps we should borrow this handy verb *gloam* from our Scottish friends.

The adjective *benighted,* "unenlightened, ignorant," is familiar to us, but the verb **benight** that gave it birth is rare. It means to overtake by darkness or night and is generally used in the passive: <Two flat tires caused us to be benighted; we didn't reach home until 9:00 P.M.>

Anyone not of legal age (for example, to vote) is in hiser **nonage:** <While still in her nonage she was married three times.> Much too soon heshe is **middle-aging** or **senescent** "growing old but not yet old." Actually, every young or middle-aged living being is senescent, but the term is most often used for someone or something beyond middle age. Opposed to *senescent* is **juvenescent,** "becoming young or youthful": <The end of his financial worries made him seem juvenescent.>

At any time in one's life, one may experience **halcyon days.** The ancient Greeks believed that a kingfisher, which they called a *halkyōn,* built its nest afloat in the sea and that it could calm the waters during the winter solstice incubation period. From this legend rose the use of *halcyon* to mean calm, idyllically peaceful; by extension, it may mean youthful, unharassed, affluent. Youthful days are also sometimes called **salad days,** a term that implies not only vigor and vivacity but also inexperience and possible indiscretion. Shakespeare referred to <"my salad days, when I was green in judgment, cold in blood">.

Sometime in each person's life may come a **climacteric,** a critical year or other period, especially one when major physical change, such as menopause, is occurring. Numerologists believe that years representing multiples of 7 and 9 are especially significant, so that the 49th year (7 × 7), the 63rd year (7 × 9), or the 81st year (9 × 9) may be the **grand climacteric.**

Influential in all our lives is the body of memories, experiences, and (to some extent) beliefs that have been passed down through the centuries from one generation to another. Collectively these are called **race memory,** "memories handed down to a race or to all mankind": <Distrust of strangers is part of race memory, no doubt dating back to prehistoric days when every stranger was a potential enemy.> Race memory sometimes represents the **dead hand** of the past, which the French call **mortmain**—a word that we, too, sometimes use for its English equivalent. To the Romans it was *mortua manus,* again "dead hand." Every generation must decide which parts of the past, which bits from the dead hand, it should keep, which it should bury. The "revolt" of each generation is an inevitable part of the decision-making.

Always we move on, rejecting and accepting. Some of us are more willing than others to endure **dailiness,** "routine; regularity; monotonous quality arising from daily repetition." **Thenness,** "the essence of a past time," changes to **nowness,** "the essence of the present; the state of existing in or for the present." <It is nowness that concerns a child —not what happened yesterday or may happen tomorrow.> The seasons still march with us or we with them; Latin *ver,* "spring," gave us the adjective **vernal;** *aestas,* "summer," gave us **estival;** *autumnus,* "autumn," gave us the familiar *autumnal;* and *bruma,* "winter," gave us **brumal.** (For good measure we got from Latin *hibernus,* "wintry," our word **hibernal,** obviously related to *hibernate.*) The ancient Romans live on in these and in the thousands of other words they have handed to us across the centuries.

Time fascinates people so much that a scientific and rather difficult-to-read book, *A Brief History of Time,* by Stephen W. Hawking, was on *The New York Times* best-seller list for more than two years.

Some Miscellaneous Words Related to Time

abruption *n* That which is abrupt happens suddenly, at a usually unexpected moment, as <an abrupt denial>. *Abruption* refers to a sudden breaking off (from Latin *ab*, "from," and *rumpere*, "to break"). It was formerly more widely used than it is now, but seems worth reviving, as in <the abruption of negotiations> <the unexpected abruption of his story>.

afterday *n*, **afterdays** *n* A later period of time: <But what of the afterday that is sure to come?> <His afterdays could never be quite so happy.>

atomic clock *n*, **atomic time** *n* An atomic clock is an extraordinarily accurate electronic instrument that uses the resonance frequency of atoms or molecules (usually of cesium). What it measures is atomic time, which differs from other time mainly in its extreme accuracy.

bang time *n* Light waves travel faster than sound waves. You see, for example, debris flying into the air from an explosion, or a puff of smoke from a distant gun, before you hear the sound. The length of time between the two is informally called *bang time*.

circadian *adj* Many or most of earth's living things are adjusted to its 24-hour rotation. People and many animals, for example, usually sleep at night, and some plants grow faster during their favored parts of the day. From Latin *circa*, "about," and *dies*, "a day," comes the word *circadian* to describe this phenomenon: <the circadian rhythms of everyday life>.

coeval *adj* Although *coeval* is sometimes used as a synonym for *contemporary*, it tends to be applied more in connection with long-lasting periods of time past—to eras, eons, geological periods, and so on. Thus ichthyosaurs and dinosaurs were coeval, because both existed in the Triassic period of some 200 million years ago.

ephemeral *adj* Here today, gone tomorrow. Lasting a very short time: <Because a mayfly usually lives less than two days, its technical name is *ephemera* or *ephemerid*.>

evanescent *adj* Disappearing gradually; fading away:

<evanescent evening light> <an evanescent jet streak> <the evanescent pleasures of childhood>.

flextime *n* To suit the needs of its employees who have family or other responsibilities, some businesses and industries are able to use flextime. Workers' hours may, within prescribed limits, be flexible, adapted to their individual circumstances.

foreverness *n* A somewhat poetic way to say "permanence" or "eternity." <The Church of Jesus Christ of Latter-Day Saints has a ceremony of "sealing," based on a belief in the foreverness of marriage of a couple who have proved their compatibility.>

futuramic *adj,* and related words. Something advanced in design, such as an experimental airplane or automobile, may be described as *futuramic.* And of late years, we have heard much from **futurologists,** who specialize in **futurology,** the careful study of the future and its perils and possibilities.

geologic time *n* Geologists think of time less in days, years, or centuries than in millions or even billions of years, ranging from the almost "modern" Pleistocene epoch of a mere two million years ago to the Archaeozoic period of some five billion years past.

horology *n* Horology is the measurement of time or the principles for building clocks or other instruments that measure time. The word comes from Greek *hōra,* "a period of time," which is also the distant source of *hour.* <Precision of measurement is essential in horology.>

lobster shift *n* Newspaper people refer, usually deploringly, to the lobster shift (or *graveyard shift*) as one that encompasses late-evening or early-morning hours. The small staff on duty between newspaper editions is also sometimes called the lobster shift.

long-term (short-term) memory *n* Our long-term memory may let us recall, even when we are elderly, things we learned or experienced as children. Short-term memories consist, for example, of recall of recent conversations.

lunation *n* On average the time between two successive new moons is 29 days, 12 hours, and 2.8 seconds. That length of time is a lunation.

momently *adv* Three slightly different meanings: (1) every moment, (2) at any moment, (3) lasting only a moment: <Explosions occurred momently.> <Disaster may strike momently.> <The engine coughed momently and then was silent.>

nowanights *adv* During these nights. A nocturnal form of *nowadays:* <Nowanights theater time is 7:30.>

perdurable *adj* Unusually durable: <as perdurable as the cliffs of Dover>.

postatomic *adj* Existing since (1) the invention of atomic weapons, or (2) the first explosion of an atomic bomb, July 16, 1945: <the postatomic world>.

primaveral *adj* Latin *primo vere* and Spanish or Italian *primaver* or *primavera* mean "in the early spring." Our *primaveral,* with the same meaning, comes from those sources: <Crocuses are primaveral flowers.> Incidentally, a *pasta primavera* consists of pasta and minced vegetables such as those of springtime.

primordium *n* Related to *primordial* (mentioned above), *primordium* means the first stage, a rudimentary form: <fins, perhaps the primordium of feet and hands>.

Subrecent *adj* Geologists say that the Recent period is the one dating from the Pleistocene era that ended about ten thousand years ago. Subrecent overlaps the Recent, but is in general earlier; it includes also the last part of the Pleistocene.

subsequence *n* A consequence is something that grows out of something that happened earlier. A subsequence is only a later event and is not necessarily a consequence of (that is, caused by) the earlier one: <In the story of Jack and Jill, Jill's tumble is a subsequence of Jack's fall but was probably not a consequence of it.>

thitherto *adv* Although *hitherto,* "up to this time," still appears in modern prose, its partner *thitherto,* "up to that time," is very rare. It could be moderately useful.

time warp *n* Probably no such thing exists, but some scientists—and especially sci-fi writers—have hypothesized a time warp, a "wrinkle in time," that may either suspend time or permit backward or forward movement in it.

trice *n* A quick-sounding word that may suggest its meaning: "instant; a very short time." Generally used after *in a*: <In a trice the lifeguard leaped into the water.>

triennium *n*, and related words. A biennium, as is well known, is a period of two years. A **triennium** is a period of three years; **quadrennium,** four; **quinquennium,** five; **septennium,** seven; and **decennium,** or *decade*, ten. For the missing numbers, **sexennium, octennium,** and **nonennium,** though not listed in dictionaries, could be used. A corresponding adjectival form with *-ial*, like *biennial*, either exists or should exist for any of these nouns. *Century, centenary, centennial,* and *bicentennial* are familiar; **sesquicentennial,** pertaining to one hundred fifty years, is a little less so.

watch night *n*, and related words. *Watch night* is another name for New Year's Eve, especially when observed at a **watch meeting** or **watch party.**

Yahrzeit *n* (*Jahrzeit* in German) In Judaism, the anniversary of the death of a loved one, observed with a candle or other light and by a special religious ceremony.

zone time *n* Ships at sea may follow zone time, a system of dividing the earth into 24 time zones of 15 degrees (one hour) each, starting 7 1/2 degrees east and west of the Greenwich meridian.

Mastery Test

Match each word with the best definition in its group.

___	1. afterdays	a. during the nights at present
___	2. thenadays	b. the essence of that time
___	3. nowanights	c. existing together

___	4. thenness	d.	at 2400 or 0000 hours
___	5. coeval	e.	before that time
___	6. midnightly	f.	a later period of time
___	7. momently	g.	permanent cyclical repetition
___	8. thitherto	h.	regular routine
___	9. dailiness	i.	at every instant
___	10. eternal recurrence	j.	in those days
___	11. cosmic year	k.	twelve moons
___	12. grand climacteric	l.	an event later than another
___	13. lunar year	m.	sleeping in the daytime
___	14. dayspring	n.	experimental in design
___	15. diurnation	o.	overtake with darkness
___	16. millisecond	p.	e.g., the seventh year times nine
___	17. subsequence	q.	unusually lasting
___	18. futuramic	r.	1/60,000 of a minute
___	19. benight	s.	start of something new that looks good
___	20. perdurable	t.	225,000,000 × 365 days
___	21. horology	u.	five years
___	22. halcyon days	v.	calm times
___	23. sesquicentennial	w.	three times a day
___	24. estival	x.	harmful inheritance
___	25. quinquennium	y.	earliest
___	26. terdiurnal	z.	youth
___	27. dead hand	aa.	pertaining to winter
___	28. primordial	bb.	measurement of time
___	29. brumal	cc.	pertaining to summer
___	30. salad days	dd.	150th birthday
___	31. flextime	ee.	a very short time

___	32. trice	ff.	in the spring
___	33. Yahrzeit	gg.	short-lived
___	34. ephemeral	hh.	service for a death anniversary
___	35. primaveral	ii.	arrangement of hours for workers' convenience

28

AND NOW OUR FEARLESS WEATHERCASTER

"Nice day!" "Think it'll rain?" "Cold enough for you?" Even though the weather is more often than anything else the topic of casual conversation, most of us don't use our linguistic resources as fully as we might in talking about it. True, English doesn't have as many words for snow as the Eskimo language does (twelve according to some Eskimos, thirty-nine according to others, or any intermediate number your informant fancies). But we have a number of words for varieties of rain and yet content ourselves with a few like *drizzle, mist, cloudburst,* and *raining cats and dogs.* Let's note a number of little-known weather terms here.

Some of these are blends, like the familiar *smog,* "smoke mixed with fog." **Smaze** looks like smog but is drier; it's a mixture of smoke and haze. A New Englander may talk about a **drisk,** which isn't quite a drizzle and not quite a mist but a cross between the two. Some Scottish people have a word of unknown origin for *drisk;* they call it **drow** (pronounced drəo͞o). **Smur** is a dialectal noun for drizzly fog or mist, and **smurry** means drizzly, foggy, nastily damp. It would seem that few words could so well suggest such unpleasantness, but another that succeeds is **haar** (pronounced (h)är), a British dialect word for a cold, damp, raw sea-fog.

Another blend is **sneet,** for a mixture of snow and sleet. Not listed in any dictionaries I've checked, but pretty useful, are **hain,** "hail mixed with rain," and **snain,** "snow mixed with rain." **Drismal** isn't listed either, but it's great for describing one of those dismal days when it's drizzling. For a quite different kind of day, specifically for those soft-looking little white clouds of midsummer, Conrad Aiken invented the name **clouderpuffs,** and with that start anyone could easily move on to "a sunny, **clouderpuffy** day."

Everybody knows about rainbows and their mythical pots of gold, but why are **snowbows** so seldom mentioned? Mightn't they have their own gold? There are also **frostbows,** white arcs formed by sunlight reflected from ice crystals in the air. There's a **white rainbow,** too, caused by sunlight and tiny drops of water, as in fog, drops that are too small to create the color bands we observe in "regular" rainbows. And at Kentucky's Cumberland Falls State Resort Park, when the moon is full and atmospheric conditions are right, you can see a beautiful **moonbow** above the waterfall.

Sometimes snow falls in the form of little white balls that are too small and not hard enough to be damaging like hail. These balls are known collectively as **graupel,** from a German word for hulled grain, which graupel somewhat resembles. The Germans borrowed the word from the Serbo-Croatian *krupa;* a later drummer by that name could play the drums so rapidly that imaginative folk could think that showers of ice pellets were doing the job. **Snow pellets** and **soft hail** are other names for graupel.

In the Far North, light coming through clouds over snow may so closely equal the light reflected from the snow that there are no shadows and no visible horizon. In such a **whiteout** even a traveler familiar with the area may become quickly and completely disoriented. By another definition, a whiteout is extremely poor visibility caused by windblown snow: <An international team of Antarctic explorers almost lost one of its members in 1990 when he became lost in a whiteout a few yards from their shelter.>

A useful word meaning pertaining to snow is **nival** (rhymes with *rival*). A nival region has much snow; a nival climate is snowy; nival plants or animals can live in or beneath snow. One of nature's nival beauties is the **snow roller,** a snowdrift in the form of a cylinder with concave ends. A **snowbreak** can be either damage caused by snow: <extensive tree destruction by snowbreak> or, more often, a barricade such as a row of bushes or evergreen trees or a fence so placed as to retard drifting snow. The word is analogous to **windbreak,** "trees or other objects that break the force of the wind." A master of **snowcraft** knows a great deal about snow: the weather conditions conducive to heavy snow, kinds of snow, and especially snow safety and ways to travel in snow.

The Greek-Roman god Zeus or Jupiter was, in one of his guises, Jupiter Pluvius, "the god of rain." *Pluvius* has given us several words related to rainfall, besides the *pluviometer* I mentioned in the chapter on measurement. **Pluviometry,** "rain measurement," and **pluviometric,** "pertaining to rain measurement," are derived from these two words. A **pluviograph** is a self-registering rain gauge, and **pluviography** is information about rainfall. The adjective **pluvial** means pertaining to rain, or having abundant rain, although it may be a bit jargonish to say "pluvial conditions" instead of "rainfall" or "a pluvial climate" instead of "a rainy climate." **Interpluvial,** "between rains," is, however, a rather handy word. An interpluvial period is any time (day, month, year, or longer) when rainfall is absent or scarce: <The interpluvial period responsible for the dust bowl lasted nearly a decade.>

Climate obviously is a large factor in ecology. The ecologies of the temperate and tropical regions, to take a simple example, differ greatly from each other because of climatic conditions. The **ecoclimate** is the climate considered in relation to ecology or, reversing the emphasis, ecology relative to climate: <The ecoclimate of the polar regions, with their intense cold, results in the development of only a small number of highly complex organisms.> **Phenology,** a semantically related word, means the study of the influence of climate on biological phenomena. A **phenologist** may study, for example, variations in plumage, fur, or nesting habits attributable to climate.

Glaclology is the study of glaciers and the physical effects of glaciers or other large icy accumulations. One who specializes in such study is a **glaciologist.** One of hiser tools, used to measure glacial motion, is a **glaciometer.** Icebergs that are chunks of ice broken away from glaciers are described as **glacionatant.**

Shippers, farmers, and gardeners are among those who can profit from information about normal freezing or thawing conditions. On a special kind of weather map prepared for their use, an **equiglacial** line connects points that have or are likely to have approximately the same conditions at a given time. Three specific kinds of equiglacial lines are:

isopag This line connects points where there is ice or freezing conditions for about the same number of days each winter.

isopectic This one joins points where ice begins to form at the same time at the start of winter—e.g., places where the first killing frost tends to come at the same time.

isotac This line connects points where ice begins to melt at the same time each spring.

Iso-, "the same," is a favorite prefix among the meteorologists who make weather maps. An **isobar** joins points with the same barometric pressure; its adjective is **isobaric** or **isobarometric.** An **isohel** (from Greek *helios*, "sun") is a line joining places that have equal amounts of sunshine. An **isotherm** (adjective **isothermal**) shows places where the same temperatures exist or are predicted; some TV national weather maps, for example, show west–east isotherms, irregular curving lines that may connect the places where the high temperatures of the day are expected to be ninety degrees, eighty degrees, seventy degrees, and so on.

The **microclimate** is the climate of a very small or relatively small area. Scientists may gather considerable information from the intensive study of weather and climate even in a plot of an acre in size. Usually, however, the term refers to a somewhat larger area than that—say, a county, a group of counties, or a state.

Miscellaneous Terms for Weather and Climate

Aprilian *adj,* **May** *vi* April is honored among the months as the father of an adjective, *Aprilian,* "pertaining to or similar to April": <those glorious, bright, Aprilian days>. May seems to be the only month that has become a verb: <Robert Herrick: "Corinna's Going a-Maying">. To May (or may) is to gather flowers in May or to take part in May Day dances or other pleasures of May 1.

Beaufort scale *n* Although no longer used by meteorologists, the Beaufort scale is still helpful in indicating estimates of wind force. It gives numerical values to different strengths of wind. For example, wind velocity in a gale is 32 to 63 mph, that of a hurricane above 72 mph. In contrast, a breeze travels 4 to 31 mph.

brontogram *n,* **brontometer** *n* The study of thunderstorms—their frequency and intensity—may save human lives. The instrument that makes measurements for that study is a brontometer, and the record it makes is a **brontogram** (or alternatively **brontograph**). Greek *brontos* means loud noise; it appears also in *brontosaurus, brontophobia,* and a few other words.

chinook *n* Named for the Chinook Indians of the West Coast, a chinook may be either a warm, moist wind that blows from the ocean on the coasts of Washington and Oregon or a warm, dry wind that flows down the eastern slopes of the Rockies. *Chinook* is also a name for the chinook salmon, known, too, as the *king salmon.*

cirrus *adj, n,* and other names of clouds. Although we see clouds nearly every day, most of us do not know the names of the various kinds. The World Meteorological Organization classifies clouds by height as follows:

A. High (mean height 5 to 13 kilometers)
   1. **cirrus** detached thin white clouds
   2. **cirro-cumulus** rather regularly arranged thin white clouds that resemble ripples
   3. **cirro-stratus** thin white veil of clouds

B. Middle (mean heights 2 to 7 kilometers)

4. **alto-cumulus** rounded masses or rolls of white or gray clouds
5. **alto-stratus** grayish or bluish cloud layer, smooth in appearance, covering most or all of the sky, sometimes thin enough to show sun faintly
6. **nimbo-stratus** dark gray, heavy cloud layer from which steady precipitation often falls

C. Low (mean heights 0 to 2 kilometers)

7. **strato-cumulus** gray or whitish clouds usually covering large parts of the sky and resembling rounded masses or rolls
8. **stratus** gray, even-looking but not thick clouds that often result in drizzle or light snow
9. **cumulus** separate clouds, clearly defined, sometimes small and drifting, sometimes fairly tall; brilliant white in sunlight; typical good-weather summer clouds
10. **cumulo-nimbus** thunderstorm clouds, tall, anvil- or mountain-shaped, rugged-looking, characterized by accompanying wind and lightning

climatography *n,* and related words. *Climatography* and **climatology** are often used interchangeably, although *climatology* is more often employed as the name of the science dealing with climates and *climatography* as describing (literally "writing about") climates. Related words that are fairly obvious in meaning are **climatographer, climatographical,** and **climatologist.**

comfort index *n* (Sometimes *discomfort index*) A figure derived by some weather forecasters to measure the comfort or discomfort of summer days, combining figures for temperature and humidity. The forecaster adds the customary dry-bulb temperature and the unusual wet-bulb (moist and ventilated) temperature, multiplies by 0.4, and adds 15.

crepuscular rays *n* Especially toward evening of a cloudy day, you may see isolated rays of light shining through cloud gaps. These crepuscular rays illuminate the atmospheric dust particles they are moving through.

dewfall *n* Although dew doesn't fall (it condenses instead), the term *dewfall* has long been in the language to signify the formation of dew, the time when it forms, or the amount of moisture formed in one period of time: <a heavy dewfall last night>.

dogwood winter *n* Dogwood trees are among the earliest to bloom in the northern United States. A spell of cold weather when dogwood trees are in bud or in blossom is dogwood winter.

foehn *n* A foehn is a warm, dry wind that blows down the lee slope of a mountain. A chinook is an example.

fire storm or **fire wind** *n* When there is a very large fire, as in a forest, or in a bombed city, or in an active volcano, the heated air rises and creates an atmospheric disturbance that may result in strong, often gusty winds and sometimes in rain. These disturbances are called *fire storms* or *fire winds.*

Scotch mist Besides being a cocktail, a Scotch mist is a combination of mist or fog with drizzle, observed especially in Scotland and northern England.

serotinal *adj* Pertaining to the latter part of summer, which is also generally the driest part: <unexpected serotinal rainfall>. The word comes from Latin *sero,* "late."

squall line *n,* **windshift line** *n* Sometimes a cold front advancing into warmer air is called a *squall line,* since storms often accompany it. Another name is *windshift line,* because (in the northern hemisphere) winds customarily shift to the northwest after passage of the front. Sometimes the squall line may precede the front by twenty-five to two hundred miles, although the windshift line is mainly delayed until the front passes.

squaw winter *n* A brief cold snap preceding Indian summer.

storm lane *n,* **tornado alley** *n* A storm lane or a tornado alley is a narrow belt that receives more than its fair share of storms, especially tornadoes: <Climatologists have demonstrated that some portions of the Midwest are truly tornado alleys.>

storm surge *n* Abnormally great increase in the shoreward flow of water, caused by a great offshore storm.

sweltry *adj* Based on *swelter* and possibly influenced by *sultry*, *sweltry* means abnormally hot and (often) humid: <sweltry days and nights in the tropics>.

windfirm *adj* Of buildings and plants: sufficiently sturdy and firm to withstand even strong wind: <Trees that don't have deep, clinging roots—that aren't windfirm—won't survive long in this area.>

Mastery Test

For each definition, supply the missing letters.

1. misty drizzle — dr___
2. smoke and haze — sm___
3. snow and sleet — sn___
4. pellets of snow — gr____l
5. cause of poor visibility in the far north — wh_____t
6. pertaining to snow — n___l
7. barricade against snow — sn________
8. self-registering rain gauge — pl_________h
9. between rains — inter______l
10. one who studies the relationship of climate to living things — ph__________
11. study of glaciers — gl________
12. line on a map, joining places with equal sunshine — i____l
13. climate of a small area — mic__________
14. instrument for measuring thunderstorms — bro________r
15. high, thin cloud — c____s
16. thunderstorm cloud — cu_____-______s
17. cold in the spring — d_____d w____r
18. wind resulting from fire — ____ ___d
19. short cold snap in autumn — s___w w____r
20. very hot, isn't it — sw____y
21. scale for naming winds — B______t

22. index of temperature and humidity c_____t
23. high waves, perhaps caused by a hurricane s___m s___e
24. mist, fog, drizzle in British Isles S____h m__t
25. "night rainbow" m_____w

29
FEATURES OF THE LANDSCAPE

Scape is a back-formation from *landscape* and means scenic view (either the real thing or a pictorial interpretation). For specificity, *scape* is often combined with another word, like *desert:* **cityscape; moonscape; riverscape; seascape; streetscape; waterscape;** as well as **miniascape,** a garden made in a dish and using pebbles and plant materials requiring no water. At least in theory, although these seem not to be listed in dictionaries, there may be *lakescapes, swampscapes,* and others.

In any scape, some one or two features are likely to attract most attention. Such a conspicuous feature is a **salient,** from Latin *salire,* "to leap or spring." For example, a salient may be a promontory along a coast. (In battle it is a wedge or bulge driven into enemy territory.) As an adjective, *salient* means prominent, jutting out or sticking up noticeably; it is now often used figuratively: <the most salient points in his speech> <salient ideas>.

Salient features have their own special qualities, which to primitive people were often equated with minor deities. The **genius loci** of a pond or any other thing in nature was its guardian spirit. Even those of us who cannot believe in this multitude of spirits recognize that every place does have its unique spirit or character, caused no doubt by its geographical characteristics and the peculiar mix of its inhabitants. This character, too, is called *genius loci:* <the somber genius loci of Egdon Heath in Hardy's *Return of the Native*>.

As a child I was revolted by the thought of **friable** soil. "Who would want to fry dirt?" I asked. Actually, friable soil is that which is easily pulverized. The adjective comes from Latin *friare,* "to crumble." **Permeable** soil is that which will permit water to pass through fairly readily—unlike clay soil, which is relatively impermeable. **Gally** soil is not usually very friable, since a gall is a barren spot of land, or one that has lost most or all of its topsoil: <Land that had been plowed near the tops of hills became gally after a few years, since water leached or carried away the topsoil.> **Sheet erosion** tends to remove topsoil somewhat more evenly over a large area instead of through the formation of gullies: <Wind and drought are mainly responsible for sheet erosion.> A **sandblow** is an area where the remaining soil is sandy and where the wind has blown away so much topsoil that little vegetation can survive: <the sandblows of western Nebraska>.

Water, too, has much influence on every genius loci. The water that is the source of springs and wells—the water that flows from faucets as well as that upon which our supplies of food largely depend—comes from beneath the earth's surface and is called **groundwater.** The **groundwater level,** also called the **water table,** is the top level at which the earth is saturated with water. When this level gets too low, wells go dry, and drought and crop shortage may result. An environment that is excessively lacking in groundwater and other moisture, as a desert, may be described as **xeric.** (The word *serene* is a distant relative; dry weather is usually clear, calm, serene.) Plants that thrive in dry places are **xerophilous;** those that don't are **xerophobous.**

To a person in the oil industry a **wellhead** is the top of a well: <the wellhead price of oil>. To a geologist, though, it is the place where a spring emerges or a stream begins. By extension it is the principal source, the fountainhead, of anything: <the wellhead of our knowledge of thermody-

namics>. A **wellspring,** in contrast, is not usually just the beginning point but also the source of continuing supply: <the wellsprings responsible for the town's water> <God is the wellspring of our blessings and our responsibilities.>

There may be too much water as well as too little. From Latin *diluvium,* "flood," **diluvial** means pertaining to a flood, especially the one that made Noah famous. (*Antediluvial,* better known than *diluvial,* usually refers to the period before that biblical flood.) **Diluvianism** is a theory of some geologists that much in geology can be accounted for by a worldwide flood long ago. A believer in that theory is a **diluvialist.**

Perhaps you have seen a branch of a stream that follows an independent path for a while and then rejoins its parent. (In dry areas it may sink away into the sand.) One meaning of *ana-* is anew, so this new branch of a stream is called an **anabranch.** Figuratively, anything or anyone that strikes off on its or hiser own way may be called an anabranch: <those most remarkable anabranches, the college freshmen>.

More Words About the Landscape

affluent *adj,* **effluent** *adj* With reference to streams or any flowing liquids, an effluent one flows out from a source, and an affluent one is flowing into something. The same stream, of course, may be effluent from the point of view of one observer, affluent from that of another, as when it moves between lakes with an observer at each lake.

boreen *n* Sure and we can say *lane* or *country road,* but Irish *boreen,* "narrow rural road, especially in hilly country," paints an especially pleasant picture even for us Irishmen by adoption.

borrow pit *n* Beside many interstate highways are small ponds every mile or so. Most of these were dug during the construction of the road; dirt was borrowed here for use elsewhere. Any such source of borrowed soil—not necessarily beside a road—is a borrow pit.

circumdenudation or **circumerosion** *n* Water or sometimes wind may erode the soil all around an object such as a tree, a rock, or an island created by division of a stream, and leave the object isolated. The process responsible is "denuding or eroding around"—that is, circumdenudation or circumerosion.

coteau n *(pl. coteaux)* Canadian French took over French *coteau,* "slope, small hill," and began using it to name the upland between two valleys and then either side of a valley. Both meanings are found in the United States, though most often in areas with French backgrounds: <a gentle Louisiana coteau with a small stream flowing at the base>.

coulee or **coulie** *n* In the Midwest and West this word may have any of these meanings: (1) a small stream that sometimes dries up; (2) the bed of such a stream; (3) a ravine or small, steep valley, often with a stream at the base of the coteaux; or (4) a (usually) solidified stream or sheet of lava.

declivity *n,* and related words. If you stand at the top of a hill or cliff and look down, you refer to the downward slope as the *declivity;* at the bottom, where you are looking up, the same slope is the **acclivity. Declivous** and **acclivous** are the corresponding adjectives. **Declivitous** and **acclivitous** are adjectives referring to an especially high degree of steepness.

desertness *n* The condition of being like a desert: <The desertness of what had once been farmland appalled us.>

detritus *n* To the geologist, detritus consists of particles of rock originally belonging to a larger mass: <detritus left by the glacier>. To the rest of us it may also be any partly disintegrated material, or debris: <the detritus of last night's party>.

disembogue *vi, vt* We derived this word from Spanish, which had built it on Latin *boca,* "mouth." To disembogue, with reference to a body of water, is to flow out through an outlet or mouth: <The Mississippi disembogues (or disembogues its water) into the Gulf of Mexico.>

escarpment *n* An escarpment is a long, clifflike ridge dating back to a long-ago break in the Earth's crust.

eutrophication *n* A lake with too many nutrients, such as contained in the runoff of farm fertilizer and certain other pollutants, gradually fills with algae and other organisms. The oxygen supply is thus reduced, and fish and many other creatures die. The process is called *eutrophication.*

hot springs *n*, **thermal springs** *n*, **warm springs** *n* The water temperature difference between Warm Springs, Georgia, and Hot Springs National Park, Arkansas, is more than just a few degrees. It's 88° F versus 143° F. Warm springs in general have temperatures below 98° F, hot springs above that figure. For both, water is heated by hot or molten rock far below the surface. Any spring that has water temperature significantly higher than the average air temperature of the area is called a *thermal spring.*

quaggy *adj* Marshy, boggy, like a quagmire. Also flabby: <His quaggy body shook like gelatin.>

scabland *n*, **scrubland** *n* Both are unattractive landscapes. Scabland is chiefly lava—rough, treeless, almost without vegetation. Scrubland is land with scrubby growth—a few small plants, unattractive bushes, and perhaps some spindly trees.

scarp *n* A line of cliffs created usually by erosion, or an oceanside low, steep slope caused by the action of waves.

spate *n* A spate is a freshet or flood, whether literal or figurative: <a spate of water, almost a flash flood> <a spate of rumors>.

stagnum *n* (pl. *stagna*) A stagnant pool, or any pool of water that has no outlet.

strath *n* Along parts of many rivers one may find wide, flat bottomland called a *strath.*

submontane *adj* (1) Lying under a mountain or mountain range: <A submontane stream emerges here from the shelter of Mount Noah.> (2) Pertaining to foothills or the lower slopes of mountains: <attractive submontane villages at the feet of the Adirondacks>.

sward *n* Grassy surface, turf, sod, especially a patch of land covered with grass and relatively free of trees and shrubs. Also called *greensward.* <The little Oxfordshire town of Witney has a beautiful sward about five hundred yards long, with an Anglican church at one end and a still-used medieval market at the other.>

topographer *n,* and related words. A *topographer* studies the terrain, the physical surface features of an area. Hiser vocation is *topography,* and heshe perhaps prepares *topographic* maps.

transmontane *or* **tramontane** *adj,* **cismontane** *adj* The first two words originally meant pertaining to the area north of the Alps but now mean pertaining to the area beyond any mountain or mountain range. *Cismontane* means on this side of the mountains: <our cismontane friends>.

tumulose or **tumulous** *adj* Characterized by or full of mounds or small hills: <The tumulose area, he suspected, might have been an Indian burial ground.>

waste bank *n* If you dig a ditch, you have to put the excavated dirt somewhere. If you merely leave it lying beside the ditch, it is a waste bank.

water gap *n* A stream over many centuries cuts its way through a ridge, leaving a water gap—a somewhat V-shaped area with the stream at its lowest point.

watersmeet *n* The place where two rivers meet: <Cairo, Illinois, is located at the watersmeet of the Mississippi and Ohio rivers.>

Mastery Test

Choose the best answer to each question.

___ 1. Where would you be most likely to see a *borrow pit?*

a. near the seashore
b. close to a highway
c. atop a hill

___ 2. What does *friable* mean?

a. easily fried
b. like clay
c. easily pulverized

___ 3. May a *scape* be seen only in a rural area?

a. yes
b. no

___ 4. What is true of a *xerophilous* plant?

a. It likes a dry climate.
b. It likes cold weather.
c. It reproduces prolifically.

___ 5. *Sheet erosion* is most likely to be caused by what?

a. heavy rain
b. steady light rain
c. wind
d. wind and drought
e. drought

___ 6. What is true of an *affluent* stream?

a. It carries a load of soil.
b. It flows away from a place we are concerned with.
c. It flows into a place we are concerned with.

___ 7. What is a coulee?

a. an ice formation
b. a small stream or ravine
c. one side of a valley

___ 8. What is *detritus?*

a. decayed rock
b. unnecessary destruction of natural resources

c. pieces of rock broken away from a larger mass

___ 9. Which way does an *acclivity* slant?

a. upward
b. downward

___ 10. Where might you most probably find a *sward?*

a. in a flat area with few trees
b. in a museum of medieval history
c. close to a large river

___ 11. At what place would a *genius loci* be likely to be evident?

a. in a forest
b. in any place with a character of its own
c. in a large city
d. in a small town

___ 12. What is most likely true of *permeable* soil?

a. It is friable clay.
b. It is hard.
c. Water penetrates it easily.
d. It is unusually long-lasting.

___ 13. *Water table* is synonymous with what?

a. groundwater level
b. groundwater
c. the table where water is available to diners
d. table water

___ 14. Where would you be most likely to find a *boreen?*

a. in a chemistry laboratory
b. on a workbench
c. in New York City
d. in Ireland

___ 15. On a *scarp* what danger might be most likely?

a. falling off
b. wild beasts
c. gunfire
d. forest fire

___ 16. The point where a warm spring becomes a hot spring is what?

a. 88° F
b. 72° F
c. 98.6° F
d. 98° F

___ 17. Which surface is most likely mainly black?

a. moonscape
b. scabland
c. scrubland
d. escarpment

___ 18. Which might you find inside a house?

a. escarpment
b. miniascape
c. crepuscular rays
d. water gap

30
THE WATER AND THE SHORE

All life, scientists tell us, derives ultimately from the sea, and man has tended to settle first along the margins of the oceans, lakes, and rivers. As a result, we have coined familiar words like *shore, coast, bank, shallows, waves, and tides,* and a number of others less well known but still important to millions of people.

The gravitational pull of the moon, which causes tides, varies from quarter to quarter. During the first and third quarters, the difference between high and low tide is relatively small; the tides with so little variation are **neap tides.** But during the time of the new and the full moon, the difference is considerably greater and we have **spring tides,** with *spring* used not in a seasonal sense but in the sense of springing up. As the word *ebb* suggests, an **ebb tide** is receding; a **flood tide** is rising. Before any turn of the tide there is a time of **slack water** or **slack tide** when the water does not appear to be rising or falling at all. During a heavy storm at sea, vast amounts of water may be moved by the wind toward the shore; this water, added to normal flood tide, creates a **storm tide,** which is abnormally high and which may occur even when onshore weather is very pleasant. A **tide day** or **tidal day** is the length of time between one high tide and the next—in most places a little less than twenty-five hours. A **tsunami,** loosely called a *tidal wave,* is Japanese for port wave, because of the damage it may do in ports; it refers to an unusually large ocean wave caused by an underwater cataclysm—an earthquake or a volcanic eruption.

Pelagic means pertaining to the open sea. Thus pelagic life is that whose habitat is the deep sea rather than close to land: <Charles Darwin: "I had a net overboard to catch pelagic animals."> Closer to shore are the **sublittoral** waters, which are always submerged but extend to the low-water marks on the shore. However, sometimes **adlittoral,** "to the shore," is used to describe the generally shallow area closest to these low-water marks. **Littoral** areas are those parts of a seacoast that are bare at low tide but covered at high tide. The word and its own derivatives come from Latin *litus,* "shore," which has been traced to a much older Indo-European **lēi,* "to flow," with reference to the daily inflow and recession of tidal waters over parts of the shore.

Water close to the shore is often frothy and foamy and is called **spume,** a word also applied to any bubbly effervescence, such as that of a boiling liquid. Fine sea spray is **spindrift.** This word, too, is more broadly applied, to anything light, airy, and windborne—even figuratively: <his spindrift ambitions, ever-changing and never based on reality>.

A shore that is extraordinarily steep is sometimes described with the adjective **steep-to:** <The boat anchored in the lee of a steep-to shore for protection against the storm.> (Less often, an inland cliff or mountainside may also be described as *steep-to.*)

On a sandy beach, as each wave recedes, it leaves a low ridge of sand, a **wavemark,** to indicate its farthest advance. Soon a sturdier wave surpasses it and leaves its own temporary signature.

On any shore, with each high tide the sea gradually submerges the land, and before it leaves, it deposits and stratifies sand, silt, and anything else carried in by the powerful waters. **Onlap** is the name given both to the process of submergence and to the newly formed strata: <Rare shells are sometimes found in the onlap at Sanibel Island.> The recession of the tide carries the sand, silt, and other objects back toward the sea; the process of ebbing and the materials left near the water's edge are both called **offlap.** On a larger scale, over a period of centuries or millenniums the sea may more enduringly rise or fall, causing more lasting onlaps or offlaps.

Latin *rivus* means stream, and *rivalis* means pertaining to a stream. People who live across a stream from each other, or close to each other on the same side, have often quarreled about fishing rights, the right to build a dam, or other privileges that one or the other has assumed. Our *rival*, from the Latin words, commemorates such competitiveness of the river people, and so do *rivalry* and **rivalrous,** "showing rivalry; pertaining to rivalry": <the rivalrous instincts of the young bull elephants>.

From Latin *ripa*, "bank, shore," the Romans derived *riparius*, "pertaining to the bank of a river." English has taken this word over as **riparian.** A riparian is a person who lives or owns property on the bank of a river. As an adjective, *riparian* means pertaining to or located on the bank of a river or (sometimes) the shore of a lake. **Riparian rights** are often the subject of legal controversy, and in some places lawyers specialize in **riparian law.** Sometimes the subject of controversy is the extent of the **foreshore**—the narrow strip of land next to the water. (On a seacoast, the foreshore is the land between the extremes of low and high tide.)

Other Words Pertaining to Bodies of Water

Arctalian *adj*, **Antarctalian** *adj* These words take in more territory than do *Arctic* and *Antarctic*. *Arctalian* is used for the marine biogeographic region, including all northern seas and as far south as the icebergs travel—generally that means farther south than Newfoundland, as icebergs sometimes force temporary changes in customary North Atlantic shipping lanes. **Antarctalian** refers to the marine biogeographic region south of a line where mean temperatures are about 44° F (4° C).

benthic *n*, **benthos** *n* The benthos is the bottom, especially the deepest parts, of a sea or lake, and also may be the organisms that live there. *Benthic* means "pertaining to the benthos." <Could benthic life survive nuclear winter?>

black mayonnaise *n* People now know that oceans can become badly polluted despite their size. On the bottom of bays and harbors and even parts of the ocean floor surprisingly far from land lies sometimes toxic black or dark brown sludge, composed typically of oil, sewage, feces, and what-have-you. Because of its color and its consistency of thick mayonnaise, someone has nicknamed it *black mayonnaise.*

cross sea *n* The choppy surface caused by waves stirred up from different directions by possibly distant storms.

HYDROLANT, *n*, **HYDROPAC** *n* The U.S. Navy Hydrographic Office issues, as needed, urgent warnings of navigational hazards such as severe storms: HYDROLANT for the Atlantic, HYDROPAC for the Pacific.

limnal *adj*, and related words. *Limnal* means pertaining to lakes: <Limnal freezes sometimes kill all the fish.> A **limnimeter** can measure the very slight tides in lakes; it makes its record on a **limnigraph.** A **limnologist,** whose speciality is **limnology,** studies the plants, animals, chemistry, and physical properties of lakes. The source of all these words is a Greek word for pool, lake.

limpid *adj* The basic meaning of *limpid*—a word derived from Latin *limpa,* "water"—is "clear, free of any murkiness": <a limpid pool>. Figuratively, though, not only water may be limpid. A style of writing, painting, architecture, or music is limpid if it is simple and clear, and a person who is calm, serene, untroubled may be described as having a limpid disposition.

maremma *n* Especially but not exclusively in Italy, a swampy area close to the seashore; the term also applies to its unhealthful atmosphere. Plural *maremme.*

rapture of the deep *n* Technically *nitrogen narcosis.* The term was invented by Jacques Cousteau for a problem sometimes encountered by deep-sea divers. Besides light-headedness and unclear thinking, the diver may experience euphoria, a carefree feeling that everything is safe and wonderful. Hence "rapture."

sea oats *n* A tall grass of southeastern U.S. coasts, useful in controlling sand beach erosion.

sea puss *n* Has nothing to do with cats. The term is from Algonquian for a tidal stream near Long Island. Oceanographers use it for a dangerous near-shore undertow.

swash *vi, vt, n* To splash, to dash water against, or (as a noun) the sound made by such movement. Swashing may range from gentle to crashing, as people who spend much time on oceanside piers can verify.

thermocline *n* In lakes and other large bodies of water, temperatures are often stratified, with a layer of similar temperature, then a layer of colder temperature, and so on. Between such strata there may be a thermocline, which is itself a layer in which temperature decreases rapidly with depth—usually one or more degrees Celsius for each meter of descent.

transmarine *adj* Existing across the sea, or coming from or going across the sea: <transmarine people> <a transmarine trip>.

twilight zone *n* To an oceanographer the twilight zone is the deepest ocean level to which light can penetrate.

Mastery Test

Is each statement *true* (T) or *false* (F)?

___ 1. The *foreshore* is the water in front of the shore.

___ 2. An *adlittoral* area is between *littoral* and *infralittoral* areas.

___ 3. A *thermocline* is water with relatively constant temperature.

___ 4. Sharks are never *pelagic.*

___ 5. If you are a *riparian,* you are likely to be interested in water levels.

____ 6. A *slack tide* is generally a low tide.

____ 7. A *tsunami* may cause considerable damage to small boats along the shore.

____ 8. *Transmarine* means sending marines across the water.

____ 9. The *Antarctalian* area extends farther north than the Antarctic area.

____ 10. A *flood tide* occurs only after a storm.

____ 11. A *limnologist* specializes in painting waterscapes.

____ 12. If one is slapped by a wave, a *wavemark* may result.

____ 13. A *tidal day* usually lasts almost twenty-five hours in most places.

____ 14. Sand and silt may be deposited ashore by an *onlap*.

____ 15. *Limpid* water is relatively easy to see through.

____ 16. *Black mayonnaise* is inedible.

____ 17. The climate of a *maremma* is probably unhealthful.

____ 18. The main use of *sea oats* is to fight cholesterol.

____ 19. *Benthos* is the name for the deepest parts of a large body of water.

____ 20. Light does not penetrate beyond the *twilight zone*.

31
FUR AND FEATHERS

The adaptability of living things is reflected in our words relating to places where they live. A **ubiquist** (from the same source as *ubiquity*, "the state of being everywhere") is an organism found throughout a region: <Among the ubiquists of our region are rabbits, raccoons, and opossums.> A **eurythermal** creature can exist in a wide range of temperatures; the word comes from Greek and Latin words for broad and heat. In contrast **stenothermal** describes plants and animals not capable of surviving except in a narrow temperature range. A **stenecious** plant or animal also can exist only in a limited sort of environment: <stenecious bacteria found only in the sputum of coyotes> <a stenecious mushroom of Lower California>.

During the Ice Age some areas were less affected than others climatically. In those places, called **refugia** (singular *refugium*), many plants and animals survived, and as the ice retreated, they spread out or back to the once-again habitable areas. Adaptation to the various environments has taken many forms. Creatures that can exist beneath the snow are **subnivean:** <subnivean burrows used by some small ro-

dents>. Organisms (for example, trout) that prefer living in moving water are described as **lotic;** others (for example, carp), which prefer still water, are **lentic.** A plant, insect, animal, or bird that lives among rocks is **petricolous.**

Any creatures that live or spend time in nests are **nidicolous.** When birds or other creatures are building a nest, they are **nidifying** or **nidificating. Nidology** is the study of birds' nests and is the occupation of a **nidologist.** All these words come from Latin *nidus,* "nest."

Some animals, birds, or insects, called **inquilines,** don't bother to make their own homes but move into the dwelling of a creature of a different species. Thus the burrowing owl, which lives in prairie dog holes, is an inquiline. Other creatures, described as **cryptobiotic,** literally "secret life," spend most of their time concealed from those not of their own kind; examples are whippoorwills and termites.

Vagile means free to move about; it comes from Latin *vagus,* "wandering." It is contrasted with **sessile** (from *sēdere,* "to sit"), which means permanently attached. <With some exceptions, animals are vagile and plants are sessile.> A vagile animal likes to have a way to escape danger, a **bolt-hole:** <In addition to the main entrance a groundhog almost always has a bolt-hole at the end of a tunnel perhaps twenty feet from the entrance.> Bushes, tall grass, and the like provide an **escape cover** (or **escape covert**) to which vagile creatures may flee when predators threaten: <Pheasants have almost disappeared from this area because of the loss of escape cover.>

The digestive systems of birds and animals have adapted themselves to various kinds of food, some being much more specialized than others. Most of the adjectives describing eating habits are based on Latin *-vorus,* "feeding on," or Greek *-phagos,* "eating."

amphivorous eating both vegetables and meat (e.g., dogs)
carnivorous or **zoophagous** eating meat (e.g., wolves)
entomophagous eating insects (e.g., swallows)
fungivorous eating fungi (e.g., people eat mushrooms)
geophagous eating dirt (e.g., earthworms). Starving

people sometimes become **geophagists**—they practice **geophagy**—because of the urge to feel something in their bellies.

graminivorous eating grass (e.g., horses). The botanical order to which grasses belong is Graminales.

herbivorous eating seeds or other vegetable parts (e.g., squirrels)

hippophagous eating horseflesh. <Many people have unknowingly been hippophagous.> The act of eating horseflesh is **hippophagy,** and one who eats it is a **hippophagist.**

hylophagous eating wood (e.g., termites)

limivorous eating mud (e.g., certain crustaceans)

monophagous eating only one kind of food (e.g., seed-eating birds)

omnivorous eating anything (e.g., chickens)

oophagous eating eggs (e.g., weasels, people)

phyllophagous eating leaves (e.g., deer, certain worms)

phytophagous eating plants (e.g., cabbage worms). If a vertebrate is plant-eating, we describe it as herbivorous, but if an insect or other lower animal is plant-eating, we call it phytophagous.

pleophagous or **polyphagous** eating a variety of foods (e.g., starlings)

seminivorous eating seeds (e.g., chickadees, titmice)

Occasionally one may want to refer to the essential quality or nature of dogs in general, or to the canine race as a whole. Obviously *doggedness* won't do, and probably not *doggishness*, so **caninity** is useful: <Rover had grown up assuming that he was a person, but inevitably his caninity emerged.> **Dogdom** may mean "all dogs," "the condition of being a dog," or "all dog-lovers." Corresponding to *caninity*, but for horses, cats, and pigs, are **equinity, felinity,** and **porcinity** (certainly not *horsiness, cattiness,* and *piggishness*). No doubt we should have similar names for cows, sheep, and goats, but I find none in dictionaries. I suggest *bovinity, ovinity,* and either *capricity* or *hircinity* (not *goatishness!*).

Just as it is handy to use the adjective *canine* instead of something more cumbersome like "pertaining to dogs," so it may occasionally be convenient to have these *-ine* words at one's disposal:

accipitrine pertaining to hawks
anserine geese
aquiline eagles
asinine asses
corvine crows
lacertine lizards
leonine lions
ovine sheep
passerine perching birds
vulpine foxes

More About Animals and Birds

acaudal or **acaudate** *adj* A caudal or caudate appendage is a tail; *caudal* means possessing a tail. <Charles Darwin, 1872: "The male . . . bird, remarkable for its caudal plumes">. The opposite is *acaudal* or *acaudate* (Greek *a-*, "without," and Latin *cauda*, "tail"). <A Manx cat is acaudate except for a few internal vertebrae.> Incidentally, *coward* is also from *cauda*, presumably because some frightened or cowardly animals run away with their tails between their legs.

bausond *adj, n* Sometime it may be useful to you, in describing a horse or other animal, to refer to hiser bausond—a white spot or streak on the dark background of hiser forehead or face. The word dates back five hundred years but still has reached only dialect status. One of Robert Burns's "twa dogs" is described as having an "honest, sonsie [pleasant], baws'nt face."

chiropodous *adj* Having feet adapted for grasping and climbing: <A squirrel is chiropodous.>

chirr *n, vi* A repetitive sound like that of cicadas and grasshoppers, made or apparently made by rubbing together two rough surfaces, is a chirr. Making such a sound is chirring. <All night the katydids chirred.> (See also *stridulation.*)

chunter or **chunner** *vi* Instead of saying "The cows, pigs, sheep, and horses uttered their respective typical sounds," it is possible to say (in some British dialects) "The cows, pigs, sheep, and horses [or any other animals] chuntered." Obviously this verb can save time for people who need to talk or write about animals and who don't object to giving wider circulation to dialectal terms.

congener *n* The derivation of *congener*—from Latin words meaning of the same race or kind—explains the meaning: <The dog is a congener of the wolf and the fox.> Persons similar to others—for example, in stinginess or in pleasant temperament—are congeners. Related chemical substances are also congeners.

couchant *adj* Some terms from heraldry might be moderately useful if better known. If, for instance, you want to say that an animal is lying down but has its head raised, the heraldic term *couchant* can save you several words: <The dog is couchant.> <In coats of arms, couchant lions were frequent.>

cynology *n,* **cynologist** *n* Cynology is the scientific study of dogs, including the history of the species and the characteristics of the various breeds. One who specializes in such study is a cynologist.

definitive plumage *n* Baby birds look very different from adults. The pattern of feathers that the babies eventually achieve remains with them and is called their *definitive plumage.*

deratization *n* Rats are sometimes numerous on ships and often in poor housing. Getting rid of them is deratization.

deserticolous *adj* *-Colous* is from Latin *-cola,* "inhabitant." *Deserticolous,* then, means pertaining to living in a desert, desert-dwelling: <Deserticolous animals are more numerous than you would suspect.>

die-up *n* In the western United States, if many cattle or other range animals die because of drought, blizzard, grass fire, or other such phenomena, stockmen refer to a *die-up.* An individual animal that perishes in a die-up is also called a *die-up:* <There's another die-up over there.>

dogie *n* The animal that is urged "Git along, little dogie" is a motherless calf.

dominance hierarchy *n*, **pecking order** *n* Earlier in this century someone discovered that in a flock of hens the dominant hen may peck all the others, No. 2 can peck all but No. 1, and so on down to the forlorn bird that is not allowed to peck anybody. So the term *pecking order* arose, and was applied to other groups, too, including people. But that designation did not seem fancy enough, and the behavior did not consist merely of pecking, so social scientists substituted *dominance hierarchy.*

echolocation *n* Even in darkness a bat can fly among and around trees and buildings without bumping into them. The bat's secret is echolocation—the steady emission of very-high-frequency sounds that echo back from solid objects and tell the bat of their presence, their distance, and their location. Submarine-hunting ships may use equipment based on the same general principle. Perhaps someday sophisticated echolocation devices will reduce some of the problems of blind persons out walking.

first cross *n*, **crossbred** *adj*, **double hybrid** *n*, **three-breed cross** *n* The offspring of a purebred collie and a purebred Irish setter—or any other pair of differing purebred animals—is a first cross. In contrast, a mongrel is a mixture of several or many different breeds. *Crossbred* is an adjective describing a first cross: <crossbred kittens>. If one first cross mates with a first cross of two still different ancestral lines, the result is a double hybrid (2 + 2). But if, say, a collie-setter offspring mates with a collie-pointer offspring, the result is a three-breed cross.

fossorial *adj*, **cursorial** *adj*, **prehensile** *adj* Fossorial animals are adept at digging, cursorial ones can run well, and prehensile ones are capable of gripping and carrying. A reason for our emergence as the dominant animal is that we possess all three skills to a fair degree.

geratology *n* The study of the approach to death of an animal or, more often, the movement of a species toward extinction: <Geratologists are now busy people, as

hundreds of species of plant and animal life vanish each year.>

hippic *adj*, **hippology** *n* As many people know, *hippopotamus* means river horse and *hippo-* is from the Greek word for horse. *Hippic*, from the same source, means pertaining to horses or horse racing: <hippic ailments>. (*Horsey* or *horsy*, another adjective, usually describes people who like horses or belong to a set wealthy enough to own riding horses.) *Hippology* means the study of horses.

liger *n*, **tiglon** or **tigon** *n* A male lion and a female tiger have been known to produce a *liger*, which may grow to a weight of nine hundred pounds. A *tiglon* or *tigon*, considerably smaller, may result from the mating of a male tiger and a female lion. The cross-breeding is generally between tamed animals. Familiarity breeds consummation.

living fossil *n* A living fossil is a plant or an animal of an ancient type that has changed but little since earlier geologic eras, even though its long-ago relatives have become extinct. An example is the gingko tree, which is virtually the same as its ancestors of some 225 million years ago.

mammillary *adj*, **mammillate** or **mammilate** *adj* Mammillary means pertaining to breasts, or shaped like breasts: <The Tetons received their name because of their mammillary appearance.> *Mammillate* has as its primary meaning having nipples or nipplelike protuberances: <mammillate warts on the Hubbard squash>.

mimetic *adj* Imitative. Besides the mimetic endeavors of actors and actresses, one may refer to mimetic animals (such as the mockingbird or the viceroy butterfly), to mimetic plants or minerals (such as certain seaweeds and crystals), or to anything else displaying intentional or natural mimicry.

nativeness *n* The state of being native: <The nativeness of this shrew is dubious, since it closely resembles an Asian variety.>

oology *n* Birdwatchers, and their perhaps more scientific cousins, the ornithologists, have their own specialties.

Those who collect birds' eggs and study the shape, size, and coloration have oology as their specialty.

ornithography *n* Greek *ornith-*, "bird," is familiar to us in a number of words like *ornithology*, "the study of birds." One of the less familiar derivatives (not in *Webster 3*) is *ornithography*, "writing about birds": <Her major fame as a writer resulted from her ornithography—two books and dozens of popular articles about birds.>

parturient *adj* Giving birth: <parturient ewes>. Like *parturition*, "the act of giving birth," the word comes from Latin *parturire*, "to be in labor."

recognition mark *n* A distinctive mark, such as a white spot, making an animal or a bird easy to recognize—supposedly by others of the same species: <the white-tufted underside of the tail—the well-known recognition mark of these American rabbits>.

stridulation *n*, and related words. On summer evenings in the country one may hear the stridulation of the katydids, cicadas, and other insects—sounds made not vocally but by rubbing together legs, wings, or other specially adapted parts of the body. These insects **stridulate** *(vi)*; their shrill, vibrating sound is **stridulant** *(adj)*; an insect that is able to stridulate is **stridulatory** *(adj)* and is a **stridulator** *(n)*. (See also *chirr*.)

tachytely *n*, **bradetely** *n*, **horotely** *n* One of the meanings of the Greek root of *-tely* is degree of completion. The three words considered here refer to the rate or degree of completion of evolutionary processes in plants and animals. *Bradetely* (*brad-*, "slow") refers to a relatively slow rate of evolution; some modern reptiles that are little different from their remote ancestors illustrate it. *Horotely* (*horo-*, "limit") means evolution within the usual speed limits for a given group. *Tachytely* (*tachy-*, "rapid") means evolution faster than usual, like that of some modern plants that have been helped along by botanical experimenters.

territoriality *n* Male birds often "sing" to warn other birds, "This is my territory, and I'll defend it." Other animals issue their own comparable signals, from puffing out their chests to emitting identifying scents. People show territoriality, too, as in "Keep Out" signs, slogans such as "Fifty-four forty or fight," or the Monroe Doctrine.

viviparous *adj,* and related words. Viviparous animals give birth to living young. **Larviparous** ones, such as certain flies, produce larvae. **Oviparous** ones, such as hens, produce eggs in which the young develop outside the maternal body. **Ovoviviparous** ones, such as many reptiles, produce eggs in which the young develop entirely or almost entirely inside the maternal body.

zoosemiotics *n* Loosely, "animal language" but inclusive of signals other than sound, such as a dog's tail-wagging, a cat's jumping into its owner's lap, or an adult bird's pretense of being wounded to distract attention from its young.

Mastery Test

Match the members of each group.

I. If it lives (1–10), it can be described as (a–j).

___	1. in moving water	a.	subnivean
___	2. almost everywhere in the area	b.	petricolous
___	3. under the snow	c.	inquiline
___	4. in nests	d.	lotic
___	5. among the rocks	e.	eurythermal
___	6. away from other species	f.	nidicolous
___	7. in another creature's home	g.	lentic
___	8. in quiet water	h.	a ubiquist
___	9. in only a limited environment	i.	cryptobiotic
___	10. in a wide temperature range	j.	stenecious

II. If it eats (11–20), it can be described as (k–t).

____ 11. dirt
____ 12. seeds
____ 13. eggs
____ 14. horseflesh
____ 15. wood
____ 16. grass
____ 17. flies and worms
____ 18. only one kind of food
____ 19. both vegetables and meat
____ 20. leaves

k. oophagous
l. graminivorous
m. entomophagous
n. hippophagous
o. amphivorous
p. monophagous
q. hylophagous
r. phyllophagous
s. seminivorous
t. geophagous

III. If it's (21–30), it's (u–dd).

____ 21. a pig
____ 22. a goose
____ 23. a lizard
____ 24. a sheep
____ 25. a perching bird
____ 26. a fox
____ 27. a crow
____ 28. a hawk
____ 29. an ass
____ 30. an eagle

u. lacertine
v. vulpine
w. asinine
x. anserine
y. ovine
z. porcine
aa. accipitrine
bb. passerine
cc. aquiline
dd. corvine

IV. If it can be described as (31–40), it may be a (ee–nn).

____ 31. acaudal
____ 32. chiropodous
____ 33. a repetitive, stridulant sound
____ 34. a white mark on the face
____ 35. of the same race or kind
____ 36. fossorial
____ 37. lying with head raised
____ 38. cursorial

ee. squirrel
ff. bausond
gg. couchant animal
hh. living fossil
ii. Manx cat
jj. chirr
kk. deer
ll. badger

___ 39. similar to its distant ancestors — mm. duck

___ 40. oviparous — nn. congener

V. If you work at (41–45), you (oo–ss).

___ 41. studying birds' nests — oo. enjoy cynology

___ 42. studying dogs scientifically — pp. enjoy oology

___ 43. studying birds' eggs — qq. are a geratologist

___ 44. studying extinction of species — rr. are a nidologist

___ 45. writing about birds — ss. specialize in ornithography

32
PLANTS IN OUR LIVES

Without plants, none of us would survive for very long. Not only do they provide us directly or indirectly with almost all our food, they also contribute to our housing, our medication, the heating and cooling of our surroundings, and the purification of the air. Yet city dwellers in particular tend to have no more than the most basic knowledge of plants or the vocabulary to talk about them.

To the farmer or gardener the **germinability** of seed—that is, what proportion of a planting may be expected to sprout—is a matter of importance. Some seed companies, on the basis of tests, indicate the percentage of germinability to be expected for each variety of seed.

For many species of plants, pollination is essential. The processes of evolution have developed a number of methods for transferring pollen from anther to stigma to accomplish fertilization. If the wind has the responsibility, a plant is **anemophilous,** "wind-loving" (cf. *anemometer*). If insects are responsible, it is **entomophilous** (cf. *entomology*). Plants that depend on birds are **ornithophilous,** and the few that rely on water are **hydrophilous.** There are a few others for which snails carry the pollen; these are **malacophilous,** from a scientific name for mollusks.

Conditions of soil and weather or climate may strongly influence plant growth. Greek *edaphos* means soil, and English **edaphic** is literally "pertaining to the soil." *Edaphic analysis* is thus a fancy way of saying "soil analysis." To the ecologist, however, *edaphic* refers to the relationship of the soil to the entire life of an area or to interaction between the soil and any parts of that life: <Edaphic characteristics here favor the growth of coniferous trees but limit the growth of most grasses.> Plants do have soil preferences, and not always for rich, friable soil. Some, for instance, called **ruderal** plants, like to grow in rubble, especially in a place disturbed and then largely abandoned by people: <the ruderal growing alongside hundreds of miles of unused railroad tracks>. Other plants, called **breakstones,** are strong enough to force their way up through cracks in stones. (One of these plants is the **saxifrage,** which in Latin means rock-breaking herb.) Plants that prefer alkaline soils may be described as **basophile** or **basophilous.** The antonym, to describe whatever prefers acid soils, is **acidophilous.**

Soil conditions change, and often for the worse unless man applies suitable treatment. In hilly farmland you may often note that soil is less deep and rich near the tops of hills than near the bottoms. Wind and water have moved some of the hilltop soil to lower levels, but some of the movement is attributed to **soil creep,** "gradual downhill movement of soil because of the pull of gravity." Lack of moisture in soil is also often detrimental to plant growth. When the earth reaches a certain degree of dryness, called the **wilting point** or the **wilting coefficient** (which varies from species to species), permanent wilting of plants results: <fields of soybeans dangerously close to their wilting point>.

On the other hand, if weather or other conditions are particularly favorable to growth, the conditions are described as **growthy:** <the growthy hot nights of July that corn loves so well>. Also, a plant especially inclined to grow may be growthy: <Hybridization has made these petunias unusually growthy.> **Half-hardy** plants, like those of cabbage and lettuce, are able to survive temperatures slightly below freezing.

Half-hardy perennials can endure moderately cold winters but not long periods of below-zero weather. *Boreas,* the Greek god of the north wind, has given us **boreal,** "pertaining to northern regions," and also **borealization,** "adaptation to life in northerly regions": <Borealization of bananas has not yet been accomplished.> Some varieties of plants—squash, say—mature early, some in midseason, and some late. One that matures in midseason is described as **semilate. Seasonality** is the quality or condition of being seasonal: <the well-known seasonality of watermelons> <Ease of transportation has decreased seasonality, which used to dictate what fresh fruits and vegetables would be available in the stores.>

Plants, like people or other animals, interact with one another in various sociological ways. Thus some plants are most often found in proximity to others, and some make constant territorial demands and try to crowd others out. The branch of ecology that deals with plant relationships is **phytosociology.** An **ecosystem** consists of all the living creatures—plants and animals—in a given area and of the interactions of those creatures with the air, water, and soil of the same area. The extent of the ecosystem is arbitrary; a cubic foot of land has its own ecosystem, and at the opposite extreme the entire planet has an ecosystem. <Donald C. Peattie in *A Prairie Grove* described the ecosystem of one square mile of wooded land.>

An **ecotone** (*-tone* coming from the Greek *tonos,* "tension") is a transitional area between two contiguous ecological communities, such as cultivated and uncultivated land, or timber and marsh. Within the ecotone there is usually tension between the inhabitants of the areas—for example, weeds from the uncultivated land cross the boundary into the cultivated. And some plants and animals tend to flourish especially in the ecotone; thus fiddler crabs abound in the sand shared by land and ocean. In general, plant and animal life near the edge of a plot of land that is unlike adjoining plots may vary considerably from that near the center. Biologists call this phenomenon the **edge effect**—a term that physicists also use, to show, for instance, that the amount of turbulence or the electric surface density near an edge of an object may be demonstrably unlike conditions in the center.

Trees, the largest living things, have resulted in the addition of many words to the language. A number of these are derived from Greek *dendr-*, "tree":

dendriform like a tree in shape or structure <a dendriform coral>
dendritic branching like a tree
dendrochronology dating events and studying variations in environment through the analysis of growth rings in old trees
dendrogram a family "tree" or other tree-shaped diagram
dendrograph an instrument for automatic measuring of tree growth
dendrometer any of various instruments for measuring heights and diameters of trees
dendrophagous tree-eating
dendrophilous tree-loving: <Virginia creeper is a dendrophilous vine.>

Latin *silva*, "wood, forest," is also the ancestor of numerous English words, dealing mainly with forest trees:

silva the forests or woods of an area (comparable to *flora* and *fauna*)
silvicolous inhabiting wooded areas: <silvicolous animals>
silvics or **sylvics** study of environmental influence on forest trees during their whole lifetimes
silvicultural pertaining to silviculture
silviculture the planting, care, and harvesting of forest trees
silviculturist one who engages in silviculture
sylvan or **silvan** pertaining to the forests or woods (especially in an idyllic sense)

Horticulture is the growing of fruits, vegetables, and flowers. **Pomology** is the science of growing fruits. One branch of it is **citriculture,** the growing of citrus fruits, such as oranges and kumquats.

Fire and ice are both enemies of trees. In forest areas you may have seen signs indicating the degree of danger of forest fires. Those signs, which may be revised daily, are based on the **burning index,** a figure determined by the relative moisture of the forest, the wind speed, and other factors. If a fire begins, one of the greatest problems for those who must fight it is the **crown fire,** which is one that leaps from treetop to treetop and often causes the fire to spread much more rapidly than it would if confined to ground level. Occasionally **crown** is used as a verb to refer to the phenomenon: <"The fire is crowning!" he shouted.> During cold weather, the frigid temperature sometimes causes a tree trunk to split. The split is called a **frost crack.** When the wound heals, a ridge called a **frost rib** or **frost ridge** is often left. Sometimes severe cold during dogwood winter (q.v.) causes leaves to fall off (with replacement leaves emerging a little later). Evidence of such a freeze is retained in **frost rings,** thin, brownish lines between the annual growth rings.

More Words About Plants

annuation *n* In one year the number of violets (or any other small plants) in a given area may be very large, the next year very small, and so on in irregular variation. These annual changes in numbers of a species of plants are caused mainly by differences in temperature and precipitation and are referred to as *annuation.*

azonic *adj* Anything not local, not confined to a particular zone: <Only a few plants, birds, and animals are strictly local; most are azonic.>

bocage *n* French *boscage,* "grove, thicket," is occasionally used in English. *Bocage* is a modification of *boscage* but refers not to groves or thickets but to rural areas cut up into rather small patches of woodland, orchards, and little fields. In the United States, especially the East and much of the Midwest and South abound in bocage.

bosky *adj* Probably most of us have heard of a "bosky dell" without knowing the meaning of *bosky:* heavily grown over with thickets, bushes, or small trees.

celeriac *n* **celtuce** *n* Two vegetables perhaps deserving more recognition are celeriac, a variety of celery in which the root rather than the stem is eaten, and celtuce, a fast-growing plant with leaves that taste like lettuce and stems somewhat like those of celery. Still being sought is a satisfactory **pomato, potomato,** or **topato,** a plant that through a graft of tomato scions on potato plants would produce tomatoes above the ground, potatoes below.

chou *n* (pl. **choux**) The French word for cabbage is employed in English as the name of a soft rosette shaped something like a cabbage and used as a clothing ornament. And since for some peculiar reason many French people use *chou* as a term of endearment roughly equivalent to *sweetheart,* some English and American people also do so, sometimes varying it by calling their beloved *choufleur,* "cauliflower." The ways of love are strange.

cryophilic *adj,* **thermophilic** *adj* Cryophilic plants or animals prefer cold or cool surroundings, but thermophilic ones are happy in warm weather or warm climates.

cuttage *n,* **graftage** *n* Two methods of propagating plants are cuttage, which is the planting of cuttings that eventually develop into complete plants, and graftage, which is the uniting of one part of a plant (called the *scion*) to another plant (called the *stock*).

dentate *adj* Leaves with toothed edges are said to be dentate.

design bedding *n.* **carpet bedding** *n* If you plant flowers or foliage plants in a design that looks like some object, word, etc., you are creating a design bedding: <In a huge design bedding, red tulips surrounded the word MOM, spelled out in white tulips.> Carpet bedding, in contrast, is more like abstract art—a patterned arrangement of low flowers or foliage but not intended to represent a specific object, etc.

diddledees *n* No one seems to know why, but some people in New England refer to fallen pine needles as diddledees: <a soft ground covering of diddledees>.

ecdysis *n,* **endysis** *n* Birds, snakes, cicadas, and some other creatures shed their garments occasionally and then grow new ones. This molting or shedding is ecdysis, and the replacement is endysis. On the basis of *ecdysis* (which goes back to Greek *ekdyein,* "to strip off") H. L. Mencken coined **ecdysiast,** "stripteaser." Since burlesque queens seldom reverse the strip act (at least onstage), there is apparently little need for *endysiast.*

espalier *n, vt* A fruit tree or some other plant that has been trained to grow flat against a wall or other flat surface is an espalier. So is a trellis, etc., on which such flat growth may occur. The word may also be a verb: <He espaliered a pear tree and a lilac bush.>

etiolation *n* If you try to grow a plant in too little sunlight, its leaves become yellow or white, and the plant loses vigor. This process or its result is known as *etiolation.* By extension, the word means any decrease in vigor, not confined to plants and not necessarily caused by lack of sunlight: <Living alone so long with almost no outside contacts had resulted in George's mental etiolation.> People who are extremely self-centered and who suffer from an unusual inability to make up their minds are also said to suffer from etiolation.

flavescence *n* Certain diseases of plants also cause a reduction of chlorophyll and a consequent change of leaf color to yellow or white. This change is known as *flavescence.* The adjectival form is **flavescent:** <flavescent foliage>.

floret *n,* also called *flowerlet.* A tiny, dainty flower, or a single small flower in a multiple head. The little flowerlike designs that printers sometimes use in borders or for purposes of separation or decoration are also known as florets.

frondescence *n,* and related words. The stage in a plant's life during which leaves are unfolding is frondescence, sometimes called *foliation.* With reference to the opening of flowers, the corresponding word is **florescence,** or sometimes **anthesis** or **efflorescence.** The period of growth of fruit is **fructescence.**

fruitive *adj* Capable of producing fruit: <Our orchard was fruitive after five years.>

fugacious *adj* From the same root as *fugitive, fugacious* means disappearing quickly: <as fugacious as yesterday's applause>. With reference to plants, leaves or petals that fall prematurely or before others do may be described as *fugacious.*

grabble *vi, vt,* **guddle** *vi, vt* The basic meaning of *grabble* is to grope, to grope for, but in the South it has more specific meanings. While potatoes are still growing, it is possible to grabble with one's hands beneath the vines to remove the largest tubers, and then replace the dirt so that smaller ones can continue their growth. It is also possible to grabble for fish, putting one's hands into hollow sunken logs or other likely hiding places. This procedure is also sometimes called *hogging* fish, although this term seems not to be included in dictionaries. Still another word for it is *guddling.*

green out *vi* When plants put out their green shoots, as in the spring or after a severe drought, they are said to be *greening out:* <"Looks like that old maple will green out again, but I never thought it'd make it.">

heel in *vt* When shrubs or trees arrive from the nursery and cannot be planted at once, they should be heeled in—that is, the roots should be given a temporary cover of wet soil to prevent their drying out.

heliotropism *n,* **heliotropic** *adj,* **phototropism** *n* Most houseplants near a window will lean and grow toward the light—a phenomenon known as *phototropism.* When a plant tries to turn toward the sun, as the well-named sunflower does, it is said to be *heliotropic* and to illustrate *heliotropism,* words that come from Greek *helios,* "sun," and *tropos,* "turn."

horizontal training *n* The gardener or orchardist who trains hiser fruit trees or grape vines to spread in a horizontal direction, as on an espalier, is demonstrating horizontal training.

market-ripe *adj* Unfortunately, *ripe* and *market-ripe* are not synonymous. Fruits and vegetables must be picked before they are ripe in order not to spoil before reaching the consumer. The degree of greenness at which they are picked is described as *market-ripe.*

offscape *n* In landscaping, the parts most distant from the central focus are the offscape.

perennate *vi* To be a perennial; to live more than one or two years: <The search went on for a marigold that would be able to perennate.>

prevernal *adj* In general, prevernal refers to the period when winter is changing to spring: <a prevernal robin>. In botany, the adjective is used to describe plants that leaf out or bloom very early: <The crocus is a prevernal flower.>

pteridography *n*, and related words. Greek *pter-* (as in *pterodactyl*) means feather. Since ferns have featherlike leaves, *pter-* appears in several words pertaining to ferns. Pteridography is anything written about ferns, or the act of describing ferns. **Pteridoid** means pertaining to or resembling a fern. **Pteridology** is the study of ferns and is carried on by a **pteridologist.** The technical name of a fern or fern ally is **pteridophyte. Pterography,** however, is writing about feathers.

side-dressing *n* Side-dressing, from the verb *to side-dress*, is fertilizer placed in or near a row where plants are growing.

site index *n* Foresters use *site index* to indicate a measurement of the capability of an area for growing trees. They measure, for instance, the average height of fifty-year-old Norway pines in the area and use that figure as a site index showing them how suitable the area is for that kind of tree. The term could well be used also to help determine the appropriateness of a given location for a factory or a dwelling, if one took various factors into account and assigned a weighted value to each; thus if one site index turned out to be seventy and another was sixty-two, the first one would presumably be the preferable place for construction.

stag-headed *adj* A stag-headed tree has dead branches, suggestive of a stag's horns, at the top.

taxonomy *n* A system of classification that divides plants and animals into the *kingdoms* Animalia and Plantae and then subdivides step by diminishing step into *phylum, class, order, family, genus,* and *species.*

understory *n* Sounds like a subplot, but in botany it refers to the low-lying shrubs and other plants beneath the tall trees (the *canopy*) of a forest.

urban forest *n* It may once have been news that "A Tree Grows in Brooklyn," but today considerable attention is given to cities' treed areas called (exaggeratedly) *urban forests:* <Including Central Park, New York now has about forty-five hundred acres of urban forest, but Chicago has sixty-five thousand.>

verdure *n* Greenness, especially green vegetation such as grass: <The verdure of the countryside attracts many city dwellers.> The adjective is **verdurous.** By extension *verdure* may mean "freshness, vigorous growth."

Mastery Test

Match each word with the best definition in its group of ten.

___	1. anemophilous	a.	shaped like a tree
___	2. basophilous	b.	shedding of skin, shell, etc.
___	3. dendriform	c.	preferring alkaline soils
___	4. sylvan	d.	heavily grown over with bushes, etc.
___	5. bosky	e.	cabbage
___	6. azonic	f.	falling prematurely
___	7. chou	g.	pollinated by the wind
___	8. ecdysis	h.	decrease of vigor
___	9. fugacious	i.	not confined to one area
___	10. etiolation	j.	pertaining to forests
___	11. grabble	k.	yellowing or whitening of leaves
___	12. side-dressing	l.	plant temporarily
___	13. fructescence	m.	dead at the top
___	14. pteridoid	n.	inclination toward light
___	15. germinability	o.	dig potatoes selectively
___	16. phototropism	p.	probability of sprouting
___	17. flavescence	q.	like a fern
___	18. stag-headed	r.	fertilizer placed close to plants

____ 19.	edaphic	s.	fruit-bearing stage
____ 20.	heel in	t.	pertaining to the soil
____ 21.	phytosociology	u.	downhill movement aided by gravity
____ 22.	borealization	v.	study of plant interrelationships
____ 23.	pomology	w.	living in wooded areas
____ 24.	dendritic	x.	tree-eating
____ 25.	dendrophagous	y.	with branches like those of a tree
____ 26.	soil creep	z.	pertaining to the growing of forest trees
____ 27.	silvicolous	aa.	adaptability to northern regions
____ 28.	silvicultural	bb.	the science of growing fruit trees
____ 29.	verdure	cc.	preferring cool surroundings
____ 30.	cryophilic	dd.	greenery

33
HEAVENLY BODIES

Primitive humans saw, as it appeared to them, the sun, the moon, and certain stars circling the earth, which appeared to them the center of the universe. This **geocentric** view, which makes our home and therefore our species itself the focal point of everything visible, is a persistent one that has not vanished even in our age of astronomical enlightenment.

Early humans learned to use the sun and the stars to help them find their way through forests or across plains or waters; today's **celestial navigation** represents mere refinements of what our ancestors discovered. For millenniums many people have also believed in some mystic connection between their own destinies and the positions of heavenly bodies; the whole pseudoscience of astrology rests on belief in such a connection. Ancient Mesopotamian rulers made crucial decisions with the advice of court astrologers, and **genethlialogy,** "the casting of horoscopes, or nativities," is basic to most astrology. **General astrology** attempts to determine the significance of the time of eclipses, planetary conjunctions, etc., to nations or large groups. **Catarchic as-**

trology recommends certain times as favorable or unfavorable for the beginning of an undertaking. And **interrogatory astrology** answers a client's question (about almost anything) by studying the positions of astronomical bodies at the time of the interrogation. **Iatromathematics** attempts to apply astrology to medicine.

The science of astronomy, as distinguished from astrology, is relatively young. Up to the seventeenth century it consisted mainly of attempts to measure positions and motions of the sun, moon, planets, and fixed stars; some eclipses, for example, were predicted with fair accuracy more than two thousand years ago. In the seventeenth and eighteenth centuries, thanks to the telescope and to some brilliant physicists, the laws of planetary motion were discovered and a reasonably accurate picture of our little corner of the universe began to evolve. The nineteenth century added to the astronomer's tools photography and **spectroscopy** (analysis of spectra to determine composition or motion), and the twentieth century has added new branches of physics, such as quantum theory, and managed for the first time to send both machines and men outside Earth's atmosphere—very far outside. As a result, astronomy and **astrophysics** have leaped far beyond what must now be regarded as a still-primitive stage of the early twentieth century.

Our nearest neighbor in space, the moon, has long attracted us, but the Apollo missions in particular have increased our knowledge of it. We now have, in fact, a science of the moon, **selenology,** conducted by **selenologists** who, of course, do **selenological** research. The study that concentrates on the physical features of the moon is **selenography.** (All these words come from Greek *selene,* "moon.") The word **gibbous,** formerly used only by astronomers, now finds its way into semipopular magazines. When you can see the moon with more than half but not all of its visible side illuminated, you are looking at a gibbous moon. (If the amount lighted is between none and half, the moon is *crescent.*) Other meanings of *gibbous* also suggest such a shape: humpbacked, swollen on one side: <Martha, already gibbous in her pregnancy>.

Astral, alternatively **asterial,** comes from Greek *astēr,* "star," and means pertaining to stars, like a star: <astral phenomena> <astral distances>. *Astēr* also gave us the name of the flower *aster; asteroid, astronomy,* and related words; and less obviously *disaster*, literally "opposed to the stars." **Sidereal** is another word meaning pertaining to the stars or constellations, especially astronomical bodies outside our solar system: <The sidereal year of the earth is measured with reference to the positions of stars.>

One of the finest tributes to human mathematical ability is that long before the computer existed, remarkably accurate measurements were made of celestial distances and the movements of heavenly bodies—so that, for instance, the precise times of planetary conjunctions (explained below) were determined far in advance. **Astrometry** is the branch of astronomy that deals with such measurements. **Astrometric** is the adjectival form.

A machine intended to illustrate planetary movement is the **orrery.** In about 1700 an Englishman named George Graham invented a clockwork device that moved a series of balls representing planets around another ball representing the sun; it was intended to show the relative and constantly changing positions of the planets. A copy of the machine was later made for the earl of Orrery and was therefore named after him; in a more just world an orrery would be called a *graham.*

The comparative location of heavenly bodies has long been of interest to astronomers and of use to them in some of their calculations. If two bodies look as though they are meeting or passing each other, we speak of their **conjunction;** thus an **inferior conjunction** occurs when Venus or Mercury passes approximately between Earth and the sun. Mercury and Venus are **inferior planets**—not because there's anything low-grade about them but because their orbits are inside Earth's; the other planets are **superior planets** because their orbits are outside Earth's. A **superior conjunction** occurs when Earth and the other planet are on opposite sides of the sun but in approximately a straight line.

A condition called **opposition** exists when Earth lies in a straight line between the sun and a planet—say, Mars. A **syzygy** (this word was a favorite in nineteenth-century spelling bees) may be any one of several straight-line configurations but most often is a condition, such as that in an eclipse, when the sun, the moon, and Earth are lined up. When two celestial bodies, as measured from a third, are separated by ninety degrees, the resulting configuration is a **quadrature;** for example, the first-quarter moon is said to be at east quadrature, the last-quarter moon at west quadrature. Or if Jupiter (or another superior planet) rises about midnight and sets about noon, its position is ninety degrees west of the sun and it is at west quadrature.

Astronomers gaze out with their mighty eyes at a universe some parts of which seem to be running down while others are just being born. They keep asking more questions than they can answer: Why do some **nebulae** (diffuse masses of interstellar gas or dust) absorb radiation, others reflect it, others absorb it and then emit it as visible light? Why does a **nova** (one type of variable star) suddenly flare up to several times its normal magnitude and then in a few weeks or months subside? How did this huge universe start? This question of beginnings is an ancient one that almost every religion has sought to answer. Modern astronomers aid the search with some of the most sophisticated instruments yet imaginable. Any theory concerning the origin of the universe is a **cosmogony,** and the branch of astronomy dealing with the theories is also *cosmogony.* A person specializing in this philosophoscientific subject is a **cosmogonist,** who performs **cosmogonic** studies.

A Few Other Celestial Words

airglow *n,* and related words. A faint photochemical luminescence in the upper atmosphere that may be visible on the Earth's surface as a dim glow. Depending on the time, airglow may be called a **dayglow, twilight glow**, or **nightglow**.

astrobiology *n,* and related words. *Astrobiology* is called **exobiology** by scientists. It is the study of life beyond Earth's atmosphere. <Exobiology includes biological ex-

perimentation in space and potentially the study of life on other planets or in other solar systems.> **Astrogeology** deals with the geological structure and components of other planets. An **astrocompass** uses stars as a navigational aid. **Astrodynamics** deals with the motion in space of spacecraft or other bodies.

cometary *adj* Like a comet; pertaining to a comet; derived from a comet: <the cometary path> <cometary in his climb to fame> <meteors of cometary source>.

cosmography *n,* and related words. "The science of everything" is one attempt at defining *cosmography.* That isn't quite accurate, but cosmography does encompass astronomy, geography, and geology. A general description of the universe and Earth's small place in it is also called a *cosmography.* A person devoted to the subject is a **cosmographer** or a **cosmographist.** The adjectival form is **cosmographic.**

cosmology *n,* and related words. One branch of philosophy, called *cosmology,* is concerned with how nature works and how the parts are interrelated. It combines both scientific knowledge and philosophical speculation. One who specializes in it is a **cosmologist.** Adjectival forms are **cosmologic** and **cosmological.**

epact *n* A lunar month is the average time between successive new, or full, moons: 29 days, 12 hours, 44 minutes. This is obviously not quite the same as a calendar month of 28 to 31 days. The numerical difference is called the *epact,* a word also used to signify the number of days' difference between a lunar year (354.37 days) and a solar year (365.24 days).

escape velocity *n* To escape from the gravity of the Earth (or a moon or another planet), an object such as a rocket must attain a certain velocity, its escape velocity. If it does not, it may fall back or go into orbit.

galactic *adj* Pertaining to a galaxy, a huge system of stars such as the Milky Way. By extension, the word may refer to a large number of prominent people: <a galactic assemblage of leading scientists>.

inner planets *n,* **outer planets** *n* The inner planets are those nearest the sun: Mercury, Venus, Earth, and Mars.

The outer planets, in order, are Jupiter, Saturn, Uranus, Neptune, Pluto, and possibly an undiscovered planet X.

librate *vi*, **libration** *n* If you weigh something on a balance scale, the scale quivers for a few moments before coming into equilibrium. The scale is librating; the movement is libration. Libration of the moon, caused in part by variations in the moon's orbital speed, permits us to see somewhat more than the "half" of the moon that is normally turned toward Earth; actually, because of libration, 59 percent of the moon's surface is visible from Earth.

light-time *n* Light-time is the time required for light to travel from a distant object to Earth: <The light-time of Sirius is about 8.6 years.> Or: Sirius is about 8.6 light-years from Earth.

occultation *n* Latin *occultare* means to conceal. *Occultation* means being concealed from public view; disappearance from public notice: <Occultation is never possible for ex-presidents.> Astronomers use the word to mean the hiding of light from one body by another, as in an eclipse: <occultation of Venus by the moon>.

twilight arch *n* Go out into an open field in the very early morning or the evening of a clear day and look toward the west (in the morning) or toward the east (in the evening). You may see an arched, somewhat pink band with a darker area beneath. This is actually the shadow of Earth on the atmosphere and is called a *twilight arch*.

Mastery Test

Fill in the missing letters.

1. sp__________y	analysis of spectra
2. se____logy	science of the moon
3. g_____s	over half illuminated
4. as________ic	pertaining to astronomical measurement
5. i_______ planets	Mercury and Venus

6. co__________	apparent meeting or passing of two celestial bodies
7. co______y	theory of how the universe started
8. co______y	pertaining to a comet
9. e____	difference between a lunar and a calendar month
10. cos________ist	one who describes the universe in general terms
11. oc______tion	hiding of light, as in an eclipse
12. cat____ic astrology	It recommends propitious times.
13. a__________ics	physics of stellar phenomena
14. o____y	working model of our solar system
15. qu______ure	apparent separation of two bodies by ninety degrees
16. g_______c	pertaining to a galaxy
17. astro________	plants and animals in space
18. astro________	rocks, etc., on other planets
19. astro_________	movement in space
20. inner ________	Mercury, Venus, Earth, Mars

34
A POTPOURRI OF ADJECTIVES

The only thing that the words in this chapter have in common is that they are adjectives deserving to be known better.

armipotent *adj*, **armipotence** *n* <"Ther stood the tempel of Mars armypotent"> Chaucer wrote. Anyone or any group or nation like Mars in fighting strength may be called *armipotent. Armipotence*, "great military power," is the noun form.

ascensive *adj* Something is ascensive if it is rising or, more often, if it has a tendency to rise: <Without yeast, bread dough is not ascensive.>

circumjacent *adj* Lying adjacent to on all sides: <They kept their building painted and in good repair despite the circumjacent ghetto.>

collocal *adj* If two things are to be found in or belong to the same place, they are collocal: <Apple trees and pear trees are collocal, but apple trees and orange trees ordinarily are not.> <In our pasture, morel and shaggymane

mushrooms are collocal, growing in the southeast corner often side by side.>

crisic *adj* We generally use *critical* as the adjective meaning pertaining to a crisis, but because *critical* has other meanings, its use sometimes results in ambiguity. For instance, does "The patient is critical" mean that the patient is at a stage of crisis in hiser recovery or that heshe is complaining? *Crisic* has no such ambiguity, meaning pertaining to a crisis—nothing more: <The patient is crisic.> <the crisic years of the Civil War, when the future of the nation was at stake>.

Cyrillic *adj* The Russian alphabet, which looks somewhat like Greek, is Cyrillic, so named because it is believed to have been invented by ninth-century Greek missionaries, one of whom was called Cyrillus (now St. Cyril).

determinate *adj* The negative *indeterminate,* "uncertain as to bounds or number," is well known, but oddly enough the positive *determinate,* "definitely limited or numbered," is rarely heard: <The tensile strength of any strand of wire is determinate.>

diaphanous *adj* Upon hearing *diaphanous,* most people think of gauzy, almost completely transparent cloth such as painters or moviemakers like to show as the costume of harem dancers. Actually, though, not only clothing but also nearly anything else that is thin or insubstantial may be described with this word. *Webster 3* uses as an example "diaphanous water through which fish may be clearly seen." In addition, *diaphanous* may mean unusually delicate in structure: <as diaphanous as a butterfly's wing> or vague and insubstantial: <The plan was still diaphanous.>

disedifying *v part* Disedifying language or actions shock or disturb someone, being objectionable to hiser religious or moral beliefs: <A recording had been made of the entire disedifying conversation.>

ectopic *adj*, **entopic** *adj*, and related words. *Ectopic* means occurring in a place other than the usual one, and its antonym, *entopic,* means occurring in the usual place. Thus an ectopic pregnancy might be one in which gestation takes place in the fallopian tubes rather than the uterus. The corresponding nouns are **ectopia** and **entopia.** The ancestral Greek *ektopos* means away from a place, *entopos* in a place. Although the medical profession has largely preempted these four words, there is no etymological or other reason to restrict them, and it might be useful to refer, for example, to a plant or animal or type of rock found outside its expected environment as *ectopic* or to comment on its *ectopia.*

factitious *adj* This unfortunate word is sometimes confused with *factual,* and no less often with *fictitious,* but it is not synonymous with either. Something is factitious if it is artificial and man-made rather than natural and spontaneous: <The symmetrically arranged holes in the ground were unquestionably factitious.> Sometimes it may mean fake, sham: <His good humor was clearly factitious.>

felicific *adj* The usual meaning of this word (which is related to the noun *felicity* and the verb *felicitate*) is "causing happiness, or intended to cause happiness": <Gifts should be chosen not for ostentation but for genuinely felicific purposes.> It may also mean hedonistic, measuring worth in terms of happiness: <Some philosophers claim that human existence can be justified only on felicific grounds.>

gravid *adj* Something is gravid if it is distended, noticeably filled: <a fish gravid with eggs> <a gravid [pregnant] mare>. Abstract things may be figuratively gravid: <theorizing that is gravid with faulty assumptions>. By further extension the word may mean portentous, as if forecasting some important event: <the spread of nuclear weapons, gravid with peril for all humanity>.

heuristic *adj* Greek *heuriskein* means to discover. In modern logic a heuristic tool is one that helps or may help in discovering a truth, even though itself incapable of proof or demonstration. For example, no one can speak with assurance about the qualities of the "ideal person," but the concept as a heuristic device may lead to constructive thinking and even to empirical research. In education, the "discovery method," in which a student learns by discovering things for himerself, is also sometimes described as *heuristic.*

inrooted *adj* A word used in certain abstractions for deeply rooted: <his inrooted jealousy>.

macro *adj,* **micro** *adj* Although *macro* and *micro* are familiar constituents of many words (e.g., *macrocosm, microscope*), few persons are aware that they may also serve as independent adjectives. *Macro* means large, thick, numerous, highly developed; *micro,* small in quantity, size, or number: <macro economic policies> <possesses only a micro conscience>.

magazinish or **magaziny** *adj* With notable exceptions, magazine writing is more superficial, more slick, and often more sensationalized than writing published in books. *Magazinish* or *magaziny,* then, is a rather disparaging word describing a writer's style.

meretricious *adj* This word is sometimes confused with *meritorious* but is actually almost an antonym. It comes from *meretrix,* "prostitute," and in one sense means like a prostitute, pertaining to a prostitute or prostitution: <Francis Bacon, 1626: "The Delight in Meretricious Embracements (where sinne is turned into Art) maketh Marriage a dull thing."> More often today it means gaudy, fake, attracting by false show of beauty or richness: <meretricious advertising of desert land> <a meretricious prose style>.

multifarious *adj* Anything that exists in many forms or varieties may be described as *multifarious:* <the multifarious grasses of virgin prairies>.

multivious *adj* Having many paths, roads, or ways: <the multivious nervous system of higher animals>.

nonpareil *adj, n* As an adjective, *nonpareil* means unequaled, peerless; as a noun, a paragon, a person with no equal: <nonpareil in both beauty and wit>.

omniphibious *adj* An amphibious plane can land on water or land. An omniphibious plane can land on water, land, snow, or ice.

outré *adj* From French *outrer,* "to carry to excess," *outré* means shamelessly unconventional, bizarre: <Even our

sophisticated set disapproved of his openly outré sexual behavior.>

pearlescent *adj* Resembling mother-of-pearl.

pellucid *adj* Glass or similar substances are pellucid when they permit a maximum amount of light to pass through. Prose or poetry is pellucid when it is extraordinarily clear. Somewhat figuratively *pellucid* may also mean shining, iridescent, or pleasing to the eye.

perspicuous *adj* Something, such as an explanation, is perspicuous if it is clear, easily understood: <The examples helped to make his technical discourse perspicuous.>

pluripotent *adj* A thing or person is pluripotent when the potentialities are numerous and not yet determined: <as pluripotent as a Renaissance man> <one of the great pluripotent ideas of our time>.

pristine *adj* *Pristine* basically means from the earliest time or condition, but has gone beyond that to mean pure, fresh, unsullied, uncorrupted, unsoiled: <pristine air> <pristine, virginal appearance> <pristine white sheets>.

privative *adj* Anything that causes privation may be labeled as *privative:* <Alcohol makes many parents unintentionally privative.> A prefix or word that reflects the negation or absence of a quality is also privative—for example, *un*certain, *non*operating, *blindness* (the absence of sight).

proximate *adj* From the same source as *proximity, proximate* means very near, next: <S. Johnson, 1755: "Words are seldom exactly synonymous . . . It was then necessary to use the proximate word."> <*Blackwoods* Magazine, 1836: ". . . some proximate village"> <*Science,* 1889: "The enormous consumption of petroleum and natural gas . . . raises the question as to the . . . proximate exhaustion of the supply.">

pusillanimous *adj* Timid, wishy-washy, contemptibly indecisive or inactive: <In retrospect, several of Lincoln's generals were downright pusillanimous.>

quinary *adj* *Quinary* means in fives; consisting of five; fifth in order: <flowerpots in a quinary arrangement>.

recondite *adj* Something is recondite if it is difficult to understand, deep, or (possibly) if it is not commonly known: <the recondite theory of relativity> <a recondite explanation> <a recondite thinker> <the recondite philosophies of ancient Indian mystics>.

recrudescent *adj,* and related words. If something undesirable, such as an indication of cancer, has abated for a while but now has returned, it is said to be recrudescent; it **recrudesces** *(vi);* its **recrudescence***(n)* is noticeable.

rejuvenescent *adj,* and related words. *Rejuvenescent* means making or becoming young again: <Dad is rejuvenescent now that the pressure of the lawsuit is over.> The noun form is **rejuvenescence. Revirescent** and **revirescence** come from Latin for "to grow green again" and are used with that meaning especially when there are references to spring: <revirescent grass> <the annual revirescence>.

rosewatered *adj* Basically *rosewatered* simply means perfumed with rose water, but by extension it means affectedly delicate, excessively effeminate, cloyingly sentimental: <a rosewatered account of the incident> <She wanted her daughter to be rosewatered like herself—to behave like the eyes-downcast maidens of early-twentieth-century fiction.>

rumorous *adj* Having the nature of rumor: <rumorous reports about an invasion>.

sedulous *adj* A sedulous person (or other creature) is persevering and diligent in hiser work: <M. Prior, 1709: "The sedulous Bee Distill'd her Honey on Thy purple Lips.">

should-be *adj* *Would-be* is a familiar expression, as in a *would-be senator. Should-be* is less known but perhaps no less deserving: <a should-be reduction in food prices>.

snippety *adj* *Snippety* may mean small, cut up into little pieces: <a snippety collection of famous arias on one recording> or unpleasantly curt: <snippety responses to my well-intended inquiries> <snippety, discourteous airs>.

soi-disant *adj* In French *soi-disant* means "saying oneself," and in English it has the parallel meaning of self-styled, so-called, or pretended: <a soi-disant statesman> <Many soi-disant biographies are in actuality hired puffery.> As the examples suggest, the term is generally disparaging.

specious *adj* Latin *speciosus* means beautiful, especially in a showy way. In English something is specious if it is superficially beautiful: <preached about the specious attractions of sin> or if it is plausible but not really true, fair, or right: <specious arguments>.

splendiferous *adj* Although *splendiferous* may mean unusually splendid, magnificent, today it most often means deceptively splendid, superficially splendid, and suggests ostentation rather than genuine beauty. It may also be used as a humorous substitute for *splendid*.

squabbish *adj* Rather fat or squat, like a squab, which is a young, lumpish pigeon: <Her father was a squabbish five by five.>

stelliferous *adj* This word, obviously related to *stellar* and *constellation*, means having markings shaped like stars: <a stelliferous dress> <the oddly stelliferous carapace of the tortoise>.

stratagemical *adj* A stratagem (not to be confused with a strategy) is a clever trick—such as a ruse or a deception—designed to gain a victory in a military or other contest—for example, a fake buildup in one sector while an invasion is planned for another place. *Stratagemical* means characterized by stratagem: <Always a wily boxer, he followed this time an even more stratagemical fight plan than usual.>

stuporific *adj* Something is stuporific if it causes stupor: <stuporific days and nights of sandbagging the levee> <a stuporific blow to the head>.

subjacent *adj* *Subjacent* may mean (1) below the surface: <a subjacent rock layer>; (2) lower but not directly beneath: <looked at the subjacent narrow ledge>; (3) causative and therefore (figuratively) underlying: <Subjacent to the accusation may be a persistent hatred of his ex-wife.>

suboptimal *adj* Something is suboptimal if it is less desirable or less satisfactory than might be hoped for: <In my judgment, the bill passed by Congress is suboptimal or even of minimal value.>

subvisible *adj* Not visible to the unaided eye: <examined the subvisible specks by means of a magnifying glass>.

supernal *adj* Anything that comes from heaven, possesses a heavenly quality, or is literally or figuratively located on high may be described as *supernal:* <supernal words sent down to Moses> <unearthly, supernal music> <The Mets reached supernal heights in July.>

talkable *adj* *Talkable* may mean either capable of being talked about or inclined to talk friendlily: <The weather is the most talkable subject the world over.> <He's quite talkable, not at all hostile or even reserved.>

tardive *adj* Something is tardive if it habitually tends to be slow in development: <Some cabbage varieties are more tardive than others.>

tensional *adj* Pertaining to tension: <Those *tensional* elements long considered essential for most fiction are also important in most poetry.> <severe tensional effect on the two bolts>.

this-worldly *n* Ministers have for centuries preached in favor of thinking about and planning for the "other world," a world beyond the grave. Instead, as they have lamented, they have kept encountering this-worldly attitudes, an interest in the comforts and luxuries and pleasures of this world.

tortuous *adj,* **tortuosity** *n* *Tortuous* means winding, extraordinarily crooked, convoluted; or by extension indirect, treacherous, lacking in straightforwardness: <tortuous mountain roads> <tortuous reasoning>. Tortuosity is crookedness, sinuousness, or deviousness: <The tortuosity of his arguments disappointed us.>

transnational *adj* Beyond national boundaries: <transnational customs shared by Canada and the United States>.

transpontine *adj* On the other side of the bridge: <the transpontine rivalry of Davenport, Iowa, and Rock Island, Illinois.>

trenchant *adj* Originally meaning cutting or trenching, *trenchant* has now become almost completely figurative in its meanings: sharply perceptive, penetrating: <trenchant insights into today's oligopolies>; effective, articulate, brisk: <trenchant criticisms>.

turbid *adj* Murky, filled with sediment, muddy, not transparent; or, figuratively, muddled, unclear, obscure, confused: <the turbid water in the creek after the rain> <turbid prose>.

two-by-twice *adj* Small in floor area: <her secretary's two-by-twice office>.

vincible *adj* Everybody knows *invincible,* "unconquerable," but most people seem unaware that there is also a *vincible,* "conquerable": <The forces to the south seemed most easily vincible.>

weariable *adj* Capable of becoming weary (especially quickly): <Since my illness I'm so weariable!>

wopsy *adj* There's a dialectal *wopse* meaning a tangled mass, from which *wopsy* is derived. It means tangled, disordered, disheveled, uneven: <My hair was wopsy and my cheeks burned.>

xenial *adj* Pertaining to hospitality, to relations between host or hostess and guest: <Xenial customs in many households changed when television arrived.>

Mastery Test

Choose the most probable adjective for each blank.

1. The camp was filled with short, fat children—all unusually ________________ (ascensive, squabbish, armipotent, multivious).
2. As a slugger, the great Hank Aaron was ____________ (omniphibious, multifarious, nonpareil, xenial).
3. He tried hard but unsuccessfully to make his explanation ________________ (perspicuous, pluripotent, pusillanimous, pristine).
4. Joshua found that the damp climate was causing his

respiratory ailments to become ________________ (rejuvenescent, revirescent, recondite, recrudescent).

5. The reports were not definitely based on fact; they were merely ________________ (rumorous, soi-disant, specious, subjacent).
6. ________________ (Trenchant, Collocal, Proximate, Xenial) customs are those referring to hospitality.
7. After the windstorm, the corn in my little patch was all ___ (tortuous, wopsy, trenchant, quinary).
8. For a week after the accident, he remained in a (n) ___ (determinate, ectopic, disedifying, crisic) condition.
9. ________________ (Factitious, Felicific, Privative, Stratagemical) accounts of wrongdoings are told about almost every Presidential candidate.
10. Unlike most of the bland, flattering reviews, Kennon's was filled with ________________ (turbid, armipotent, gravid, trenchant) and not always kind analysis.
11. Many rulers have chosen to ignore the fact that most of the praise they received was ________________ (fissile, factitious, multivious, sedulous).
12. She was chided for wearing a blouse that her mother considered too ________________ (stelliferous, ectopic, pellucid, diaphanous).
13. A (n) ________________ (collocal, Cyrillic, sedulous, entopic) employee is one who works unusually diligently.
14. His slick, readable, but sometimes shallow articles were criticized as ________________ (crisic, magazinish, snippety, splendiferous).
15. ________________ (Meretricious, Rosewatered, Supernal, Heuristic) advertising deceives many purchasers of new cars.

35 OLLA PODRIDA

A national dish of Spain and of a number of other Spanish-speaking countries, **olla podrida** is a stew consisting of a mixture of meat, chicken, and assorted vegetables and seasonings—or sometimes just any edibles that happen to have been left lying around. It's cooked in an **olla,** which in the American Southwest is a large, wide-mouthed container. Since the olla podrida is such an unpredictable assortment, the name has been taken over to represent any miscellaneous mixture, not just of foods. This chapter, then, is olla podrida—hash, if you prefer—consisting of words that didn't fit well anywhere else.

abrade *vi, vt,* **abrase** *vi, vt* Both verbs come from Latin *abradere,* "to scrape off," and may be used interchangeably in the sense of to erode, rub off or out, smooth off. *Abrade,* however, more often has the meaning of to roughen, irritate, chafe.

airy-fairy *adj* May be used in either the sense of delicate, fairylike, or visionary: <a thin, Persian medallion with airy-fairy patterns in the silver> <Who could support a

candidate with such airy-fairy ideas about international relations?>

asperse *vt* The noun *aspersion* is well known, as in *to cast aspersions.* An aspersion is a defamatory statement. The verb *asperse,* though, is oddly enough seldom heard. It means to make a defamatory statement about, to attack with insulting reports or hints: <Jones maliciously aspersed Brown's political record.>

bitt *n* On the deck of a boat there may be a post called a *bitt,* to which mooring lines or other lines can be fastened. Reportedly the phrase *to the bitter end* originally referred to reaching the bitt end of a rope.

bollard *n* In areas of highway construction or repair you have seen inverted cones standing on or beside the road to mark places not to be entered. The British, and increasingly the Americans, call these posts *bollards.* The word also refers to posts or piers where boats may be tied up.

bonification *n* Literally "making or doing good," *bonification* is generally narrowed in meaning to the improvement of housing and of agricultural practice in an area: <American professors in southern India contributed considerably to its bonification.>

borrowed light *n* If you are in a room with no windows or other direct sources of light, and if light enters from an adjoining lighted room, the indirect illumination is borrowed light.

by-end *n* Some goals are more important than others. A short name for a subordinate goal is *by-end.*

centesimal *n,* and related words. *Centesimal* refers to marking a division into hundredths, like the centesimal markings of the Centigrade thermometer. To decimate, as is well known, is to punish or execute every tenth person, but to **centesimate** is only one tenth as severe, since it refers to the punishment or execution of every hundredth person. **Centuriation** is division into hundreds or centuries: <Centuriation could not develop until after general adoption of the decimal system.>

Cloud-Cuckoo-Land *n* People in the Middle Ages called it the land of Cokayne, Sir Thomas More called it Utopia, and a twentieth-century song called it the Big Rock-

Candy Mountain. It's an imaginary paradise, equipped with whatever the dreamer likes best—twenty-dollar bills hanging from bushes, cigaret trees, thinly clad houris, a never-ending dance, fountains of youth, castles in the air.

creephole *n* Basically a creephole is only a hole into which an animal may creep so as not to be seen. By extension, it is any subterfuge or excuse that a person may use to cover one of hiser failings, mistakes, or misdemeanors.

decrement *n* "There will be an annual increment in your salary," said the employer. In an inflationary spiral, heshe did not need to know the opposite of *increment,* which is *decrement,* "a gradual or regular decrease," but during the Depression of the 1930s, workers gladly accepted decrements in preference to layoffs and firings.

dormition *n* A peaceful, painless death, like falling asleep, is called *dormition:* <He prayed for dormition.>

esoterica *n pl.,* **exoterica** *n pl.* Esoterica are items that only a specialist or a native knows about: <When Carl left the army and became a sailor, he was, of course, unfamiliar with the esoterica of shipboard life.> Exoterica, on the other hand, are widely known items, familiar to those in the "outer circle" and not just those in the "inner circle." Perhaps the word is seldom used because of possible confusion with *exotic.*

extrapolate *vt* To interpolate is to insert (something), as <an interpolated remark>. *Extrapolate,* sometimes confused with *interpolate,* is quite different. It means to extend or project what is known into what is at present unknown. Thus if one extrapolates from the numerical series 0, 1, 3, 6, 10 . . ., heshe gets 15, 21 . . . Or one may extrapolate from a series of U.S. Supreme Court decisions concerning monopolies the possible decision about the next Court case involving monopolies.

fire flow *n* When a fire breaks out in a city, most people continue using water at their normal rate. The quantity of water left over for fighting the fire is called *fire flow.* If, as sometimes happens, the fire flow is too low, pressure drops and the fire fighting is less effective.

flannel board *n.* **flannelgraph** *n* Familiar in schools but useful also in homes for decoration or for holding messages, a flannel board is a board covered with flannel or felt to which appropriately backed lightweight materials will adhere; an illustration, message, etc., suitable for a flannel board is a flannelgraph.

fusty *adj* Mainly British, *fusty* is a handy word for stale, musty, smelly, old, and damp: <the fusty smell of the ancient dungeon>. By extension, someone who clings unyieldingly to the past may be described as *fusty:* <a fusty old fellow who still wore garters and suspenders>.

gambit *n* In chess an opening in which one contestant intentionally risks one or more inconsequential pieces is called a *gambit.* By extension, a conversational opening or transition designed to help prove a debatable point is also called a *gambit,* and so in other circumstances is any move or maneuver that one hopes will gain himer an edge: <One of his gambits was to pretend lack of interest in buying any property.>

googol *n,* **googolplex** *n* An American mathematician, Dr. Edward Kassner, in 1955 coined *googol* for the number represented by 10^{100}, which is 1 followed by 100 zeroes. Few of us have occasion to refer except hyperbolically to such an incomprehensibly large number: <A googol of gnats swarmed around us.> But there are words for even larger numbers. For example, a centillion is 10^{303} (or in England, 10^{600}). And if you added a googol of zeroes to 1, the result ($10^{10\ 100}$) would be a googolplex—a number so large that it would require many years just to write.

haply *adv* *Haply,* an old word, is more appropriate than *accidentally* when something good may happen by chance: <Haply the children may have reached the cabin before the storm.> "Perhaps by good luck" may be considered a synonym.

hatching *n* The use on maps and charts of close parallel lines to show differences (for example, in rainfall) is called *hatching.* In engravings hatching may give the effect of shading. Weavers also use hatching, achieving a shading effect by weaving threads of one color into an adjacent area of a different color.

hypertrophy *n,* **hypotrophy** *n* Hypertrophy is excessive growth, whether of a bodily organ or an institution: <hypertrophy of the heart muscles> <America may fall victim to corporate hypertrophy, with only a few huge corporations dominating all aspects of life.> Hypotrophy is subnormal growth: <the hypotrophy of the arms and legs of an invalid child>.

logogram or **logograph** *n* A logogram or logograph is a written symbol representing a complete word, as "+" means plus, "$" means dollar or dollars. Most international highways signs are logograms.

marginalia *n pl* Some readers delight in writing comments in the margins of what they read—comments understandably called *marginalia.* In addition, marginalia are nonessential or noncentral parts of anything: <His lectures abounded in the marginalia that in print would have been relegated to footnotes.> <the dentist, the TV repairperson, the one-night-standers, and other people who represented the marginalia of her life>.

minify *vt* To make small or smaller: <Lawn mowers became minified tractors.> <The secretary tried to minify her influence on company policy.>

multivalence *n,* **multivalent** *adj* In chemistry, *multivalence* is a synonym of *polyvalence,* "having multiple valence." More generally, though, it is useful in the sense of the state or quality of having many values, appeals, or other characteristics: <the great diversity and multivalence of Shakespeare's characters> <multivalent arguments concerning remedies for our economic ailments>.

near-hit *n* A near-hit is customarily called a *near-miss,* a word that Margaret Bryant, a linguist, once described as "the most illogical of the wartime compounds."

nullibicity *n* *Ubiquitousness* means the state of being everywhere. Its opposite is *nullibicity,* "the state of being nowhere": <Nothing is more remarkable than the nullibicity of taxicabs in bad weather.>

occasional cause *n* A mental state, physical phenomenon, or other circumstance that triggers an action without being its root cause is called an *occasional cause*—that is, it is the "occasion" that brings about the action:

<The occasional cause of World War I was the assassination of Archduke Francis Ferdinand.>

paleography *n*, **paleology** *n* *Paleo-* is from a Greek word for ancient. *Paleography* may mean either ancient writings, an ancient way of writing, or the study of ancient writing. *Paleology* is broader in meaning, referring to the study of ancient times in general, especially prehistoric times.

palindrome *n* A word, group of words, or group of numbers that reads the same either forward or backward: <Hannah> <a man, a plan, a canal, Panama> <2647462>.

pararescue *n, vi,* **pararescuer** *n* If a parachutist attempts the rescue of someone (for example, a victim of storm, flood, or battle), heshe is trying a pararescue. The word *pararescuer* is not yet in dictionaries but does appear in newspaper stories.

pictograph *n* Early cave drawings were pictographs—line drawings, usually intended to tell a simple story. Some of the precursors of alphabets may also have been pictographs; thus *aleph*, the Hebrew ancestor of our *A*, may have been a simplified pictorial representation of an ox. Hieroglyphs appear to have been stylized pictographs.

possibilitate *vt* To make possible: <Any of a dozen types of weapons can possibilitate the end of civilization.> <Strong plastic possibilitates much less expensive automobiles.>

previse *vt,* **prevision** *n* To previse is to foresee or to plan ahead, and prevision is foresight, prognostication, or planning ahead: <Prevision in writing is superior to revision.>

protohistory *n* *Proto-* means first in time. *Protohistory* refers to the times just before recorded history, or the study of that period: <The tools of the protohistorian are necessarily different from those of the historian, since the former can use no written records, no engravings, no pictures, no still-surviving myths.>

provenance *n* Source or place of origin: <words of literary provenance> <the provenance of Ingersoll's atheistic beliefs>.

reify *vt,* **reification** *n* To reify is to treat something abstract as if it had concrete, physical qualities: <The speaker reified democratic ideals by giving specific examples from history.> *Reification* is the noun form: <When one personifies an abstraction—"Father Time," "blind Justice"—heshe illustrates reification.>

repristination *n* Repristination is restoration of something to its original, pristine, pure form: <Repristination of democracy's early ideals was what he longed for but believed impossible.>

rubric *n* In old manuscripts, pages or sections were often headed by an ornate letter, design, or title, often in red, and called in Middle English *rubrike,* "red ocher." Today a rubric may still be a section or chapter heading, though use of red is likely to be only coincidental. More often today, however, the term has no direct connection with a book but means only the name of a class or category, or (sometimes) a governing rule or direction: <This type of offense falls in law under the rubric *tort.*>

sentence sense *n* Teachers often lament that some of their students lack sentence sense, "the ability to recognize a grammatically complete sentence." As a result of such a lack, students often punctuate fragments as sentences, or run two or more sentences together without punctuation or with only a comma as a divider. In speaking, the lack does not show up, so perhaps the lack of sentence sense is only a lack of mastery of some conventions in writing.

show-how *n* A show-how is a step-by-step demonstration of how some action should be performed: <a show-how for assembling bicycles>.

sine qua non *n* Latin for "without which not." Something is a sine qua non if it is absolutely essential, if whatever is being talked about could not exist or operate properly without it: <Horses and a carriage were regarded as a sine qua non for anyone to be considered as "high society.">

snit *n* An informal expression for the condition of being upset or agitated: <The coach was in a snit because what

would have been the winning touchdown was called back.>

sociatry *n*, **sociatrist** *n* Sociatry is group psychotherapy that employs such techniques as psychodrama, sociodrama, and sensitivity sessions. One who practices such therapy is sometimes called a *sociatrist.*

sociocentric *adj*, **sociocentrism** *n* Sociocentrism is typified by the attitude "My group is better than other groups. My group is right in what it says and does." A person with such an attitude may be described as *sociocentric:* <The sociocentrism of a street gang often results in conflict with another equally sociocentric group.>

subfix *n*, **subscript** *n* A number, letter, or sign written below or lower than a line of type or script; thus H_2SO_4 has two numbers as subfixes or subscripts, and the French *leçon* uses a cedilla as a subfix.

superscript *n* A character, number, or sign written or printed above (or above and to the side) of another—for example, $x^2 + y^3$.

supervene *vi, vt* Something supervenes if it happens (usually unexpectedly) after or during something else and affects the consequences: <We had been planning to marry in early May, but my mother's death in late April supervened and caused a delay.>

theory of games *n* The application of mathematical logic to intellectual games or gamelike real-life situations, such as a problem in education or business. A person well versed in game theory is likely to be able to outmaneuver hiser opponents and thus win.

thought-read *vt* A person thought-reads when heshe observes another's facial expressions and draws conclusions about what is being thought: <Although she didn't say a word, I knew her well enough that I could thought-read every movement of her facial muscles.> Telepathy is also known as thought-reading.

traditionate *vt* You traditionate a child if you teach, imbue, or indoctrinate himer in the traditions of your family, group, community, or nation: <A usually unavowed purpose of teaching history in elementary schools is to traditionate the children, so that all will know about the

Pilgrims, John Smith and Pocahontas, and little George Washington's cherry tree.>

ukase *n* One of the small number of Russian words that have found their way into English. A ukase is an edict, a decree—originally an imperial proclamation equivalent to a command.

white list *n* People seldom want to have their names on a blacklist, which is a list of persons disapproved of for some reason. But businesses—or families, or almost anyone—may also have a white list of approved or favored people, companies, items: <That store treated me so well it's going right to the top of my white list.>

Zeitgeist *n* A German word, sometimes used in English, for the spirit of the times; the existent moral, intellectual, religious, or cultural state: <The twentieth century is so varied that no one can catch its Zeitgeist in a few words.>

zoophobe *n,* and related words. People who dislike or fear animals are zoophobes, who are described as **zoophobous,** and whose fear of animals, if it becomes morbid, is labeled **zoophobia. Zoophilia,** "love of animals," must be used with care, because it sometimes refers to erotic attachment between persons and animals. **Zoophilous** is the adjectival form.

Mastery Test

Indicate whether each statement is *true* (T) or *false* (F). For each correct answer give yourself an extra ______________ (fill in whatever you like) if you can also explain *why* your answer is correct.

____ 1. An *olla podrida* is more likely to have hot seasoning than a *Zeitgeist* is.

____ 2. For people who love life, even a *decrement* in salary is better than a *dormition.*

____ 3. It is generally better to be on a *white list* than to be *fusty.*

____ 4. *Protohistory* is of particular interest to the *sociatrist.*

___ 5. *Subfixes* are small injections of narcotics.
___ 6. *Decrements* are likely to play rock music on their *ukases.*
___ 7. Every science, including *haplography*, has its *esoterica.*
___ 8. *Paleology* is broader in meaning than *paleography.*
___ 9. "Madam, I'm Adam" is a *palindrome.*
___ 10. A *sine qua non* is one form of *reification.*
___ 11. *Prevision* looks toward the future, but *repristination* looks to both past and present.
___ 12. "Under the rubric" earlier was equivalent to "under the red-lettered chapter heading."
___ 13. A *theory of games* may sometimes be concerned with *gambits.*
___ 14. You will probably not hear much about *googols* in a meeting of *sociatrists.*
___ 15. *Haply* means about the same thing as "Maybe by good luck."
___ 16. If muscles are not exercised, *hypertrophy* is likely to result.
___ 17. An example of a *logogram* is the square-root sign used in mathematics.
___ 18. *Hatching* is a term used by poultry raisers, chartmakers, and weavers.
___ 19. When some people read a book, they scribble *marginalia* on some of the pages.
___ 20. A *zoophobous* person is more likely to run away from a growling dog than a *bollard* is.
___ 21. If during a blackout a neighbor lends you a candle, *borrowed light* is the *by-end* of hiser kindness.
___ 22. Your apparent *nullibicity* could come in handy when the bill-collector comes around.
___ 23. Lawyers sometimes cast *aspersions* and sometimes *skepticize.*
___ 24. It would be possible to *abrade* your skin by rubbing against a *bitt.*
___ 25. *Airy-fairy* people could well be among those who live in *Cloud-Cuckoo-Land.*

ANSWERS TO MASTERY TESTS

CHAPTER 1

1. j	6. b	11. p	16. l	21. v	26. x
2. a	7. d	12. s	17. n	22. u	27. w
3. f	8. e	13. k	18. m	23. y	
4. c	9. g	14. q	19. r	24. aa	
5. h	10. i	15. t	20. o	25. z	

CHAPTER 2

1. h	6. i	11. s	16. o	21. v	26. u
2. d	7. f	12. q	17. l	22. z	27. w
3. a	8. c	13. k	18. n	23. dd	28. y
4. j	9. e	14. m	19. p	24. x	29. aa
5. b	10. g	15. t	20. r	25. bb	30. cc

CHAPTER 3

1. F	6. T	11. F	16. F	21. F	26. F
2. T	7. T	12. F	17. T	22. F	27. T
3. T	8. T	13. T	18. F	23. T	28. F
4. F	9. T	14. F	19. T	24. T	29. T
5. F	10. T	15. F	20. T	25. T	30. F

CHAPTER 4

1. f
2. i
3. j
4. g
5. b
6. e
7. c
8. h
9. d
10. a
11. q
12. k
13. s
14. t
15. l
16. o
17. m
18. p
19. n
20. r

CHAPTER 5

1. heterosexism
2. demi-vierge
3. epicene
4. impuberty
5. Rabelaisian
6. philogyny
7. altrigenderism
8. amorist
9. canoodle
10. alliciency
11. alloerotism
12. beefcake
13. ambosexual (or ambi-)
14. Cytherean
15. desexualize
16. androcentric
17. succubus
18. sapphist

CHAPTER 6

I.
1. d
2. c
3. e
4. b
5. b
6. b
7. b
8. a
9. b
10. c
11. b
12. c
13. d
14. a
15. c
16. b
17. a
18. a
19. a
20. d

II.
1. T
2. F
3. T
4. F
5. T
6. T
7. T
8. T
9. F
10. F

CHAPTER 7

1. d
2. c
3. a
4. a
5. b
6. c
7. a
8. d
9. a
10. c

CHAPTER 8

These answers are a matter of personal preference or opinion.

CHAPTER 9

1. T
2. F
3. F
4. F
5. T
6. T
7. T
8. T
9. F
10. F
11. T
12. F
13. T
14. T
15. T
16. F
17. F
18. F
19. T
20. T
21. F
22. F
23. T
24. T
25. F

CHAPTER 10

onomatist, euonym, patronymic, ananym, anonym, pseudandry, allonym, anthroponymy, toponymy (or toponomy), surnominal, paraph, day name, numeronym

CHAPTER 11

1. d
2. h
3. c
4. g
5. b
6. f
7. a
8. j
9. e
10. i
11. s
12. k
13. o
14. l
15. t
16. r
17. m
18. p
19. n
20. q

CHAPTER 12

1. edentulous
2. dol
3. heliotherapy
4. synergism
5. somniferous
6. hypersomnia
7. bruxism
8. minimus
9. elastosis
10. embolus
11. collywobbles
12. subhealth
13. ablactation
14. anile
15. bimanual
16. demulcent
17. dermatosis
18. ingest
19. afferent
20. laterality
21. narcosis
22. percuss
23. encephalitis
24. psilosis
25. afterpain
26. arrhythmic
27. cellulitis
28. crymotherapy (or cryo-)
29. thermotherapy
30. cephalic index

CHAPTER 13

1. determinist
2. deteriorist
3. egoistic
4. universalistic
5. energist
6. axiology
7. shu
8. tychism
9. chapter of accidents
10. dharma
11. latitudinarian
12. mystagogue
13. negativism
14. Panglossian
15. agathist
16. ephectic
17. anthropocentric
18. pseudodoxy
19. selectionist
20. ultraism
21. teleology
22. nihilist
23. dogmatic
24. bioethics

CHAPTER 14

1. polytheistic
2. ditheism
3. diabolist
4. theophany
5. theomorphism
6. theocentric
7. theological
8. plutolatry
9. numina
10. ecclesiolatry
11. creationist
12. fideism
13. totemism
14. hamadryad
15. pantheism

16. sin money
17. psilanthropy
18. theogony
19. theologue
20. pyrolatry
21. schism
22. Sabbatarian
23. manitou, manito
24. irenics
25. bat (or bas) mitzvah

CHAPTER 15

1. i
2. d
3. a
4. j
5. b
6. g
7. c
8. f
9. h
10. e
11. k
12. q
13. n
14. s
15. l
16. t
17. m
18. o
19. p
20. r
21. y
22. u
23. x
24. w
25. v

CHAPTER 16

1. c
2. a
3. d
4. b
5. d
6. a
7. c
8. b
9. d
10. a
11. a
12. c

CHAPTER 17

1. f
2. i
3. a
4. c
5. e
6. g
7. j
8. b
9. d
10. h
11. r
12. k
13. t
14. o
15. l
16. q
17. m
18. s
19. n
20. p
21. x
22. bb
23. z
24. u
25. cc
26. v
27. w
28. y
29. aa
30. dd

CHAPTER 18

These answers are a matter of personal preference or opinion.

CHAPTER 19

1. barrator
2. allograph
3. a street offense
4. abjudge
5. probatum
6. testate
7. allide
8. jetsam
9. mandatory injunction
10. subreption
11. true bill
12. Draconian

CHAPTER 20

1. tetrarchy
2. ideocracy
3. technocracy
4. psephology
5. immobilism
6. civicism
7. duumvir
8. heteronomous
9. juridical
10. patrial
11. syndicalism
12. statism

13. sansculotte
14. gynarchy
15. androcracy
16. oligarchy
17. stratocracy
18. graveyard vote
19. capitation
20. laborism
21. spinnish
22. defalcation
23. gerontocracy
24. narcokleptocracy
25. centrist

CHAPTER 21

1. F
2. T
3. F
4. T
5. T
6. T
7. F
8. T
9. T
10. T
11. F
12. F
13. F
14. T
15. T
16. T
17. F
18. F
19. T
20. F
21. T
22. F
23. F
24. T
25. T

CHAPTER 22

1. casement
2. jalousie
3. strip
4. abatvent
5. cinerarium
6. demountable
7. gazebo
8. wellhole
9. gambrel
10. shed
11. gable
12. tectonics
13. cenotaph
14. effloresce
15. riser
16. possum trot plan
17. loggia
18. lightening holes
19. oriel
20. Palladian
21. entablature
22. ogee
23. clerestory
24. corbel
25. skirt

CHAPTER 23

1. anemology
2. hydrosphere
3. photophone
4. speleologist
5. apiary
6. aviculture
7. thermotropism
8. conchitic
9. heterosis
10. biophysics
11. green
12. a drill
13. motion pictures
14. archaeologist
15. rising . . .
16. becomes thin
17. is probably . . .
18. an attractor of the opposite sex
19. wind velocity
20. the curvature

CHAPTER 24

1. quincunx
2. napiform
3. ectomorph
4. trifurcate
5. claviform
6. decussate
7. hexagram
8. ostreiform
9. cordate
10. obrotund
11. palmate
12. pyknik
13. bifurcate
14. mesomorph
15. topiary

16. arcuate
17. biform
18. cuneiform
19. dolioform
20. excurvate
21. deltoid
22. duodecagon
23. cruciform
24. nonagon
25. whorl

CHAPTER 25

1. T
2. T
3. F
4. T
5. F
6. F
7. F
8. T
9. T
10. F
11. T
12. F
13. T
14. T
15. T
16. T
17. F
18. F
19. F
20. T
21. T
22. T
23. T
24. F
25. F

CHAPTER 26

1. cephalometer
2. manometer
3. sphygmomanometer
4. hemometer
5. inspirometer
6. tactometer
7. odometer
8. hypsometer
9. telemeter
10. echograph
11. bathythermograph
12. fadeometer
13. launderometer
14. elastometer
15. colorimeter
16. hygrometer
17. chronograph
18. gravimeter
19. infiltrometer
20. phonometer
21. salinometer
22. spherometer
23. tonometer
24. chartometer
25. flexometer
26. Geodimeter
27. hemometer
28. cusec
29. skosh
30. clinometer

CHAPTER 27

1. f
2. j
3. a
4. b
5. c
6. d
7. i
8. e
9. h
10. g
11. t
12. p
13. k
14. s
15. m
16. r
17. l
18. n
19. o
20. q
21. bb
22. v
23. dd
24. cc
25. u
26. w
27. x
28. y
29. aa
30. z
31. ii
32. ee
33. hh
34. gg
35. ff

CHAPTER 28

1. drisk
2. smaze
3. sneet
4. graupel
5. whiteout
6. nival
7. snowbreak
8. pluviograph
9. interpluvial
10. phenologist
11. glaciology
12. isohel
13. microclimate
14. brontometer
15. cirrus
16. cumulo-nimbus
17. dogwood winter
18. fire wind

19. squaw winter	22. comfort	24. Scotch mist
20. sweltry	23. storm surge	25. moonbow
21. Beaufort		

CHAPTER 29

1. b	4. a	7. b	10. a	13. a	16. d
2. c	5. d	8. c	11. b	14. d	17. b
3. b	6. c	9. a	12. c	15. a	18. b

CHAPTER 30

1. F	5. T	9. T	12. F	15. T	18. F
2. T	6. F	10. F	13. T	16. T	19. T
3. F	7. T	11. F	14. T	17. T	20. T
4. F	8. F				

CHAPTER 31

I.	1. d	3. a	5. b	7. c	9. j
	2. h	4. f	6. i	8. g	10. e
II.	11. t	13. k	15. q	17. m	19. o
	12. s	14. n	16. l	18. p	20. r
III.	21. z	23. u	25. bb	27. dd	29. w
	22. x	24. y	26. v	28. aa	30. cc
IV.	31. ii	33. jj	35. nn	37. gg	39. hh
	32. ee	34. ff	36. ll	38. kk	40. mm
V.	41. rr	42. oo	43. pp	44. qq	45. ss

CHAPTER 32

1. g	6. i	11. o	16. n	21. v	26. u
2. c	7. e	12. r	17. k	22. aa	27. w
3. a	8. b	13. s	18. m	23. bb	28. z
4. j	9. f	14. q	19. t	24. y	29. dd
5. d	10. h	15. p	20. l	25. x	30. cc

CHAPTER 33

1. spectroscopy	3. gibbous	5. inferior
2. selenology	4. astrometric	6. conjunction

7. cosmogony
8. cometary
9. epact
10. cosmographist
11. occultation
12. catarchic
13. astrophysics
14. orrery
15. quadrature
16. galactic
17. astrobiology
18. astrogeology
19. astrodynamics
20. planets

CHAPTER 34

1. squabbish
2. nonpareil
3. perspicuous
4. recrudescent
5. rumorous
6. Xenial
7. wopsy
8. crisic
9. Stratagemical
10. trenchant
11. factitious
12. diaphanous
13. sedulous
14. magazinish
15. Meretricious

CHAPTER 35

1. T
2. T
3. T
4. F
5. F
6. F
7. F
8. T
9. T
10. F
11. T
12. T
13. T
14. T
15. T
16. F
17. T
18. T
19. T
20. T
21. F
22. T
23. T
24. T
25. T

INDEX OF WORDS AND PRONUNCIATION GUIDE

PRONUNCIATION KEY

ă as in h**a**t
ā as in **a**te
âr as in c**are**
ä as in f**a**ther or h**o**t
ĕ as in p**e**t
ē as in b**e**
ĭ as in s**i**t
ī as in h**i**de
îr as in t**ier**
ô as in l**aw**
ō as in **o**de
au as in **ou**t
oi as in p**oi**se
o͝o as in t**oo**k
o͞o as in b**oo**t
ŭ as in r**u**t
ûr as in **ur**ge
zh as in vi**si**on
ə as in **a**bout, lin**i**ment, sof**a**

The mark ″ following a syllable indicates strong stress; the mark ′ indicates less strong stress.

Parentheses within a word enclose a sound that is optional: făm″ (ə) lē.